THE DISTRIBUTED
SYSTEM ENVIRONMENT

THE DISTRIBUTED SYSTEM ENVIRONMENT
SOME PRACTICAL APPROACHES

Grayce M. Booth
Honeywell Information Systems Inc.

McGraw-Hill Book Company

*New York   St. Louis   San Francisco   Auckland
Bogotá   Singapore   Johannesburg   London
Madrid   Mexico   Montreal   New Delhi
Panama   Sao Paulo   Hamburg
Sydney   Tokyo   Paris
Toronto*

Library of Congress Cataloging in Publication Data

Booth, Grayce M., date.
  The distributed system environment.

  Bibliography: p.
  Includes index.
  1. Electronic data processing—Distributed pro-
cessing. I. Title.
QA76.9.D5B66   001.64   80-13494
ISBN 0-07-006507-1

1234567890   KPKP   8987654321

The editors for this book were Barry Richman and Susan Thomas,
the designer was Mark E. Safran, and the production supervisor
was Teresa F. Leaden. It was set in Baskerville by the Fuller Organization.

Printed and bound by The Kingsport Press.

CONTENTS

PREFACE

An important trend toward the distribution of computing resources is under way. One facet of this trend involves the interconnection of hitherto independent computer centers, while another facet involves the creation of complex information systems consisting of large-scale, general-purpose computers, minicomputers, and large numbers of terminal devices—often intelligent terminals.

Many industry buzzwords are being used to describe this trend toward distributed functionality: *distributed systems, distributed processing, distributed databases, distributive processing,* and so on. Unfortunately, these buzzwords have no generally understood definitions, and so they mean many different things to different people. One of the goals of this book is to provide a common set of terminology to describe distributed information systems so that the reader can grasp the fundamental principles which lie beneath the buzzwords.

This book will provide the information system analyst, designer, or programmer with a good understanding of this new distributed system environment. Through the presentation of numerous examples, the reader will learn how distributed systems can be configured and used. The reader will also learn how to evaluate the advantages and disadvantages of distributed systems.

Major sections are devoted to distributed processing and distributed database structures, as well as to the network or data communications structures used to interconnect the component elements of distributed systems.

Using the above basic descriptive material, this book analyzes the network or system architectures of several vendors, describing how each vendor attacks the distributed system problem and which system structures each supports.

The reader will also be given a thorough grasp of how to design distributed systems, including how to make strategic decisions about whether to distribute or centralize computing facilities.

The emphasis throughout is on providing a practical understanding of workable methods for the implementation of distributed systems. Advanced concepts such as dynamic load leveling are described, but in the perspective of what can generally be implemented today at a reasonable cost. Pitfalls and problems are also described, so that the reader can avoid these by benefitting from the experience of others.

Perhaps the most important function of this book is to bring together all of the pieces of the emerging technology for the distributed system environment and to present them in a logical, coherent manner. Most readers will have encountered many of the concepts presented—in trade journals, computer conferences, and so on. Viewed independently and in fragmented form, however, many of these concepts are quite confusing. This book brings them all together and puts distributed systems into clear focus—perhaps for the first time.

With this thorough grounding in the subject, the designer, analyst, or programmer will be able to make an intelligent decision about whether a distributed system would best serve the needs of his or her own organization.

GRAYCE M. BOOTH □

ACKNOWLEDGMENTS

The material collected in this volume reflects not only my experience with the analysis of distributed systems but also the results of many, many discussions with people involved in various aspects of system design and use. Since I cannot individually acknowledge all of these contributions, I will simply thank the three people who gave me the most help.

First, I must thank Michel Godard, of Cii Honeywell Bull in Paris. I first became interested in distributed systems in 1974, when Michel invited me to visit a large Paris-based bank engaged in the design of a complex system. That introduction to distributed processing in the real world set me on the path which led to this book.

I would also particularly like to acknowledge the contributions of Hal B. Becker and of Walter O. Bailey, Jr., both of Advanced Computer Techniques Corporation. A number of the ideas presented in this volume are Hal's or Walt's. I have simply collected and arranged them, adding my own contributions. Without our many discussions over the years, this book would not have been the same.

THE DISTRIBUTED
SYSTEM ENVIRONMENT

SECTION • 1

INTRODUCTION

1

BACKGROUND

Distributed information systems are built upon the principle of functional distribution. This means that not all processing functions are performed by a single element; rather, they are distributed to multiple elements, and some of these elements may be moved close to where the users of the functions are located. This contrasts strongly with the concept of centralized functionality, in which all computing power is located in one processing element. Centralized functionality requires users to come to the computer or, at best, to have remote access to centralized computing resources.

1-1. TRENDS

Looking back over the last twenty years, we can see how distributed systems evolved. During the late 1950s and early 1960s, when computers were coming into general use, many organizations acquired first one computer, then another, and another, and another. . . . Each was an independent entity, and often these *decentralized* systems led to duplication of staffing, to duplication of hardware and facilities costs, to incompatible procedures and methods, and far too often to lack of management control.

Starting in the mid-60s and continuing to the early 1970s, computer *centralization* for economy of scale became popular. Larger and larger computers were being built, and "Grosch's law"* stated that for twice as much money you could buy a processor with four times as much computing power as a smaller machine. In addition, duplicate staffs and facilities were no longer needed and—most important—management control could be exercised more easily.

Although attractive in terms of cost and control, centralization sometimes led to lack of responsiveness. The centralized data processing (DP) department served many user groups (e.g., engineering, accounting, marketing . . .) with conflicting needs. When trade-offs between those needs were made, none of the users might be completely happy with the

*Stated by Herb Grosch, noted industry personality.

results. User groups began to say, in effect, "If only we could have our own computer. . . ."

It was difficult, however, for departments other than data processing to acquire computers, because all purchase or lease requests above a certain dollar value typically had to be approved by the central DP staff. Naturally, it was hard to get this approval except in special cases such as process control.

This situation was changed by the advent of inexpensive minicomputers. With minis such as Digital Equipment's PDP-8, it became possible to buy a fairly significant amount of computing power for a relatively small amount of money. Small enough, in fact, to be within local management approval authority—without central data processing management review.

So, the "minicomputer revolt" began, in an attempt to return responsive computing to individual using departments. However, many things had changed since the early 1960s. Business, government, and other organizations had become far more complex, leading to greater need for integrated information-processing systems. In most cases, it was no longer feasible to install truly independent decentralized computers, because each computer needed data available from some other computer.

Distributed information systems, which evolved as a result of this situation, consist of multiple computers and/or intelligent terminal or device controllers interconnected to form a coordinated system. For example, a user who has a large central system such as an IBM 370 might expand by installing minis in remote locations, connected to the 370 for the exchange of data to coordinate the operations of the maxi and the minis. Or a user with two independent data centers, both using large-scale general-purpose computers, might interconnect the two centers—again for data exchange.

These are the two basic trends in distributed systems:

1. To expand an existing central system by connecting intelligent remote devices to it.

2. To interconnect previously independent decentralized computers for greater coordination and cooperation.

Looking at a single computer system, we can also see that the trend to distributed functionality has been under way for some time. Early computers such as the IBM 650, 305 RAMAC, and 1401 were fully integrated: the processor performed I/O (input/output) operations as well as computations, and so these functions could only proceed alternately. However, this situation soon changed. Peripheral controllers (also called peripheral processors) were given their own logic for performing I/O in parallel with computation. This was the first step toward the distribution of functionality.

Front-end network processors (or *front-ends*) evolved next to perform remote I/O functions, interfacing with terminal devices, in parallel with local I/O and processing. Further distribution in the form of a database processor, or *back-end processor,* has been implemented in some systems. This trend toward functional distribution within a single computer system is shown in Figure 1-1.

This type of functional distribution can be called horizontal, in the sense that there is generally no master-slave relationship among the elements. All cooperate at an equal level, logically, to perform a complex set of tasks. Such functional distribution within a single computer system has been commonplace for some time—so much so, in fact, that it tends to be taken for granted. In general, these techniques are not included when the terms *distributed processing* or *distributed systems* are used.

A more recent trend, emerging from the evolution described earlier, is vertical distribution. In this case, functionality is distributed across relatively independent but interconnected elements that form a hierarchy. These elements share tasks in a structured way. Each component either is controlled to some degree by the higher-level member(s) of the hierarchy—or is at least limited to a given set of functionality by its position in the hierarchy.

The trend toward vertical distribution usually involves multiple separate elements—information processors of various sizes, concentrators, terminals, and perhaps real-time devices. Because these elements are logically related in the form of a hierarchy, vertical distribution is called *hierarchical distribution.* This form of distributed functionality is shown in Figure 1-2.

Hierarchical distribution often results when minis and/or intelligent terminals are attached to an existing central information processor in accord with one of the trends mentioned earlier.

Horizontal distribution, which began within a single computer system (as in Figure 1-1), is now expanding to encompass multiple computer systems, as shown in Figure 1-3.

Horizontal distribution usually results from the interconnection of computers which were previously free-standing or decentralized. The

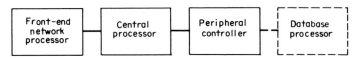

FIG. 1-1 Intrasystem functional distribution.

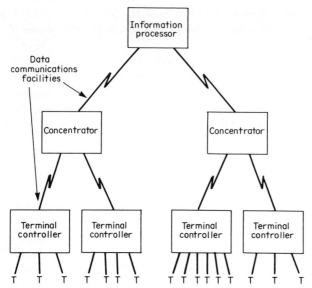

FIG. 1-2   Hierarchical distribution. T = terminal device.

difference between this form of distribution and the hierarchical form shown in Figure 1-2 is that these horizontally distributed computers cooperate as equals, or peers, sharing the total workload. In contrast to the hierarchical system, no concept of "level" exists to specialize the functionality of the information processors.

The widespread use of distributed functionality is relatively recent. Programmable logic formerly existed only in central computer systems. Devices such as terminals were hard-wired to perform a specific set of functions, because any additional logic for added flexibility would increase the cost of these devices unacceptably. Today, however, low-cost technologies such as large-scale integration (LSI) and the coming very large-scale integration (VLSI) make it feasible to include intelligence in

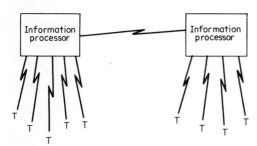

FIG. 1-3   Horizontal distribution. T = terminal device.

devices which were formerly hard-wired. The explosive growth in the use of minicomputers, one result of today's low-cost technologies, provides a major impetus for the growth of distributed systems.

Another reason for the growth of distributed functionality is the increasing use of communications-based systems. These systems are by nature physically distributed, although initially it is usually the *human* functions which are distributed, rather than the *computer-based* functions. The trend, however, tends to favor evolution from distributed access (distributed users) to distributed computing functionality.

Remotely oriented systems are often larger and more complex than the average batch system, because they are designed to handle large and complex real-world problems.

1-2. BENEFITS

All of these trends lead toward increased use of distributed systems because, in the right circumstances, these systems offer significant benefits as contrasted with centralized or decentralized information systems.

Coordination can be better in a distributed system than in a decentralized system. This means that the information system will serve its users more efficiently, often at a lower cost.

Response—how quickly a terminal user can get an answer—is often better in a distributed system than a centralized system. This is particularly true as the centralized system becomes larger and larger, serving more and more on-line users. At some point these users interfere with each other so much that response degrades unacceptably. Moving functions out of the central system (often called the "host" in a distributed system) lessens interference and improves responsiveness.

Availability or more accurately *survivability,* is an inherent characteristic of most distributed systems. Because system components are distributed, and relatively independent, it is extremely rare for any problem to cause failure of the entire system. In a branch banking system, for example, with a mini in each branch, failure of one mini affects only one branch. If the branches were all connected to a single central computer system in contrast, failure of that computer would affect all branches. Survivability is very important where on-line computer systems are tied directly into the day-to-day operations of the organization, and survivability may be achieved more economically in a distributed system than in a centralized system.

Lower cost of data communications facilities can result from moving processing—and perhaps databases—close to system users, instead of transmitting large amounts of data to and from a central computer site.

Flexibility and adaptability result from the modularity of the distributed system. It is often easier to meet evolving needs via distributed computing than with a monolithic centralized system.

These distributed system attributes translate to benefits for the using organization, whether business, government, educational institution, health care entity, or other. These benefits include:

- Better service to customers or users, because of greater computer system responsiveness and lower costs.
- Increased workforce productivity, also due to system responsiveness.
- Lower overall costs, because of lower data communications costs and increased workforce productivity.
- Ability to respond to competition and/or to changing social conditions, due to improved system flexibility and adaptability.

Of course, all these benefits are only potential. Realizing the potential benefits of distributed systems depends upon fitting the system to specific needs, evolving a practical, workable design, and implementing it. The purpose of this book is to provide guidelines for achieving these goals.

2

TERMINOLOGY

An evolving technology always leads to the use of new terminology, and distributed system technology is no exception. Because this terminology is relatively new, it is often ambiguous. Different people may have different mental images to which they apply the same term, or they may apply different terms to the same image. This chapter defines the most important terms to be used in describing distributed information systems. It also provides basic insight into how the book is organized and how distributed systems will be analyzed and described.

This book is organized around the functional approach to information systems, first defined by Hal B. Becker.* The functional approach views each information system as being formed of some combination of these three major function sets:

- Information processing
- Database management
- Network processing

Information processing includes hardware and software functions to provide computation, decision making, and data manipulation, supporting the execution of computerized applications.

Database management supports the semipermanent storage of user-owned data and provides the hardware and software functions necessary to access that data.

Network processing provides the hardware and software functions necessary to control the transfer of information between the other two function sets. Such information is usually transferred over data communications facilities.

The separation of function inherent in this approach provides modularity, and therefore flexibility, in designing and implementing distributed systems—and centralized systems as well. The functional approach and its three function sets will therefore be used throughout the remaining sections of this book.

Functional Analysis of Information Networks, Hal B. Becker, Wiley-Interscience, 1973.

The most basic term used in the following chapters is *distributed information system*. A distributed information system is an integrated set of information-processing facilities implemented in two or more relatively independent resource centers such as computer sites, terminal locations, and so on. For convenience, the phrase *distributed information system* is often shortened to *distributed system.*

If the resource centers which make up the distributed system are geographically dispersed (not always the case) and interconnected by use of data communications facilities, the system may also be called an *information network.* An information network, however, is not always a distributed system. If the information-processing and data-management functions of the network are centralized, the information network is considered centralized even though widely distributed access from remote terminals to centralized computing may be provided.

A *decentralized information system* exists when multiple resource centers (computer sites) are operated by the same organization, but are not interconnected for data exchange. A distributed system is sometimes formed by interconnecting previously decentralized facilities.

Distributed processing, or *distributed information processing,* refers to the implementation of one logically related set of application functions within more than one physical device—such as multiple information processors, an information processor and intelligent terminals, etc. ("Distributed processing" is often used synonymously with "distributed system." In fact, the term refers to only one part of the total distributed system spectrum—network processing and database management form the other two parts. This usage of "distributed processing" leads to confusion and ambiguity. It should therefore be avoided.)

Distributed processing can exist within one resource center, as when a loosely coupled multiprocessor system (two cable-connected computers) handles a center's workload. More often, distributed processing means that information-processing functions exist in multiple geographically separated locations.

Both of these forms of distributed processing require multiple intelligent components (software- or firmware-controlled) within the information system. This book will concentrate on the geographically dispersed form of distributed processing, but many of the same principles apply to the local form as well.

Distributed information systems are almost always database-centered. A *database* is a generalized collection of data belonging to an organization, company, or installation rather than an individual. A database is typically organized to reflect data relationships which exist in the real world; thus, the database structure mirrors reality. A database is typically shared by many applications, and its length of existence is independent of the execution of any particular application.

Distributed processing may lead to the formation of a *distributed database,* which is a single logical database either segmented or copied, and placed at more than one physical location within a distributed system. In the broadest sense, all the stored data of interest to an organization could be considered to form a distributed database. For practical purposes, however, a distributed database exists only when related data elements have been distributed in a structured manner (as discussed in Chapter 6) or when data elements stored at one location can be accessed by application programs executing at one or more other locations.

An important element of any information system, centralized or distributed, is the *information processor* (IP). An IP is a computer which provides computation, data-storage, and data-manipulation services in support of application requirements. IPs are available in many sizes, ranging from microcomputers and minicomputers to general-purpose large-scale and super computers. In a discussion of distributed systems, however, size is only one attribute of an IP. Another interesting attribute is the role which each IP plays within the system. The two possible roles are host processor or satellite processor.

A *host,* or host processor, is an IP—of any size—which provides supporting services and/or guidance to users and/or to satellite processors, terminals, and other subsidiary devices. A host processor is generally assumed to be self-sufficient and to require no supervision from other processors.

A *satellite,* or satellite processor, is an IP—of any size—which is arbitrarily assigned a subsidiary role in a distributed system, communicating with—and perhaps depending to some degree upon—a host for supporting services and/or guidance.

For example, a host processor may provide cross-compilers so that programs for the satellite can be developed on the host. The host may also maintain libraries of satellite programs and/or subroutines and transmit these to the satellite for use on request. A host supports terminal users by providing services such as computational timesharing, transaction processing, database inquiry, and so on.

A single IP can play both roles, acting as a satellite in relationship to a higher-level host and also acting as a host in relationship to lower-level components. This situation, which is quite common, is shown in Figure 2-1. It is common practice in this situation to refer to the lower-level component as a satellite, even though it fills both roles.

Most distributed information systems also include one or more *network processors,* or NPs. An NP is a computer devoted to the control of

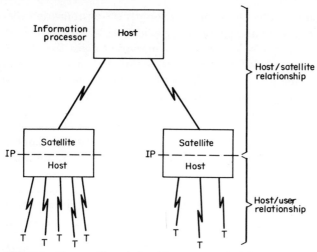

FIG. 2-1   Host-satellite relationships. T = terminal device.

data communications facilities, performing functions such as routing, concentration, and link/terminal control.

A network processor may provide an information processor with interfaces to the data communications facilities. In that case, it can be called a *front-end network processor* (FNP), or simply a *front-end*. A network processor may also be located remotely from any IP, in which case it can be called a *remote network processor* (RNP).

The *node* is another important component of distributed systems. A node is an end point of any branch of a network, or a junction common to two or more branches. When distributed systems are discussed, the term *node* is used generically to refer to information processors, network processors, terminal controllers, and terminals—and also to real-time device controllers and devices, if these are included. Nodes are interconnected by *links*. A link can consist of a data-communications circuit or a direct channel (cable) connection. Various types of nodes and links are shown in Figure 2-2.

Although it is common practice to refer to communications *lines,* this volume uses the more generic term *link*. A telephone cable (line) is a link, but a communications-satellite channel or a microwave channel is not a line. Because more and more data communications facilities make use of these new technologies, the generality of the term *link* makes it the most suitable one to use in all cases.

To summarize these definitions, Figure 2-3 shows a distributed system configuration which includes a number of the component elements and illustrates the concepts described. This example shows the use of distributed processing: the total set of information-processing functions is distributed among two host processors and one satellite processor. If the terminals shown are intelligent (have flexible logic capabilities), they may also perform information-processing functions. A distributed database is also present, composed of the data elements stored at the three IP locations. Finally, network processing functions—communications circuits and network processors—are present to tie together the processing, database, and terminal facilities.

Until recently, computer system users have been discussed as though they formed a monolithic group, with uniform requirements and uniform capabilities. In the more complex environment of on-line systems, including distributed systems, this is no longer adequate. Instead, users must be grouped according to their specific needs and their views of the information system. This volume categorizes system users as follows:

- End users
- Application developers
- System administrators

An *end user* is an individual whose normal duties include utilization of an information system. Examples of end users are bank tellers, engineers, retail store clerks, managers, and factory workers. The typical end user knows little or nothing about computers and looks on the terminal

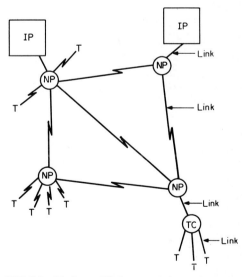

FIG. 2-2 Nodes and links. IP = information processor; NP = network processor; TC = terminal controller; T = terminal device.

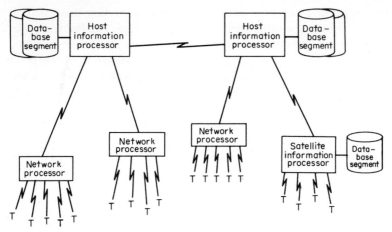

FIG. 2-3   Distributed-information-system elements. T = terminal device.

(and the information system which supports it) as simply another tool, very much like an adding machine or a typewriter.

Adequate support for end-user needs is a real challenge to information-system designers. Because of the variety of end-user requirements, many different specialized interfaces must be provided. The subject of end-user needs will be discussed at various points, especially in Chapter 18, which deals with total system design.

An *application developer* is an individual who is responsible for tailoring the basic capabilities of the information system into a form suitable for the end users. Application developers include system analysts, programmers, and coders. Their major means of meeting end-user needs is through the design and implementation of application programs.

A *system administrator* is an individual who defines, controls, and manages the information-system environment within which the activities of the enterprise are handled. System administrators include database administrators, network administrators, administrators of security and privacy, and data processing department operations personnel (console operators, tape and disk librarians, etc.). As in the case of end-user needs, the requirements of system administrators are becoming increasingly complex. How to meet these requirements will be discussed in later chapters.

The terms defined here will be used throughout the following chapters. Other terms which may be unfamiliar will be defined in the context in which they are used. A glossary is provided at the end of the text for quick reference to any term.

S E C T I O N • 2

USER EXPERIENCE

This section provides a sample of user experience with distributed information systems to date. This sample is necessarily small, because experience with distributed systems is still relatively limited, at least when compared with centralized system experience. However, a considerable body of knowledge is being built up.

Chapter 3 describes several information systems which embody various aspects of distributed functionality. Most of these examples are drawn from applications which are already operational or which are now in the process of being implemented. A few details have been omitted or changed, either to make an example more general or to preserve the anonymity of the enterprise which operates a specific system.

Chapter 4 discusses the advantages and disadvantages of distributed systems, as viewed by the owners and users of these systems. The material in this chapter was distilled from numerous conversations with the personnel of enterprises who are operating, are in the process of implementing, or are planning to implement distributed systems. The views presented therefore reflect the practical experience of these organizations.

3

EXAMPLES OF DISTRIBUTED
INFORMATION SYSTEMS

An easy way to begin a discussion of distributed systems is to describe information systems which use distributed functionality. These descriptions are based upon existing systems, systems being implemented, and systems being considered for implementation. Using this background of practical examples, later chapters will first discuss the advantages and disadvantages of the distributed approach and second examine the underlying techniques and principles which these systems embody.

3-1. ORDER-ENTRY SYSTEM

The first example is an order-entry system in which only a few functions have been distributed. A schematic of the configuration of this system is shown in Figure 3-1.

In this system an intelligent, mini-based terminal controller is placed in each cluster of terminal devices. These terminals are relatively simple, consisting only of a cathode-ray tube (CRT) screen and keyboard, with a single shared hard-copy printer available within each terminal cluster.

The terminal controllers (TCs) are programmed to support data-entry operations by providing an appropriate screen format when the terminal user depresses a function key on the device. After the user has filled in the blanks shown on the screen with the necessary input data, the TC edits the information for errors such as alphabetic entry in a numeric field, too many characters in a field, and so on. Errors are reported back to the terminal user immediately, so that corrective action can be taken at once.

In normal operation, each correct transaction is sent to the host IP on completion of data entry. Each response returned by the host is formatted by the TC and output to the appropriate screen and/or to the shared hard-copy printer. If connection to the host is lost, either because of communications-link failure or because of host failure, the TC can store transactions locally on its diskette, informing the terminal user of the temporary off-line status. These accumulated transactions are sent to the host whenever it becomes available; the TC can switch between off-line, or local, mode and on-line mode as circumstances change.

Although only the terminal-device control, screen-format management, input/output handling, and editing functions have been distributed, this is a very realistic illustration of a distributed system. A considerable amount of processing has been removed from the host, and the functions removed—terminal control, editing—are those least suited to the capabilities of a large-scale IP. In contrast, these functions are very well-suited to a minicomputer or microcomputer configured as a terminal controller. Often this type of system structure is a first step toward the greater distribution of functionality. The next step might be to supply the TC with limited application logic, and perhaps later with a local database. The TC would have then evolved into a satellite processor, removing still more of the workload from the host.

3-2.   INVENTORY-CONTROL SYSTEM

The next example is a distributed system used primarily for inventory control and secondarily for other miscellaneous applications. Two large-scale information processors, located in different cities, are linked using data-communications facilities to form a horizontally distributed structure. A simplified diagram of this system is shown in Figure 3-2.

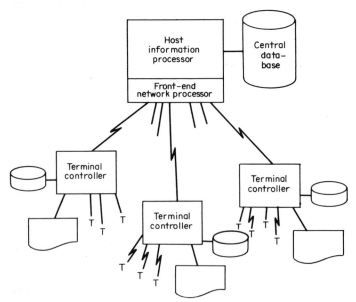

FIG. 3-1   Order-entry system. T = terminal device.

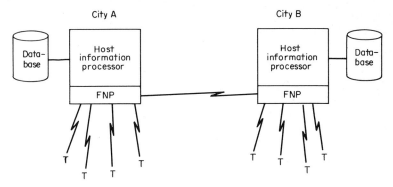

FIG. 3-2   Inventory-control system. FNP = front-end network processor; T = terminal device.

The two IPs in this distributed system communicate by exchanging files. One type of file contains a source-level program. Most program development in this company takes place in City *A*, where new programs are implemented, tested, and debugged. A copy of each new program is then transmitted to City *B* for storage and use there.

Another type of file contains a job, consisting of an executable program, the necessary job-control language (JCL), and the accompanying input data. Jobs are occasionally transmitted from one host to the other for load-leveling purposes, to smooth out a peak workload in one location by offloading work to the other. (The principles of load leveling are discussed in Chapter 15.) In this example system the two processors are of the same type, running under the same software, so there are no compatibility problems associated with moving the workload.

Each of these hosts performs an inventory-control function for a different division of the company, which has a decentralized management structure. This arrangement makes the two centers largely independent of each other, so that they exchange data only occasionally. A distributed database is not required to support the mode of operation used in this system; each center maintains an independent database.

3-3. PRODUCTION-CONTROL SYSTEM

A production-control system forms the next example. In this case a hierarchically distributed system structure is used for an integrated application which includes production scheduling, factory feedback, and semiautomatic control of the manufacturing process. A schematic of this system structure is shown in Figure 3-3.

In this system the large-scale host at the top of the hierarchy main-

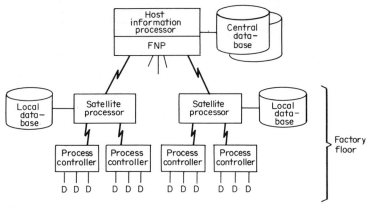

FIG. 3-3 Production-control system. FNP = front-end network processor; D = device.

tains a complex central database and performs the functions associated with overall scheduling and control of the manufacturing process. For example, parts explosions (also called bill of materials) are maintained by the host. It also maintains factory resource (personnel, equipment) data and performs scheduling operations to allocate available resources in the optimum manner. The host is not directly involved in the real-time aspects of process and production control.

At the next lower level in the hierarchy, there are several satellite processors, built around minicomputers. (Only two of these are shown in the Figure 3-3 schematic.) Each satellite handles that part of the manufacturing process assigned to the factory devices to which it is connected.

Many of the satellites also maintain local databases, each of which is a partial copy of the host database, containing only the information applicable to the local production tasks. These local databases are used for dynamic control of the manufacturing process. Whenever the master schedule at the host is updated, a new copy of any relevant changed data is transmitted to the appropriate satellite, reflecting its new schedule.

The lowest-level microcomputers monitor and control the factory equipment. These micros receive control commands from the satellite processors—and/or from the factory workers—to guide the manufacturing process as it progresses.

For example, a micro might control a pair of semiautomatic wire-wrap machines. As a factory worker keys in the identity of the next panel to be built, the micro obtains the necessary information for that panel from the satellite mini. The process-control micro then interacts with the worker to complete wire-wrap of that panel, notifies the satellite of its completion, then waits for the next human input to determine the next task.

As the situation changes, the process controllers all send process-status information up to the satellites. Each satellite processor thus remains continually aware of the status of the processes which are indirectly under its control.

Production-control distributed systems of this type are typically implemented "from the bottom up." Process-control equipment is installed first, with each process controller operating independently. Often, a large-scale computer is used, completely independently, for production scheduling. The move toward formation of a distributed system occurs when the controllers are connected to minicomputers which perform satellite processing, and these minis are then connected to the large-scale host. The result is a hierarchically distributed information system.

3-4. FINANCIAL SYSTEM

The next example is a hierarchically distributed system used for financial applications. The hierarchy of this system, shown in Figure 3-4, is much less complex than the one in the preceding example. It consists of only three levels: the host, intelligent terminal controllers, and unintelligent terminal devices.

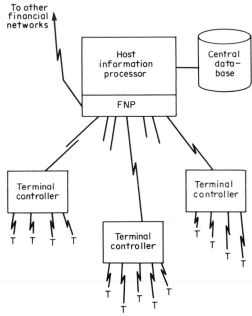

FIG. 3-4 Financial system. FNP = front-end network processor; T = terminal device.

In this system the host handles a central database containing the records of all customer accounts. The host also handles interfaces to other financial networks, such as the Interbank National Authorization Service (INAS) credit card net. Each bank branch, or group of branches, is served by a mini-based terminal controller (TC), which handles the local bank teller terminal devices and/or point-of-sale terminals in related establishments such as supermarkets. This example differs from the preceding production-control system in the area of database management. The database remains centralized in this financial system. This is because of the difficulty of finding a pattern of database use which will allow partitioning or copying of the data at the TC locations.

In the preceding example, in contrast, the central database contains all the operating information, with selective copying used to create the local, working databases at the satellite minis. Database distribution proved practical in that example because the information needed at each satellite can be identified on the basis of which devices each satellite is controlling. Therefore, a natural partitioning of data exists, and the distributed system structure is built around this pattern. A later example, in Unit 3-8, will show how a similar pattern allowing database distribution was established in another, somewhat different, banking environment.

In banking and finance, in contrast to manufacturing applications, distributed systems are most often built "from the top down," usually as part of a move from batch-mode to on-line computer operation. Intelligent terminals and/or satellite processors are installed as part of a hierarchy dominated by a large-scale host processor. Often, the host is one formerly used for batch processing. The result is a hierarchically distributed information system.

3-5.   AIRLINE RESERVATION SYSTEM

Most airline reservation systems follow a pattern of hierarchical distribution. All information processing is centralized at one location, usually on one large-scale host processor with a second host in reserve. The second host performs batch processing unless the on-line host fails. In that case the second host discontinues its batch workload and picks up the on-line reservations processing. Functional distribution in this case affects only the network-processing functions. Control of the terminals (generally unintelligent hard-copy devices) and the associated links takes place in the concentrators rather than in the host. The reservation terminals are often on *multidrop* links, meaning that more than one terminal is attached to a single link, to minimize link costs.

The concentrators also multiplex traffic between the host and the terminals, to achieve savings in transmission-link costs and also to decrease the communications-handling load on the host. Figure 3-5 shows a simplified schematic of a typical airline reservation system.

It might be a temptation to call this example a "centralized," rather than a "distributed," system. However, it *is* a distributed system: certain logical functions which would otherwise be performed by the host (or by its front-end network processor) have been distributed to the concentrators.

3-6. FUTURE AIRLINE RESERVATION SYSTEM

Future airline reservation systems may well involve the distribution of additional functions. There has been discussion concerning the use of two or more regional hosts, instead of one centralized host, for reservation processing. These hosts would be interconnected in a horizontally distributed structure, and each host might also be the apex of a hier-

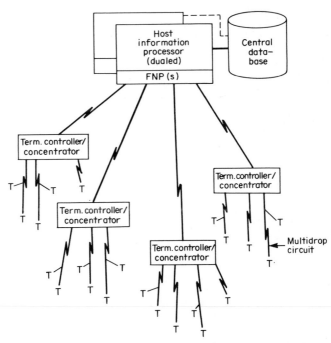

FIG. 3-5 Airline reservation system. FNP = front-end network processor; T = terminal device.

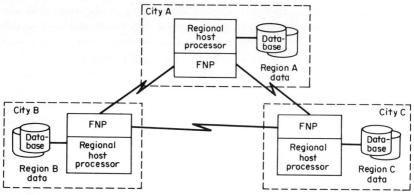

FIG. 3-6 Future airline reservation system. FNP = front-end network processor.

archy of concentrators and terminals as at present. Figure 3-6 shows how such a system might be interconnected.

The rationale for this system structure is the fact that reservation inquiries and requests originate most often in the same geographic region as the specific flight in question. For example, inquiries and requests for flights which originate in Chicago are most often made from the area immediately surrounding Chicago. This is especially true in regard to inquiries, which are often made in connection with the return portion of a round trip after the passenger has completed the outbound flight. Of course a fairly heavy volume of data would still have to be exchanged among the regional hosts, mainly to handle the booking of passenger flights originating in other regions. However, these exchanges can be minimized if the regional boundaries correspond to the most common combinations of flight patterns.

Although this system structure is more complex than the existing reservation-system structures, it has the potential of providing important savings in communications-link costs. It also has the potential of improving overall system availability by making host failures less traumatic and by providing built-in redundancy for many components. The fact that the reservation systems of the largest airlines are outgrowing the most powerful available computer equipment further encourages a trend toward functional distribution.

3-7. HOSPITAL SUPPORT SYSTEM

Health care services are being increasingly computerized in order to provide important benefits such as increased efficiency and cost savings. Often, however, individual hospitals cannot justify the investment in equipment necessary to computerize their operations. The next example, shown schematically in Figure 3-7, illustrates how a service bureau overcomes this problem by means of a distributed health care system which can be shared by many hospitals. The cost to any one hospital is kept within acceptable limits, but all enjoy the benefits of computerization.

This system structure is a hierarchy. At its apex is the service bureau's large-scale host, which provides centralized services. The shared host provides batch services such as patient billing, accounts receivable, inventory control, and related functions for all the hospitals involved. (A second host is available for back up, in case the main host fails.) Each hospital forms one or more branches of the hierarchy, with satellite minicomputers and terminals installed on the premises. The terminals are used to record patient admissions, patient-care orders, patient status, and so on.

The terminal input is acted upon immediately by the local satellite processors whenever possible. For example, if a physician orders a test for a patient, that order is entered through a terminal, usually by a nurse or nursing aide. At the same time the test request is recorded, it is also printed out on the terminal in the appropriate laboratory, x-ray department, or other section of the hospital. This eliminates the time delays which often occur in manual hospital systems, and also eliminates the risk that the test order will be lost or forgotten—this cannot occur once the order has been entered at the terminal.

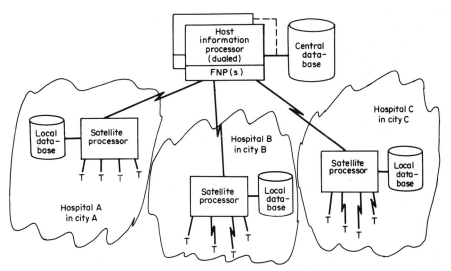

FIG. 3-7   Hospital support system. FNP = front-end network processor; T = terminal device.

This example may indicate a pattern for future shared systems in other application areas. A distributed system structure which shares the high cost of a powerful host needed for reporting, forecasting, and other similar functions is very suitable for providing low-cost, potentially customized local services.

3-8. BANKING SYSTEM

The final example, whose structure is shown in Figure 3-8, is a large European banking system which exhibits both the horizontal and hierarchical distribution of functions.

The geographical area served by the bank is separated into two regions, each of which is served by a large-scale host. Each host is placed at the apex of a hierarchy consisting of satellite processors, terminal controllers, and banking terminal devices. Each satellite processor serves either one large bank branch or a group of smaller, physically adjacent bank branches. Each maintains a local database which includes information for the accounts of the regular local customers. These data represent a working copy of part of the information in the master databases maintained by the hosts.

The terminal controllers also perform application-related functions. For example, they supply screen formats on user request and edit input data to determine that input transactions are in the correct format before being passed to the satellite processors.

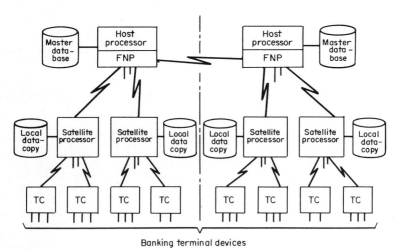

Banking terminal devices

FIG. 3-8   Banking system. FNP = front-end network processor; TC = terminal controller.

Each satellite is equipped with application logic to handle all "normal" transactions, such as deposits and withdrawals, entered at the local terminals. Because the remainder of the processing—loan requests, requests for bank credit cards, and so on—is much more complex, the transactions which require this type of processing are passed up to the host.

This system takes advantage of natural patterns of usage and is structured around those patterns. For example, the fact that bank customers normally bank at their "home" branches makes it possible to distribute customer account information to the branches. (In the banking example discussed in Unit 3-4, in contrast, customers use various branches almost at random. It was therefore found to be impractical to distribute the database to the bank branches.)

This system also takes advantage of a natural pattern of transactions. A large number of normal transactions require only simple processing and so are assigned to the satellite minis. The number of transactions which require complex processing is much smaller; these are assigned to the host processors. Finding patterns of the types and taking advantage of them in the design of the processing and data management functions are the keys to success in distributed systems.

This banking system is a good example of a complex distributed information system and of a distributed database. This same example will be used to illustrate distributed system principles in later discussions.

4

ADVANTAGES AND DISADVANTAGES OF DISTRIBUTED SYSTEMS

Distributed information systems have—in appropriate circumstances—definite advantages over centralized and decentralized systems. This chapter discusses first the benefits and then the drawbacks of distributed functionality.

4-1. ADVANTAGES

Distributed functionality can, in certain cases, provide the following advantages.

- Improved performance and response relative to cost
- Additional options for control
- Improved availability and system survival
- Decreased communications costs
- Flexibility and adaptability

Each of these potential advantages will be discussed in some detail, both to expand upon the meaning of the concepts involved and to define generally the circumstances in which the potential advantage can be achieved.

Improved performance/response for a given cost can sometimes be achieved by using a distributed system structure. This statement contradicts the often-discussed *economies of scale* which have contributed so strongly to computer centralization. In fact, for many years larger and larger computing systems have provided ever-increasing performance at a relatively lower increase in cost. Experience has appeared to show that the larger the computer, the more economically it has been able to perform each function.

Today economies of scale are not as consistent as in the past. A minicomputer can use the same 16k (16,000 bits) or 64k memory-chip packaging as a large-scale computer; the cost per bit of storage is therefore the same and economy of scale is not a factor. In some other cases, economies of scale are still evident, especially in components such as mass storage devices. The cost of a storage controller is quite significant, so it is less expensive to attach new storage devices to an existing controller than to add new controllers when more storage is needed. With current technological trends toward lower and lower component costs, it is therefore realistic to consider distributing some components rather than centralizing them.

Another factor is that computer-using enterprises are beginning to implement very large applications which cannot be handled satisfactorily by a single central IP, regardless of its size and power. Information systems are being built today which will service thousands of terminals by the 1980s. Connecting so many terminals individually and directly to a single host of any size is impractical. (Even if this were practical, the reliability of a single host in so large a system would very likely not be high enough for practical purposes.) It can be expected that future applications will service ever-larger numbers of terminals and users, and the impracticality of handling these on a centralized basis will grow.

Response can be improved in many systems by moving functions close to the end users' terminals. This avoids delays in the communications facilities, which can add a second or two to response in large, geographically dispersed systems. (Propagation delays are a basic fact of life in data communications and can be reduced only by using higher-speed circuits —which may increase costs too much to be practical.) Moving functions into multiple processors also provides more parallel facilities to operate simultaneously on the users' problems, eliminating contention and queuing delays which exist in a single central system. In addition, minicomputers and microcomputers can easily be specialized for functions such as terminal control, network processing, and real-time process control, providing more attractive price/performance ratios, in many cases, than a large-scale IP can achieve when performing these same functions.

These factors of improved performance and/or response do not apply to all systems, however. In small, simple systems the cost benefits of resource centralization still apply. It is only in systems larger than some (as yet poorly defined) "break-even" point that economies of scale may not result from centralization. The benefits of functional distribution for these large systems, should be weighed carefully.

Control options are extended in distributed systems, as contrasted to both centralized and decentralized systems. *Control* concerns who makes decisions on what the computer system will do—that is, design and implementation of applications—as well as dynamic decision making during system operation.

The psychological aspects of centralization versus decentralization or distribution can be very important, and are associated with control and responsiveness. Centralized computing is often viewed by its end users—and their management—as a faceless monster, totally out of their control and demanding more in user charges than it returns in value of services provided. In contrast, local satellite processors, terminal controllers, and process controllers can be placed entirely or partially under the control of the management where the devices are located. Individual shop supervisors might have their own minicomputers, and individual bank branch managers might control their own satellite processors and teller terminals. Even physical control over processing facilities such as satellite processors can be important, psychologically, in reconciling local management and users to the information system.

In addition to these psychological aspects, practical benefits can accrue from more extensive local control. Satellite processors can be customized to produce reports and/or to provide processing which is specific to local needs, without interfering with central-office requirements. To achieve this balance between local and headquarters needs, certain processing and reporting procedures can be developed centrally and specified for use at all locations—ensuring that headquarters-level needs are met. Local management can then be left free to meet its own additional information-processing needs as it sees fit. Local managers can thus use the computing resources effectively to support their profit-and-loss responsibilities.

The use of a distributed system structure, as contrasted to a decentralized structure of dispersed but uncoordinated components, makes it practical to achieve the degree of control that headquarters needs. Decentralized computing, in which the computer resources are independent and not interconnected, forces top management to exert control over remote computers administratively, i.e., through manually executed procedures and standards. This type of administrative control is often difficult to enforce effectively. In contrast, remote processors which are part of a distributed system are much less independent. Reporting programs specified by headquarters can be prepared centrally and transmitted directly to each remote site ("downline loaded") for execution. Such programs, available at remote sites only in object form, cannot be modified locally. This ensures adherence to procedures that have been established centrally.

Finally, centralized monolithic information systems are almost always at odds with the organizations they serve. The organization of most enterprises is best described, both formally and practically, as a hierarchy or a set of interrelated hierarchies. The ability to structure the computerized information system in the same way is inherently attractive because it increases the probability that the system will be responsive to the needs of the organization.

Improved availability or, more realistically *survivability,* can often be achieved in a distributed system. As in the case of performance and response, this factor applies to systems larger than some "critical-mass" size. Below that point, the simplicity of centralization is better suited to achieving high availability.

As in administrative control, the question of availability has both psychological and practical aspects. Psychologically, in very large systems "vulnerability" and "failure-visibility" syndromes appear. Failure of a centralized system affects all users of that system; as the number of users grows failure becomes less and less acceptable, and more and more expensive methods are used to avoid it. This is particularly true of on-line applications, such as reservation systems and others which are closely related to the operations of the enterprise. Even an occasional failure—such as once a month—of this type of system is extremely visible and causes considerable disruption of the operations of the enterprise.

In a distributed system, in contrast, failure of any component generally affects only a small number of users. The pressure to avoid *all* failures is therefore lessened. It is much more acceptable, for example, to experience a satellite-processor failure which affects 25 tellers at one bank branch than to experience a host failure which affects 2,500 tellers at all branches simultaneously. This is true, in practice, even though one large system may fail relatively infrequently, while a large number of minis may collectively fail quite often. Each failure disrupts only a small portion of the enterprise, and the *perceived* availability of the system is therefore greater even though the *computed* availability might be less than in a centralized configuration.

Survivability in a distributed system, provided the system design is a good one, is inherently improved through the use of multiple, relatively independent processors. It is very unlikely that any type of problem—hardware, software, power failure, flood, riot, communications outage—will bring down more than a small part of the system. A substantial portion should therefore be operational at all times.

Another aspect of availability is the avoidance of failures through the use of redundant elements. A distributed system usually consists of multiple components, such as minis and micros. Because each of these components is relatively inexpensive, those which are vital can be dualed at low cost so that crippling failures can be avoided. The flexible structure of the distributed system allows flexible approaches to availability.

These systems also contain large amounts of built-in *redundancy,* in the sense that there are usually multiple information processors (such as hosts and satellites) and often multiple intelligent components of other types. With careful system design, a host can provide backup to a satellite processor in case of failure, one satellite can back up another, a satellite can back up at least part of a host's functions, and so on. These capabilities are not easy to provide, and they call for complex software logic, but they can achieve significant increases in overall system availability. Moreover, it is important to note that the *overall* system availability of a distributed system may be unimportant. What *is* important is the availability of the segment of the system needed to provide service to each group of users. Failures which can be masked from some or all of the systems users are relatively unimportant.

Decreased communications costs can result from the distribution of functions to locations close to the end users. In a centralized system, every transaction or job entered at every terminal must travel to the central IP, and every response must travel back to the terminal. In some cases additional traffic is caused by sending terminal forms from the host to remote locations. In a distributed system, on the other hand, much of the processing is handled close to the terminals, sometimes on direct-channel connections rather than via telephone circuits. Only exception and/or summary data must be transmitted to a central location, and the distributed system structure usually provides a natural concentration of the paths to and from that location. In this way communications-link costs are often significantly reduced from those of a centralized system serving the same number of users. The only general exceptions are those distributed systems in which all components are physically close together, as in a production-control system located within a single factory building.

General cost trends make it attractive to offset data-communications costs with computer hardware costs. Technology and competition are providing quite significant improvements in cost/performance ratios for computers and related equipment. These improvements are on the order of 20 percent or more per year, so that each year it is possible to purchase roughly 20 percent more computer power than the year before for the same amount of money.

Data-communications costs, however, are rising in almost every country except the United States—often at the same rate as inflation or even faster. Since competition is not allowed, technology has little impact on transmission costs. In the United States, the cost of long-haul (interstate) traffic, where competition exists, has been falling. But because less competition exists and it takes longer to apply new technology, it is falling more slowly than computer costs. In intrastate traffic, where monopoly conditions exist, costs have been rising at rates which vary because they are set by different local regulatory agencies. However, the general trend is for these rates to rise to equal the rate of inflation.

All of these factors merit consideration when analyzing the potential advantages of functional distribution.

Flexibility and adaptability are attractive features of many distributed systems, particularly those made up largely or entirely of minicomputers. The modularity inherent in such systems allows functional specialization. For example, one mini might be used to provide computational time-sharing services, another mini might handle batch-mode financial processing, and another might support an on-line order-entry system. The operating system, hardware configuration, and operational use of each of these minis will be much simpler than those of a single large-scale system capable of handling all of these functions concurrently. This consideration applies most often to multipurpose information systems, which handle many different and unrelated applications. If each type of use can be isolated, the components needed to support these usage modes may be relatively simple.

All distributed systems are, by definition, modular because of the multiple components involved. Generally, modularity improves flexibility. For example, it is possible to implement one geographical or functional area at a time—settling it down to satisfactory operation before moving on to another area. Similarly, changes can be applied one area at a time, making them less traumatic than wholesale changes.

It is usually easier to expand the capacity of a distributed system, by adding new modules, than to expand a centralized system. It is important to note, however, that flexibility and adaptability are only achieved through careful planning, design, and implementation.

4-2. DISADVANTAGES

Offsetting these very significant advantages of distributed systems, the following potential disadvantages exist:

- Structural and system complexity
- Unresolved technical issues
- Replicated hardware, software, people . . .

Structural and system complexity is a characteristic of distributed systems which is too often overlooked or underestimated. There is a tendency to believe that because individual system elements (such as minicomputers) are simple and easy to program, a system built of these components will also be simple. There is also a tendency to believe that the physical modularity of the hardware ensures logical modularity of the software and of the system. Unfortunately, neither of these beliefs is necessarily justified. Complexity results as soon as so-called simple components are interconnected. All of the elements of a distributed system must work together in a coordinated way to be successful. The coordination of processing among diverse system components requires good design. The control of access to distributed databases can be very complicated. Processing coordination and database access control functions exist in centralized systems also, but there they are much simplified because they take place within a single computer rather than across multiple computers.

The proper handling of failures within a distributed system also requires very careful consideration. If one component fails, it may cause other components to fail, in the "domino syndrome" made familiar by the power blackouts in the northeastern United States over the last few years.

Avoiding the pitfalls of undue complexity requires complete planning of all aspects of the system, top-down design techniques, and structured implementation and testing methods. This book provides the information necessary to plan a distributed system and supplies many of the facts needed for system design. Questions of design and implementation techniques (structured programming, etc.) are not covered, because they are adequately discussed elsewhere in the literature.

Unresolved technical issues still exist concerning the design, implementation, and management/operation of distributed system. Problems can be encountered for which technical research has not yet provided generally applicable solutions. It is therefore necessary to build distributed systems to avoid these problem areas. Some unresolved issues include coordinated systemwide error detection and correction, restart/recovery methods, security/privacy protection, and methods of distributed database design, system design, performance prediction, and implementation. These problem areas are discussed in Section 5, and methods are provided for working around these problems in planning a distributed system. If the problems cannot be avoided, it may be necessary to discard the idea of distribution.

Replication means that distributed systems involve multiple sets of hardware, software, data, extra space to locate the hardware, and possibly additional people to operate the hardware. Cost trade-off studies are used to determine whether or not a given distributed system configuragion is acceptable. It is important to include *all* costs, not just hardware costs. If remote locations do not have adequate space, power, or air conditioning for equipment installation, the costs to provide these must be estimated. Of course minis usually operate in an office environment—without special air conditioning, power, or raised flooring—but it is well to be sure that this is the case.

It is equally important to ensure that the remote devices, such as satellite processors, terminal controllers, and network processors can operate without a DP operator in attendance. This topic will be raised again in the discussion of distributed system operational control in Chapter 20.

4-3. TRADE-OFFS

The key to success in designing a distributed information system is to identify the potential advantages which apply to a particular application environment. For example, in a geographical area where communications tariffs are very high, the potential advantage of cost savings may be most important. In a retail point-of-sale application, fast response may be the most attractive potential advantage—contributing both to better customer service and to increased productivity for the sales force.

It is then important to evaluate the potential disadvantages which may also apply. If it is determined that none directly apply to the case in question, then design and implementation can proceed. If, on the other hand, one or more potential disadvantages do apply, it must be determined whether or not these can be bypassed. If not, the system is probably impractical. Often, however, potential disadvantages can be bypassed through careful design. Much of the focus of this volume is on techniques for doing so.

DISTRIBUTED SYSTEM STRUCTURES

As Chapter 1 pointed out, there are two basic ways—hierarchical and horizontal—in which distributed systems can be structured. This section expands upon this concept, and discusses three types of structures; those for distributed information processing, those for distributed databases, and those for network processing.

Every distributed system includes the three function sets described in Chapter 2—information processing, database management, and network processing. However, each system may have a different combination of specific functions, and each may have a different combination of functional centralization and distribution. For example, information processing and database management may remain centralized, while network processing is distributed. Or both network and information processing may be distributed, with data management remaining centralized. Typically, the database is the last of the three major functions to be considered for distribution.

Studying information-system distribution in terms of these three relatively independent function sets provides much greater modularity—hence flexibility—than considering it in monolithic terms. This section is therefore organized around the three function sets.

• Chapter 5 describes the structures used in distributing information processing. It formalizes the types of system configurations illustrated in Section 2 and highlights fundamental similarities which are apparent across different systems.

- Chapter 6 approaches distributed database structures in the same way, reducing these to two generic forms and a combination of the two.

- Chapter 7 describes the two structures commonly used for network processing, with some of the possible variations. Networking, while complex, is presented simply as the underpinning needed to support the other two function sets.

The structures described in this section will form the template against which, in Section 4, several network architectures provided by computer vendors will be measured.

5

DISTRIBUTED PROCESSING STRUCTURES

Distributed information processing—or *distributed processing,* for brevity —structures are the first topic in this section on distributed system structures. How the information-processing functions of a distributed system are assigned to components, how these distributed functions are logically related to each other, and how they are interfaced to coordinate their activities—all these are defined by the processing structure.

There are two basic distributed processing structures, horizontal distribution and hierarchical distribution, which can be combined in complex systems. In the descriptions which follow, the structures discussed are *logical* structures, which define logical relationships. These are not necessarily identical with *physical* structures or with the physical interconnections of components. In the illustrations, component relationships are shown by straight lines between components. Actual connections via data communications are illustrated by zigzag lines. Relationships of logical and physical structures are discussed in Unit 5-4.

5-1. HORIZONTALLY DISTRIBUTED PROCESSING

The horizontal distribution of processing functions involves the interconnection of two or more components which are logically equal. The use of the term *logically* in this context indicates that the components may be physically unlike one another and/or have different capacity and/ or functionality. Regardless of their physical characteristics, the important point is their equality within the distributed system. No component exercises control over any other component; rather, all cooperate in an "equal partnership" or "peer" relationship.

The example system from Figure 3-6 (a hypothetical future airline reservation system) is repeated in Figure 5-1. This example shows a typical horizontal system structure.

The hosts within horizontal systems are interconnected for one or more of the following purposes:

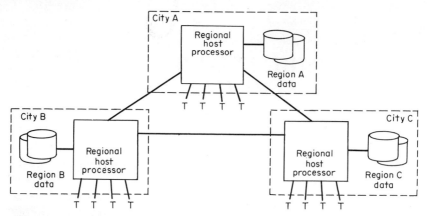

FIG. 5-1 Typical horizontal system structure. T = terminal device.

- Data exchange
- Load leveling
- Resource sharing

Data exchange is by far the most common use of the horizontal structure today. An organization which maintains multiple computer centers is very likely to require consolidated reports using input from all centers. If the centers are not linked, data are usually exchanged on magnetic tape, or even in the form of hard-copy reports. By linking the centers via data-communications facilities this data exchange can take place more rapidly and under tighter control.

Load leveling is the process of spreading a given workload evenly over a number of information processors (or network processors, in networking). The goal is to make more effective use of available processing resources, thereby avoiding the acquisition of additional resources for as long as possible.

Each information processor within a horizontal structure normally handles jobs and transactions which originate in its local area (its input is from terminals connected to that center). If an overload situation develops at any one of the hosts—that is, if the host is not processing rapidly enough to meet the response and "due date" requirements of the users —work is offloaded to another host. Candidates for load leveling could range from simple compilations to complex jobs which require that the referenced database element(s) be transferred between centers with the jobs. Load leveling, including compatibility considerations, is discussed in detail in Chapter 15.

Resource sharing allows unique resources which exist at only one or selected locations to be accessed by users or applications at other locations. For example, if a specific database is located in City *B* in the Figure 5-1 system, requests for access to that database must be filled by the City *B* host. It may fill these requests by moving only the exact data needed to the requestor, by moving the entire database to the requestor, or by causing the requesting process to be transferred to City *B* and executed there.

Resource sharing applies to many different types of resources, such as unique programs or subroutine libraries, high-speed (nonimpact) printing equipment, magnetically encoded document-handling equipment, computer output on microfilm, and so on. Resource-sharing techniques are discussed in detail in Chapter 15.

Horizontal systems are often formed through the interconnection of previously independent (decentralized) computers in order to gain the advantages of load leveling and common access to stored data (which may form a distributed database). Quite often, however, the computers connected in this way are of different models and/or have been supplied by different computer vendors. Because of this, their ability to cooperate in load-leveling activities may be limited by their incompatibilities.

Horizontally distributed processing systems today often include only a limited subset of the total possible functionality. In general, the functional capability of the total system is defined by each host's hardware and software limitations, because each IP was designed independently and not as part of a distributed system.

5-2.   HIERARCHICALLY DISTRIBUTED PROCESSING

Hierarchically distributed systems are given this name because the logical-relationship structure of the components forms a graded series, or hierarchy. This type of structure involves the vertical distribution of processing functions among a variety of components, typically large-scale hosts, minicomputers, sometimes microcomputers, as well as terminals and/or real-time devices. A hierarchical structure usually develops as a result of the expansion of an existing host system. Often, this expansion has been undertaken to enable the system to perform new online applications. Instead of simply supplying the host with greater processing power, intelligent terminals or perhaps satellite processors are installed close to the terminal users of the system. A typical hierarchically distributed structure is shown in Figure 5-2.

The most obvious characteristic of this type of system is that it follows a tree-structured form. The "root" of the tree is at the top of the hierarchy, and the "branches" fan outward and downward in an orderly and balanced way. The structure may, however, not always be completely balanced, as it is in Figure 5-2. A hierarchical structure may have a number of branches, and not all of these need be identical. An unbalanced hierarchical system is shown in Figure 5-3.

Regardless of whether the structure is balanced or unbalanced, there are seldom links between elements on lower levels of the hierarchy. Data exchange tends to flow up and down the hierarchy, not across. This is discussed further in Unit 5-4.

Perhaps the most typical hierarchical structure involves the use of a medium-scale or large-scale host processor at the apex of the hierarchy. Either multiple mini-based satellite processors are used to perform subsidiary or local processing functions—or intelligent terminal controllers and devices are used. Sometimes the latter are replaced or augmented by real-time process controllers and devices.

Hierarchical structures having two levels of intelligence are probably most common today, although it is easy to configure hierarchical structures with more levels. A three-level hierarchy would probably include both satellite processors and terminal controllers, as in Figure 5-2. A four-level hierarchy might separate the functions of each satellite processor into a local information processor and one or more network processors. The latter would perform functions such as concentration and routing of traffic between the end points and the information proces-

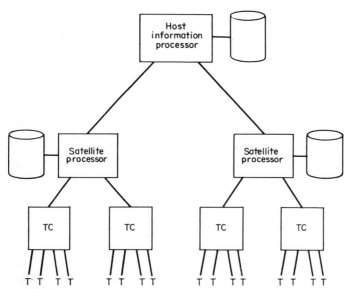

FIG. 5-2 Typical hierarchical system structure. TC = terminal controller; T = terminal device.

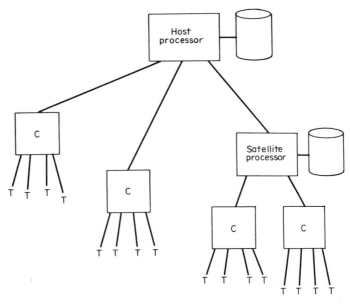

FIG. 5-3 Unbalanced hierarchical structure. C = concentrator; T = terminal device.

sors. Alternatively, a four-level hierarchy might include two levels of satellite processors, with the lower-level satellites less powerful and more specialized than the higher-level ones.

A basic rule in designing hierarchically distributed systems is to spread the processing load up and down the hierarchy in order to locate functions where they can be carried out with the best cost/performance ratio. Functions which are required repeatedly and must exhibit quick response are moved out (down) into the hierarchy as close to the users as is feasible. Other functions less often executed and/or with less stringent response requirements are moved upward toward the center of the hierarchy.

For example, input editing and error detection are best performed very close to the end-point device. This has two advantages: it improves response to the end user, and it avoids having any other component handle erroneous input. As another example, complex functions such as database browsing do not typically require fast response but do require a large database and powerful supporting software. This type of function is most often performed by a large-scale host at the top of the hierarchy. Chapter 15 discusses in more detail methods for determining how best to allocate functions among distributed system components.

This allocation of functions within a hierarchical system leads to the observation that components which are high in the hierarchy become

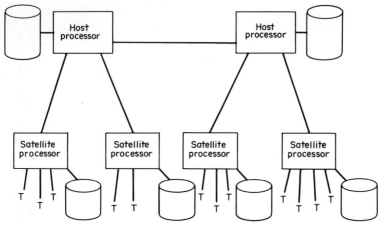

FIG. 5-4 Hybrid distributed-system structure. T = terminal device.

more powerful, but more generalized, than lower-level components. Moving down in the hierarchy, each level is less powerful and more specialized than the level above. In this respect information-system hierarchies mirror organizational hierarchies, whose "components" are people.

5-3. HYBRID DISTRIBUTED PROCESSING

Some complex distributed systems combine the horizontal and hierarchical distribution of processing functions in a structure best called *hybrid*. In the system illustrated in Figure 5-4, two hierarchies are interconnected at the top. The two host processors are involved in the horizontal distribution of information-processing functions.

Whether a distributed system includes one or multiple hierarchies may depend on geographical dispersion, the application(s) served, and/or the organization of the enterprise which owns the information system.

If the functions of the enterprise are tightly clustered geographically, then a distributed system serving that enterprise will generally consist of only one hierarchy. In contrast, an enterprise in which activities are widely dispersed geographically may create multiple hierarchies, one to serve each major geographical area. Interconnection of the hierarchies then allows data exchange and perhaps load leveling and/or resource sharing.

If the application served by the distributed system is relatively (or entirely) isolated from the other information-system applications of the enterprise, it will generally be served by a single hierarchy. For example, a factory-control system might be implemented independently of all other computerized applications. On the other hand, applications interdependent with other computerized applications tend to be best served by linked hierarchies. A manufacturing-control system, implemented as a hierarchy, might be linked to an order-entry hierarchical system handling orders and shipment of the finished goods from the production system.

If the organization of an enterprise is heavily centralized, its information system will often consist of a single hierarchy—or of a centralized, rather than a distributed, system. If the organization has multiple semi-independent major subdivisions, then each of these may be served by an individual information-system hierarchy. The individual hierarchies would be interconnected at the top as necessary.

This flexibility of processing structure, in contrast to the relatively rigid centralized system structures most used today, makes it possible to fit the information-system applications very closely to the needs of the enterprise.

5-4. LOGICAL AND PHYSICAL SYSTEM STRUCTURES

The distinction between the *logical structure* of a distributed system and the *physical interconnection,* or *linking scheme,* is very important. The discussions so far in this chapter (Units 5-1, 5-2, and 5-3) have dealt with

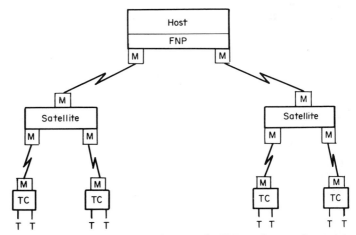

FIG. 5-5 Hierarchy with simple network. FNP = front-end network processor; M = modem; TC = terminal controller; T = terminal device.

logical structures, or how the component elements *relate* to one another. The following example will serve to put logical structures and physical structures into a unified perspective.

Physical structures are determined by how the processing and database elements are actually linked into a system. Perhaps some which are close together will be connected using cables (interface channels or buses). Those which are farther apart are usually linked via data-communications facilities. The specific facilities used are chosen based on analyses of cost/performance ratios and can range from very low-speed circuits to channels on orbiting communications satellites. To illustrate the possibilities of different physical structures, Figure 5-5 shows a hierarchical system connected in a very straightforward manner using telephone links and modems.

These same system components are show again in Figure 5-6, this time linked by a meshed network structure such as that of a value-added network (VAN) carrier service in the United States or a public data network (PDN) in another country. The network interconnections now form a complex structure with a link from each processor and terminal controller into the network.

This type of network is controlled by mini- or micro-based network processors, so not only links and modems but NPs have been used to provide the network-processing functions which interconnect the component elements. The logical structure remains the same, even in the

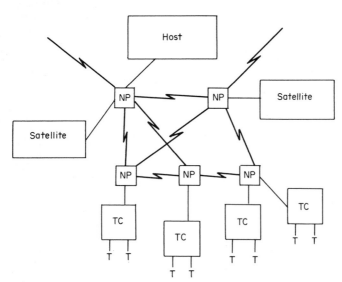

FIG. 5-6   Hierarchy with complex network. NP = network processor; TC = terminal controller; T = terminal device.

Figure 5-6 system; the host interfaces mainly with the satellite processors, which communicate with the host and with the terminal controllers.

The major difference in this alternate interconnection scheme is that the host is able to communicate directly with the terminal controllers, since transmission paths are now available. In the Figure 5-5 version of this system, data-communications economies dictate that low-volume message interchange between the host and the terminal controllers be via the satellites. The logical relationships remain the same; the physical implementation varies.

The discussion in Chapter 6 of distributed database structures is phrased in terms of logical structures and interconnections. Chapter 7, which discusses network processing, returns to the question of physical interconnections.

6

DISTRIBUTED DATABASE STRUCTURES

The distribution of information-processing functions often causes the data which support those functions to be distributed. When related data elements are stored at two or more locations and the data relationships cause interlocation access and/or coordination among the locations, these data elements form a distributed database. There are two basic structures for database distribution; partitioned and replicated. Complex systems may combine both partitioned and replicated structures.

6-1. PARTITIONED DATABASES

A *conceptual database* is a collection of all of the data of interest to an enterprise. Often only part of a conceptual database is implemented in the form of computerized data storage; other parts may be maintained manually. A *partitioned database* is formed when a conceptual database is separated into nonredundant sections—*partitions*—and spread across two or more information processors. In the case of a partitioned database, the conceptual database is generally designed and thought of as a single entity. However, the database (or that portion of the database which is computerized) is created only in the form of its partitions. These partitions, each attached to a different information processor, logically form a single database.

A partitioned database consists of nonredundant data elements. That is, a specific piece of data is stored at only one location within the distributed database. The logical database *structure* can be either nonredundant or redundant. For example, consider a distributed system formed by interconnecting a host in each of a company's major divisions. Payroll data might be stored at each location, and the structure (records, fields, interrecord linkages) of data storage might be identical at each location. However, the data concerning any one employee would appear in only one of the locations. This would therefore be a distributed payroll database with nonredundant data but common (redundant) structures. On the other hand, one of the interlinked hosts might be performing an

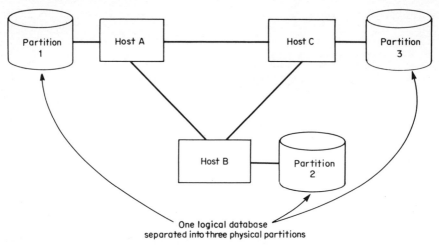

FIG. 6-1 Generic partitioned-database structure.

order-entry application while another performed production control. The data stored at the two hosts would form a distributed database in which the data elements and structure were both nonredundant. The generic structure of a partitioned database is illustrated in Figure 6-1.

Partitioning may be chosen in a distributed database to move data elements close to where access requests for those elements originate and/ or to improve privacy and security by separating sensitive data from public data.

The methods by which a database is partitioned and decisions about locating each partition are very closely related to the information-processing structure of the distributed system. In many cases processing functions are moved as close as is feasible to the users of those functions, and this often forces the movement of the stored data which support those functions. Partitioning is one form of data movement—a static form which takes place during system design and implementation. The example systems presented in this chapter show the close relationship between processing and database structures in distributed systems.

Databases can be partitioned in any of several ways, either within a horizontal or a hierarchical processing structure. Some possible methods of partitioning include: 1) via geographic boundaries; 2) across a hierarchical structure; 3) for purposes of security or privacy.

Geographically Partitioned Databases

One company, which operates two information processors interconnected to form a horizontally distributed system, provides an example of the use of a geographically partitioned database. The company's total (conceptual) database is split into two partitions, one attached to each host. Thus, both the processing load and the database accesses are separated between the two locations. The company operates nationwide within the United States; its computer centers are located as shown in Figure 6-2.

This company's system locates database elements in a logical way. Database elements heavily accessed by East Coast users are located at the Eastern host, those most heavily accessed by West Coast users at the Western host. Elements accessed from intermediate locations must be equitably distributed between the two centers. The type of database partitioning this company uses is only practical if there is a natural geographic grouping of database-access requirements. If there is not— if, for example, access to all data elements occurs equally from all geographical areas—then partitioning will cause too much traffic between centers to be practical. In that case a different database structure and/or a different system structure must be chosen.

An important reason for the geographical grouping of data elements is the fact that the cost of transmitting data among remote locations is generally high. In most cases it costs less to obtain telephone facilities in the United States when the transmission distances are shorter, more when they are longer. Even in cases where transmission costs are insensitive to distance, as in some packet-network services, transmission volume remains an important factor. Local access to desired data can in many cases reduce costs by eliminating the use of carrier facilities. However, tariff-cost trends must be studied in some depth to determine where it is

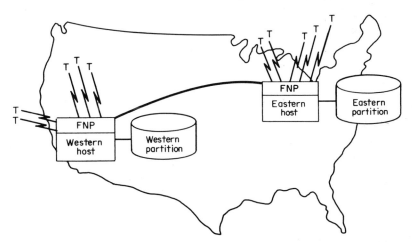

FIG. 6-2 Geographically partitioned database. FNP = front-end network processor; T = terminal device.

most important to minimize data transmission. This topic is discussed in more detail in Chapter 17.

Figure 6-2 illustrates a system in which provision must be made for at least some databases access from outside of the area where the data partition is located. The East Coast database partition will sometimes be accessed from West Coast locations, and vice versa. Such access must be allowed in a distributed database. However, the great majority of the accesses to each section of the database will originate locally. If this is not the case, the database has been partitioned incorrectly and/or the system structure has been poorly chosen.

Hierarchically Partitioned Databases

Another method of forming a partitioned database is to distribute the data elements across a system hierarchy, as shown in Figure 6-3.

This system consists of a processing hierarchy which corresponds to the organizational hierarchy. Such correspondence is fairly typical. The host handles corporate-level processing, and a corporate database partition is attached. Each division has its own satellite processor; two of these are shown. Each divisional satellite maintains its own local database partition. There is no duplication of information among the database segments shown. In effect, therefore, the data elements at all locations form a corporate database which has been partitioned across the processors within the hierarchy.

Information is exchanged both up and down the hierarchy. Corpo-

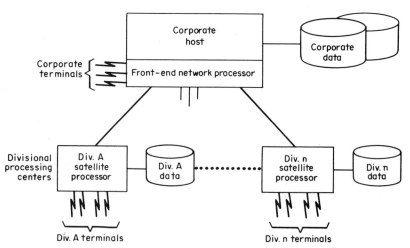

FIG. 6-3   Hierarchically partitioned database.

rate-level reports must consolidate information from the divisional locations with corporate-level information. Data also travel down the hierarchy, as goals and budgets are established at the corporate level and passed down to the divisional level for storage at the satellite processors. These interrelationships are the basis for classifying this system as one having a partitioned distributed database, rather than separate, independent databases.

The system structure shown in Figure 6-3 is fairly common, although in many enterprises the divisional or departmental computer centers are not directly connected to the corporate-level center. In such enterprises data exchange is often accomplished via magnetic tape or even via output on printed reports at one level and reinput via terminal or key-entry at another level.

Coordination of database elements at the corporate and divisional levels in these decentralized systems is typically very difficult. Although the corporate-level database often includes summaries or copies of divisional data, these may be inaccurate or out of date. Without direct and dynamic communication among the IPs, it is difficult to determine which data are accurate.

The Figure 6-3 system structure with its distributed database eliminates these problems. Data are not summarized or copied; instead, they are maintained at the level to which they directly relate—corporate data at the corporate level and data pertaining to each division at the appropriate divisional center. The distributed-processing relationship among these centers allows any processor to access data at any location, subject to whatever security or privacy controls have been imposed.

Indeed, it is important to realize that even within a single business or governmental entity, sensitive data must be protected against misuse. The definition of which data are sensitive varies widely and may be quite subjective. In one large, multidivision U.S. corporation, for example, each division operates very much like an independent company. In fact, the divisions compete with each other as well as with other companies. Each of these divisions sends financial data to the corporate-level computer system, but none exchange these data with the other divisions. In this company's hierarchical system, therefore, data move mainly up the hierarchy, and occasionally down, but *never* across. There is no technical reason why data movement between divisions is impractical, but each division wants to protect its data and share them only with the corporate level. Situations of this kind are common, and they occur in almost every type of organization. They must be watched for carefully so that distributed systems can be planned in a way that will allow them to satisfy the need for data protection.

Database Partitioning to Improve Security and Privacy

The use of database partitioning to improve security or privacy protection is shown in an example system schematic in Figure 6-4. This example shows a hierarchical system in which the host handles a wide variety of applications and maintains a large database. This large database can

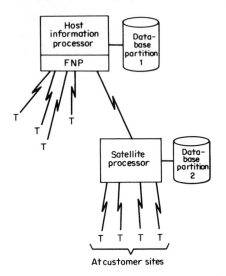

FIG. 6-4 Database partitioning for security protection. FNP = front-end network processor; T = terminal device.

be viewed as partition 1 of the partitioned database. A mini-based satellite is also configured. It has its own nonredundant database partition.

The satellite is dedicated to an order-entry application in which this company's customers are given direct access, via terminals, to the satellite-based order-entry system. Customers can enter orders via their terminals and can inquire on the status of their orders at any time. (This system represents an evolution from earlier methods in which customers sent in orders via telegram which were then keyed in on terminals attached to the host. The double keying, once by the customer and once by the vendor, caused a duplication of effort and a loss of time. It was also a potential source of errors.)

If all applications were consolidated on the host information processor, it would be very difficult in the current state of the art to guarantee security and privacy protection. Partitioning this application, and the supporting database elements, prevents customers from accessing the host system or its database. Database and application partitioning thus ease the problem of security and privacy enormously. Protection can be concentrated at the link between the host and satellite processors.

6-2.   REPLICATED DATABASES

The other method of creating a distributed database is to place copies of all or parts of the data at two or more locations. This structure is called a *replicated database*. The generic replicated database structure is shown in Figure 6-5.

As in database partitioning, replication serves to move the data elements close to where requests originate. The difference is that when replication is used to create a distributed database, only a duplicate rather than the original of the data is moved.

In a replicated database, multiple copies of the data improve availability. In a carefully designed system the replicated data can serve the same purpose as database journals, providing a backup copy of the data. (This advantage will, of course, be minimized if the various copies are at different stages of updating and must be synchronized prior to use as backup.)

Selective data replication can also increase privacy protection for data. Publicly available data elements can be replicated and made easily accessible, while sensitive data are retained at a single location where strict privacy-protection procedures can be enforced. This is a variation of the kind of privacy protection, discussed in Unit 6-1, obtainable through partitioning.

A replicated database can be formed in several ways; for example, by copying data within a hierarchy or by copying data within a horizontally distributed system.

Hierarchically Replicated Databases

An example of database replication within a hierarchy is shown in Fig-

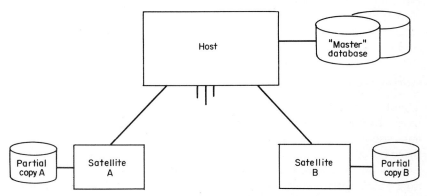

FIG. 6-5 Generic replicated-database structure. Each satellite has a copy of the data needed to support the local processing.

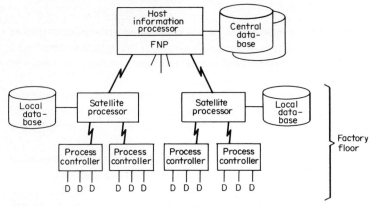

FIG. 6-6 Hierarchically replicated database. FNP = front-end network processor; D = device.

ure 6-6. This is the same production-control system illustration used in Chapter 3.

In this system the host maintains a master database containing the production schedule for the entire factory. This database supports the host's function of scheduling factory operations for a relatively long-range period—usually for several weeks and often for several months.

Each satellite maintains a copy of part of the host's master database. Each local data copy contains only information pertaining to the factory devices which are under the control of that specific satellite. Therefore, each satellite's local data copy differs from all other local data copies. It is also important to note that the local data copy at each satellite contains only the short-range schedule for the factory devices which the satellite controls. Each local data copy thus replicates only the data needed for short-term scheduling and control of the devices. New schedule information may be transmitted from the host to each satellite daily, thus allowing each satellite to update its database copy for the next period of factory operation.

Horizontally Replicated Databases

The next example, shown schematically in Figure 6-7, includes a database which is horizontally replicated (and partially partitioned). This database is used in an inventory-control application which is shared by three horizontally distributed hosts.

Each host maintains stock-balance information only for its locally produced items. (In other words, this part of the distributed database is partitioned.) For items manufactured and/or stocked at other locations the host maintains only basic descriptive information, including a record

of the location(s) where the item is stocked. Each host's data thus partially replicate every other host's data. Such an arrangement allows orders
for items not stocked locally to be checked for validity and to be priced
for credit checking before requests concerning item availability are sent
to the stocking locations. Nonexistent items are detected as input errors
and rejected at once. In effect, the replication in this database is an
example of a global directory or catalog of stocked items. A general
discussion of global database directories is provided in Chapter 16.

Database replication is most often used in hierarchically distributed
systems. Horizontal system structures most often employ database partitioning or even use a separate, independent database at each host
location.

6-3. COMBINATION PARTITIONED AND REPLICATED DATABASES

Although database partitioning and database replication are distinct
techniques which can be used separately, they are often combined in
order to achieve the optimum distributed database structure. (The system just discussed illustrates one type of combination.) In combining
these techniques, frequently used static data are replicated for easy access at all locations. More active data, whose replication would cause
severe synchronization problems, are partitioned, and each partition is
located where the activity against it is greatest.

Databases combining partitioning and replication might be employed
in the future airline reservation system illustrated in Figure 3-6 in Chap-

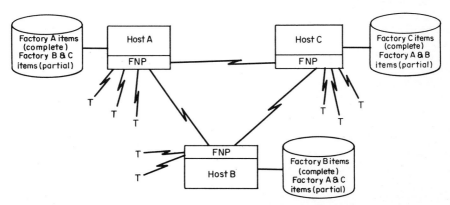

FIG. 6-7 Horizontally replicated database. FNP = front-end network processor; T =
terminal device.

ter 3. In that example system, the most active data—flight bookings—would be partitioned geographically. The records for any specific flight would be maintained at only one regional host, and all bookings for that flight would be processed at that host. Schedule and rate information, on the other hand, is relatively static in comparison to booking information. It would be replicated at all of the regional hosts. Inquiries for available flights, ticket prices, and so on, could therefore be handled locally by each host. Such a combination of database replication and partitioning will probably become quite common in distributed systems in the future.

7

NETWORKING STRUCTURES

Network-processing functions support data movement among system elements which are not physically close enough together to be cable-connected. Most often, network-processing functions connect geographically remote elements. Occasionally, they connect elements which are in adjacent rooms, or even in the same room. The principles of network processing are the same no matter what the distances involved. This chapter discusses commonly used network structures. Although there are only two basic structures, they offer a wide variety of methods for interconnecting information-system elements to meet specific application requirements.

The logical structure of a distributed information system is determined by the relationships among the elements—host and satellite processors, terminals, etc.—which make up the system. The task of network processing is to provide a communications network formed of physical network-processing hardware and facilities and of network-processing software functions which will support these logical relationships.

Network-processing hardware and facilities include the following elements:

- *Transmission facilities:* telephone lines and trunks, microwave links, communications-satellite links, etc.

- *Coupling facilities:* modems and other devices used to interface terminals and processors to transmission facilities.

- *Multiplexors:* used to combine the traffic from multiple slower-speed links onto a single higher-speed link.

- *Network processors:* used for concentration and/or switching, and/or to provide an interface between an information processor and the surrounding network.

Network-processing software controls the intelligent network processor(s) of a network and provides functions such as concentration, link management, terminal control, routing, and sometimes journalization. Together, the network-processing hardware, facilities, and software make up the communications network. Communications networks link together the processor and terminal components of a distributed system (or of a centralized system). A network is designed in order to achieve three goals:

- To provide the necessary data paths among elements
- To support the system response and throughput goals
- To minimize the cost of transmission facilities

The network design must therefore trade off system requirements against the cost of availability facilities until an optimum combination of cost and level of service is attained.

One of the reasons that the design of communications networks is so complex is that transmission costs are set by a variety of different regulatory agencies. Each such agency—at the national, regional (state, in the U.S.), or local level—approves a set of tariffs for each communications carrier. These tariffs define the classes of service offered and the cost of each class. Tariffs are generally based upon the speed of transmission allowed and the length of the transmission path. For example, in the U.S. a coast-to-coast voice-grade link—basic 2400 bps (bits per second) capability—costs a given amount. A broadband link (19.2 kbps and up) of the same length costs a different amount. So does the cost of a circuit on a communications satellite; it is usually much lower per bit for large volume transmission. However, there are no straightforward relationships between different tariffs. Intrastate tariffs in some locations are much higher than in other locations. Interstate tariffs are often lower, for a comparable service, than intrastate tariffs.

These complexities mean that it is difficult to arrive at the most effective network configurations except through repeated attempts at optimization. And, all cost-optimization techniques operate within the framework of the two major categories of network structure: hierarchical networks and meshed networks.

7-1.   HIERARCHICAL NETWORKS

The most common class of network structure is the hierarchy, in which the communications facilities form a tree structure. The simplest form of hierarchical network is often called a *star network*. Figure 7-1 shows an example of a star network.

Star networks are so named because of the structure of "rays" radiating from a single central point: the information processor. However, as later examples show, the star structure can equally well be considered the basic form of hierarchical network.

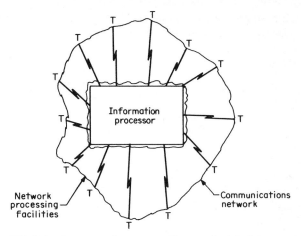

FIG. 7-1 Star network structure. T = terminal device.

In an information system which includes distributed processing, and perhaps a distributed database, the network structure becomes more complex. An example of a hierarchical network supporting a hierarchically distributed system is shown schematically in Figure 7-2.

In this illustration the physical structure of the network-processing facilities exactly mirrors the logical relationships among the processing and terminal elements. There are direct connections between closely

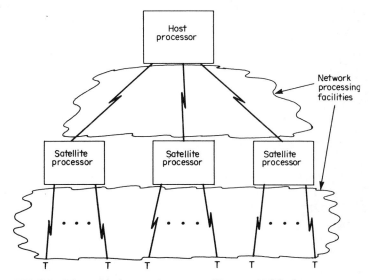

FIG. 7-2 Hierarchical network structure. T = terminal device.

related elements; elements which are only indirectly related–in this case the host and the terminals–have no direct interface and must communicate via the satellite processors.

These examples illustrated in Figures 7-1 and 7-2 show the simplest possible network-processing structures. Transmission links are shown, but they are only one of two elements needed to establish the desired data-movement paths. Also required, but not shown are coupling devices such as modems. Such coupling devices are needed to connect the links with the processors and terminals. Even in these simple cases, the physical facilities must be supported by logical network-processing functions which control the links. These logical functions may be incorporated into the host and satellite information processors and the terminal elements and thus be co-resident with information-processing and database functions. They may instead be embodied in independent network processors. Figure 7-3 illustrates the first of these alternatives by showing network-processing functions integrated into information-processing components. Figure 7-4 illustrates the second alternative. It shows the same system configured in such a way that independent front-end network processors (FNPs) handle the data-communications functions.

The terminals in these examples are presumed to be hard-wired devices, and their network-processing functions are therefore built-in. If intelligent, firmware- or software-driven devices were used, these devices would include logical network-processing functions to enable them to handle the linkage between the terminal and other system elements.

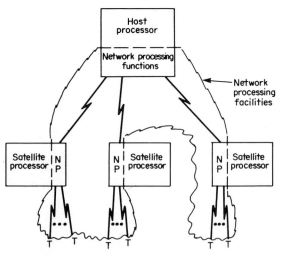

FIG. 7-3 Integrated network-processing functions. NP = network processor.

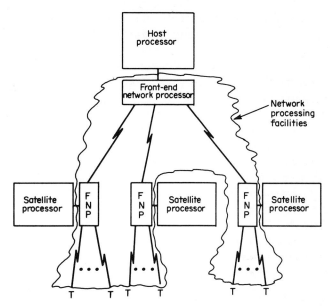

FIG. 7-4 Independent network-processing functions. T = terminal device.

The examples in Figures 7-1, 7-2, 7-3, and 7-4 illustrate only the most straightforward use of physical data-communications facilities and the logical network-processing functions needed to control those facilities. However, the need to minimize communications-link costs often calls for the consideration of alternative network configurations.

In general, the greater the number of communications links used, and the greater their lengths, the higher the cost of the transmission facilities. To minimize the number and distance of the links needed, multiplexors and/or concentrators are often used.

A *multiplexor* is a device, usually unintelligent, which multiplexes data from multiple links onto a single higher-speed link; a *concentrator* is an intelligent, programmable device which performs the same function. The main difference between the two is that a multiplexor cannot accept input link speeds with greater total capacity than the output link—since the multiplexor does not buffer data it must dispose of it instantly. A concentrator, in contrast, can buffer traffic and can therefore handle unbalanced input and output link capacities.

A fairly recent product innovation is the *statistical* or *intelligent* multiplexor. Such multiplexors include a microprocessor and usually a small buffer. They can therefore handle small differences in input and output capacities and can pack data on the output link for efficiency.

Multiplexing or concentration is useful because of the rate structures usually found in communications tariffs. These rates make it more attractive to obtain a smaller number of higher-speed links than a larger number of lower-speed links. For example, it might be assumed that a link capable of handling 2400 bps is eight times as expensive as a link capable of handling 300 bps. This is not the case. Often, in fact, the higher-speed link is less than twice as expensive as the lower-speed link. Similarly, a broadband link (19.2 kbps and up) may be less than twice as expensive as a voice-grade link (2400 bps and up), although it may handle far more than twice as much data throughput. Multiplexing and concentration take advantage of these rate structures by using a single higher-speed link to replace a number of lower-speed links.

To illustrate the use of these devices, the example network from Figure 7-4 is repeated, with variations, in Figure 7-5.

In this figure a concentrator has been used to connect some of the terminal links to one of the satellite processors, thus reducing the mile-

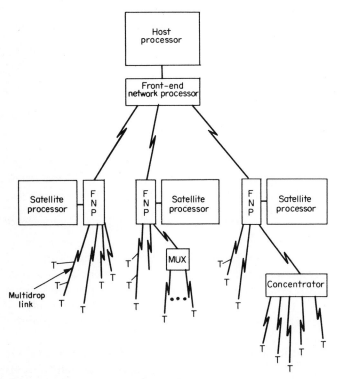

FIG. 7-5 Link cost-reduction techniques. MUX = multiplexor; T = terminal device.

age and number of links required. The use of a multiplexor is also shown.

Figure 7-5 illustrates another cost-reduction technique: the use of multidrop links. A multidrop link connects several terminals to the same communications link. The terminals involved in multidropping must have special logic to avoid interference among them; generally only one or two of the terminals on a multidrop link can be active at one time. The use of multidrop configuration reduces costs in the same way that the use of multiplexors and concentrators does: the number and lengths of communications links are minimized. All network-processing structures must allow for cost-minimization techniques such as these. The techniques do not affect the basic network structure; they simply change the specific configuration.

7-2   MESHED NETWORKS

The other major class of network structure is called meshed. A meshed network, unlike many hierarchical networks, is intended to interconnect directly all of the elements (or at least all of the intelligent elements) of a distributed system. (Sometimes meshed networks are called *distributed.* This choice of terminology is poor, because of the potential confusion with the phrase, *distributed system.* However, since this use of *distributed* is fairly widespread, it is mentioned here. Further discussion of this type of network will use the term *meshed.*) The simplest case of a meshed network is a fully connected network such as that shown in Figure 7-6.

Because there are four hosts in this distributed system, each host has three links, one to each of the other hosts. The total number of links necessary in this case is six, quite a reasonable number but larger than the minimum necessary to connect each site to all other sites. In a meshed-network structure, terminals usually access the network via the nearest host, thus avoiding the very large number of connections which would be necessary if each terminal end point were directly connected to every host and to every other terminal. In general, a terminal most often accesses one host, so connection to other locations via that host is reasonable.

Although the fully connected form of meshed network is the simplest, and provides a great deal of redundancy for availability and load-leveling purposes, it is not usually cost-effective. An alternative network structure for the example used in Figure 7-6 is shown in Figure 7-7.

Each host is still able to communicate with every other host, but in some cases the connection is via another location. To avoid traffic, particularly through traffic, passing through the hosts, the logical network-

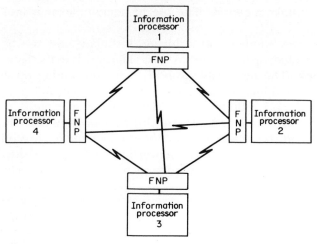

FIG. 7-6 Fully connected network structure. FNP = front-end
network processor.

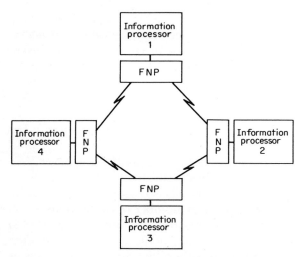

FIG. 7-7 Meshed-network structure. FNP = front-end network processor.

processing functions are implemented in independent front-end network processors. These FNPs route data as necessary among the host
locations.

The meshed-network structure has one fairly significant advantage
over the hierarchical-network structure. It provides redundant paths, so

that the loss of any one link does not usually isolate any component. In Figure 7-7, for example, the link between the FNPs for Host 1 and Host 2 might be lost. These two hosts could still communicate, however, via the links to the FNPs for Hosts 3 and 4.

The most common form of meshed network falls somewhere between the "minimum links" approach of Figure 7-7 and the "fully connected" approached of Figure 7-6. An example of a meshed network designed for packet switching is shown in Figure 7-8.

The intelligent network processors control the links in this type of meshed network. Messages from the host, satellites, and terminal controllers are broken into fixed-length packets—typically 100 bytes or less —for transmission. Since each packet may be routed independently through the network, it is possible to allow for load leveling of the traffic. But since each packet may travel independently, the packets which make up a message may arrive out of sequence at the destination NP. In most packet networks, the destination NP reassembles the packets into the correct sequence; occasionally, this function is performed by the receiving processor or controller.

Packet networks such as the one illustrated in Figure 7-8 provide redundancy and therefore high availability. Depending on the specific configuration, there may be various numbers of alternate paths between any two end points, and there is almost always a minimum of two possible paths between any two locations. Thus the network's vulnerability to

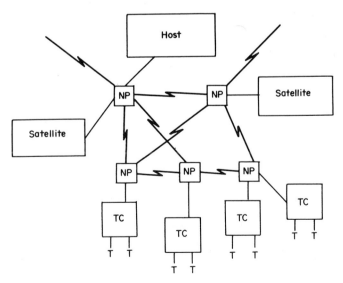

FIG. 7-8   Packet-switching meshed network. NP = network processor; TC = terminal controller; T = terminal device.

link failure is reduced. The routing methods used in packet networks can also provide a high degree of load leveling, so that, in general, a smaller number of links are required than would otherwise be the case.

Packet networks use one of two methods for routing traffic: datagrams or virtual circuits.

Datagram methods require that each packet carry its destination and packet identifier in a packet header. This allows complete freedom of routing–each packet can take a different route through the network and be reunited with related packets on exit from the network. If messages typically consist of multiple packets, the datagram approach requires that packet-to-message reassembly logic be provided—either in the network processors or in the information processors and terminal controllers.

The datagram technique is very well-suited to cases in which short messages are sent between end points dynamically—that is, cases in which relationships between pairs of end points are established and broken off frequently. As an example, messages from one computer researcher to other researchers at multiple locations would be well served by a datagram system.

Virtual circuit methods establish a logical connection between two end points (e.g., two IPs, an IP and a terminal controller) and retain that connection during a session or exchange of messages. The protocols of data exchange usually prevent packet out-of-sequence conditions and may not require packet ID in every packet. A given logical connection may imply a fixed physical route through the network or may allow routing flexibility.

The virtual circuit approach is well-suited to cases in which pairs of end points stay logically linked for relatively long periods of time. Bank teller terminals linked to a host processor for transaction input/output throughout the business day provide an example of a situation suited to the virtual circuit approach.

In general, packet networks are very well-suited to interactive traffic and to mixtures of batch (jobs, file transfer, etc.) and interactive traffic. It may be necessary, however, to use a larger packet size to achieve adequate throughput for high-volume traffic. On the other hand, packet approaches are ill suited to continuous high-volume data transfer. If two processors regularly exchange files, jobs, or other data, a dedicated high-speed link or links will provide more satisfactory service than packet transmission. And although some form of meshed network will probably be the best choice in a large distributed system, the simple hierarchical structure is the more suitable choice for small-to-medium size distributed (and centralized) systems.

DISTRIBUTED SYSTEM AND NETWORK ARCHITECTURES

An *architecture* is a framework or structure which dictates how something is constructed. An information-system architecture defines two things:

• Modularity
• Interfaces for communication among modules

The term *architecture* is used in many different contexts when information systems are discussed. For example, a computer hardware architecture determines the major modules from which the computer is constructed and the way in which these modules interface to work together. Some hardware architectures are integrated, processor-centered; in these architectures all input/output (I/O) passes through the processor. Some hardware architectures are memory-centered; in these architectures all active modules access a shared memory system via a controller which resolves access conflicts. Both processor-centered and memory-centered architectures define a computer's major hardware modules and their interactions.

The term *architecture* is also used in discussing the software of information systems. In this context, *architecture* refers to the way in which the code is modularized and the interaction of the various modules. For example, an operating system can be designed to be *event-driven*—to react to each event (such as receipt of a transaction) when the event occurs. This requires a different module structure and set of interfaces than are needed in a batch-oriented operating system.

Architectural concepts are extremely important in the context of distributed systems. Because these systems are complex, a logically organized structure is needed to reduce this complexity to manageable proportions.

Distributed system architectures begin at the "total system" level, covering both hardware and software. These high-level architectures define the broad structure of the system hardware and software elements and the relationships and interfaces among these elements. Lower-level architectures define the specific hardware or software architectures of individual system components.

This section explores system architectural concepts and several applications of these concepts. Chapter 8 describes the concept of layered functions. This is a concept which is being applied almost universally in system architectures. Chapter 8 also explains the difference between protocols and interfaces and describes how architectural concepts relate to implementation and to the degree of flexibility allowed for alternative implementations.

Chapters 9 through 12 analyze several architectures for networking and/or distributed systems. Because it was the first system-level architecture announced and has influenced—to a greater or lesser degree—all subsequent architectual approaches, the Systems Network Architecture (SNA) of International Business Machines Corporation (IBM) is described first. Architectures used by Digital Equipment Corporation (DEC) and Honeywell Information Systems (HIS) are also discussed in some detail, and shorter descriptions of the architectural approaches of several other vendors are provided. Each architecture is presented in terms of its basic structure and/or concepts, its visible protocols (as contrasted to internal interfaces known only to those who implement the system), the parts of the vendor's product line currently encompassed within the architecture, and the types of structures (as defined in Section 3) which it is designed to support.

Since all of these vendors' architectures and product offerings are evolving, Chapters 9 through 12 represent, at best, a snapshot of current developments. Within that constraint, however, the information provided will allow evaluation of an architecture for use in specific applications or within a particular environment.

8

SYSTEM ARCHITECTURAL PRINCIPLES

It is important to understand the principles and concepts which are common to all system architectures. The concepts described in this chapter represent today's state of the art in the design of complex information systems and are used in all of the vendor-supplied architectures discussed in Chapters 9 through 12.

8-1. LAYERED FUNCTIONS

A layered structure involves a hierarchical concept of functions at multiple logical levels. Generally, levels progress from the physical to the logical; that is, from close association with the computer or communications hardware to complete independence from the hardware. The general idea of layered functions is not new; it has been in use—particularly in operating-system development—for some time. However, it is currently being applied more formally than in the past. An example of layered functions is presented in Figure 8-1, which shows how the concept could be applied to database management.

At the bottom of Figure 8-1, Layer 1 handles the device-specific I/O functions. Only this layer is concerned with the detailed characteristics of the storage media; at the higher levels data are simply read from or written to storage space.

Layer 2, the next level up, handles the logical functions of reading and writing, without regard to physical characteristics. Layer 3 manages the database structure. For example, in an indexed structure this layer would create and update the indices. Layer 3 also maintains awareness of the data formats, so that it can unpack fields from records on user request. Layer 4 maps the various specialized user interfaces of Layer 5 to common system functions. Layer 5 consists of a variety of different user interfaces, each tailored to meet the needs of a specific class of users.

The Figure 8-1 illustration does not represent any specific database management system, and in fact most software systems today are less

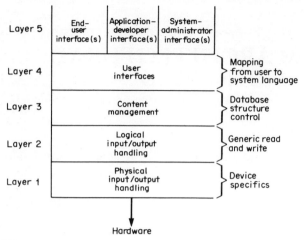

FIG. 8-1 Layered functions.

rigorous than this example in their stratification of functions. However, the example shows how progression from "low" functional levels to "high" functional levels is achieved by means of the layered approach.

The main reason for layering functions is to increase the modularity of the software, so that parts of it can be changed without affecting other parts.

In the Figure 8-1 structure, for example, it would be possible to add a new type of storage device, changing only Layer 1, unless the new device type provided totally new logical capabilities. Similarly, new interfaces for specific classes of users could be added in Layer 5 without affecting the remaining layers, unless these interfaces called for new functions not previously provided.

One reason for using database management to illustrate the layered function concept is that the concept is too often thought of only in the context of network architectures—i.e., the movement of messages across a communications network. In fact, these same principles can be, and are being, applied to any or all areas of information systems.

8-2. PROTOCOLS

According to *Webster's*, a *protocol* is "a code of diplomatic or military etiquette or precedence." In computer systems, *protocol* has come to mean a set of rules (a *code*) for the exchange of information between two or more components. *Protocol* and *interface* are often used interchangeably. However, in system architectures the two terms are used differently. A protocol provides for information exchange between two copies of the same functional layer and may be formally defined, often by a national or international standards group; an interface provides for requests for service between adjacent functional layers and is usually limited to use within one vendor's product line or even within one product. This section discusses protocols; Unit 8-3 discusses interfaces. Protocols and interfaces are shown graphically in Figure 8-2.

Protocols, like functions, tend to be layered. When discussing protocols, however, the term *level* is generally used instead of *layer,* although the concept is the same. Each protocol defines:

- Formats for data exchange
- Commands and responses for data exchange

The components involved in any exchange of data must use and understand the same formats, as defined by the protocol. They must also use a mutually agreed-upon sequence of commands and responses (SEND, ACK, ERROR, . . .) to accomplish the data exchange.

To illustrate how protocols work, Figure 8-3 shows the structure of functions and protocols defined by CCITT (the International Consultative Committee on Telephony and Telegraphy) as its recommendation* X.25 for interconnection of computer equipment to packet-switched networks.

The physical-level protocol defines the modem connection methods allowed. In the case of X.25, these include the CCITT X.21 and X.21 *bis* and EIA (Electronics Industry Association) RS232C specifications. Level 1 of X.25 is embedded in the hardware implementations of the DTE/ DCE (data-terminal equipment—including computers and/or data-com-

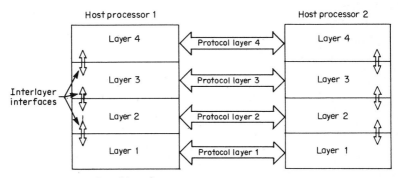

FIG. 8-2   Protocols and interfaces.

*CCITT is an association of communications carriers and does not issue "standards." Instead, its proposals are called *recommendations.* In general, however, these recommendations are widely adhered to by PTTs and in effect have the same status as standards.

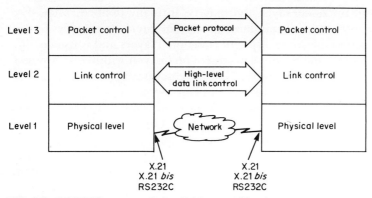

FIG. 8-3 CCITT Recommendation X.25 protocol levels.

munications equipment) connection devices. Electrical interfaces of this type have been well standardized for years, since communication would be impossible without this degree of standardization. This level of X.25 can be treated independently of how the link is logically controlled. This is defined by the higher-level protocols.

Level 2 of CCITT X.25 manages the link interface of the user's equipment (such as computers or intelligent terminal controllers) to the network. The link-control protocol used in X.25 is high-level data link control (HDLC), a bit-oriented protocol defined by the International Standards Organization (ISO). HDLC has many of the same characteristics as IBM's synchronous data link control (SDLC) protocol, which is described in Unit 9-2. The HDLC standard contains a wide range of classes of procedures; CCITT chose a specific subset of these to incorporate as Level 2 of X.25.

The link-control protocol defines the formats of the link header and trailer, as shown in Figure 8-4.

This level of header and trailer serves to delimit a transmission on the

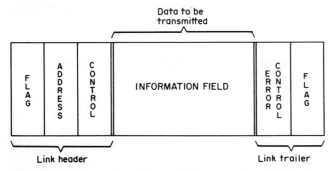

FIG. 8-4 High-level data-link control header and trailer. FLAG = the unique framing byte (content 01111110) which delimits the transmission.

link. In HDLC beginning and ending bytes of a unique pattern (bits 01111110) delimit the *frame,* or transmission increment. The address field determines where the data are to be sent if there is more than one end point on the link (as in a multipoint configuration). The control field contains status, command, and response information related to link control. The link-control protocol also defines the command and response sequences needed to exchange data and to handle error detection and recovery.

Link control receives information from the next higher-level protocol. In X.25 this protocol is packet control. The packet-control protocol provides the end-to-end addressing needed and separates logical messages into packets or frames for use at the link-control level. It also defines an (indirect) interface between the point at which a message enters the communications network and the place at which it leaves. The packet-control protocol includes the definition of the commands and responses by which a message is sent and received. Finally, packet protocol defines a packet header used for addressing, status, and other necessary information.

The relationship between the packet header and the link header and trailer in X.25 is shown in Figure 8-5. In multilevel protocols, header information is typically added in each functional layer and stripped off again when the corresponding layer at the destination location is reached.

In the packet header, an identifier (ID) field determines which of the possible destination types (terminal, computer, cluster controller) the packet is addressed to. The logical channel number is in effect a virtual circuit number and indirectly identifies the desired destination.

The CCITT X.25 recommendation is concerned only with the interface to and from packet-switched networks, such as public data networks

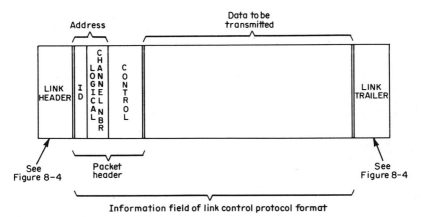

FIG. 8-5   Packer-level header. NBR = number.

(PDNs). It therefore defines only the protocols needed to input data to the network and receive data from the network after transmission. In general, higher-level protocols, which for the sake of convenience can be called *message-level* protocols, are required in order to enable the two entities (computer and terminal controller, for example) at the two ends of the data exchange to understand the data content. Later chapters in this section describe some examples of message-level protocols provided by certain computer vendors.

A hypothetical example of how multiple levels of functions, protocols, and headers can be used when transmitting data between two end points —such as two information processors—is shown in Figure 8-6.

8-3.   INTERFACES

Interfaces are the means by which different functional entities, when resident in the same location, communicate. An interface allows one functional layer to request services from the next lower layer, and receive those services. (This is illustrated in Figure 8-2 on page 73).

Generally, interfaces define formats and commands/responses just as protocols do. The major difference is that the commands and responses may be implicit and rather informal as contrasted to the explicit, formal nature of commands and responses defined in protocols. Figure 8-2

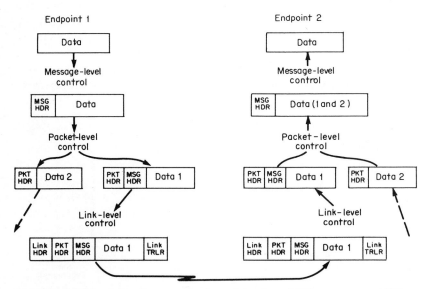

FIG. 8-6 Multilevel functions, protocols, and headers. MSG = message; HDR = header; PKT = packet; TRLR = trailer.

illustrates one reason for this. Interfaces normally occur between sets of functions residing in the same processor or controller, so there is usually no requirement to move the data being exchanged physically across a link. In contrast to interfaces, protocols incorporate the assumption that the two functions exchanging data can only communicate via some type of link—communications circuit or direct-connect cable. This difference encourages more specific and formal definition of protocols than of interfaces.

Interproduct rather than intraproduct interfaces occasionally occur. Most often this happens when a vendor has implemented the same set of functions differently in two or more products. For example, in a large-scale information processor, link-control functions are usually implemented in an independent front-end processor. In a minicomputer the same link-control functions may well be implemented in the information processor itself. In one case, the interface between link control and higher-level functions would cross the boundary between the front-end processor and the host processor, while in the other case the interface would be internal to the mini.

One of the concepts associated with the layered-functions approach is that only adjacent layers can communicate via interfaces; layers which are not adjacent (e.g., Layer 2 and Layer 4 in Figure 8-1 on page 72) can only communicate via the intervening layer(s). A specific implementation of an architecture may, however, violate this concept to improve efficiency.

8-4. PRINCIPLES VERSUS IMPLEMENTATION

One of the strengths of the layered-functions and protocols approach is that a given set of functions can be implemented in multiple ways while retaining compatibility among the various implementations. For example, layered functions were first discussed using database management as an example (Figure 8-1, page 72). Today general-purpose information processors usually include the functions shown, although perhaps not in as orderly a structure as the example. But it is perfectly possible to implement these functions in other ways. For example, Figure 8-7 shows an independent storage controller used with an information processor.

Layer 1, physical I/O handling, has been moved to the storage controller, while Layers 2 through 5 remain in the information processor. It may be necessary to revise the interface between Layer 1 and Layer 2 somewhat, because these layers now communicate via cable rather than in memory. However, if the original design was clean and modular, only relatively minor changes would be needed to accomplish the revision.

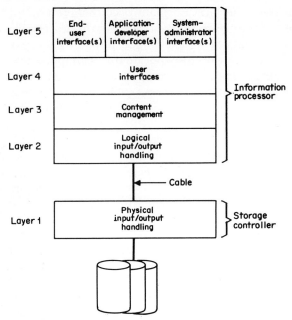

FIG. 8-7   Alternate implementation of database management.

Another way to partition these same functions is shown in Figure 8-8, which illustrates how a free-standing database processor could be constructed.

Finally, Figure 8-9 illustrates a further step in physically separating the functional layers. The database processor has been geographically separated from the information processor, so that it is now necessary to include network-processing functions to handle the interface link. Only the message-control and link-control functions are shown, since these may be adequate in a simple network.

All these examples deal with database management, but the same concepts apply to any set of well-designed functional layers. The layers can be implemented in different products, some can be provided by software, some by firmware, some by hardware. As long as a functional layer is not split and well-defined interfaces are provided, there is a great deal of flexibility in implementation.

The following chapters consider the ways in which several computer vendors are applying the architectural concepts presented here. The terminology used in the chapter or section on a vendor's architecture is, so far as is feasible, the one chosen by the vendor. When the definitions pertaining to these terminologies are not obvious, cross-references to the terminology used in the remainder of this book are provided. Many of these vendor-specific terms are also defined in the glossary.

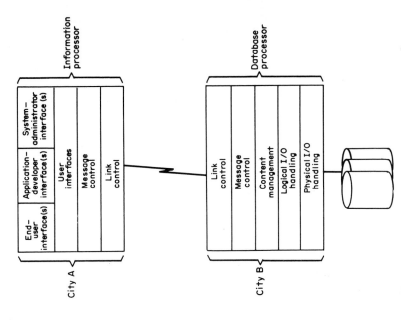

FIG. 8-9 Geographically separated database functions.

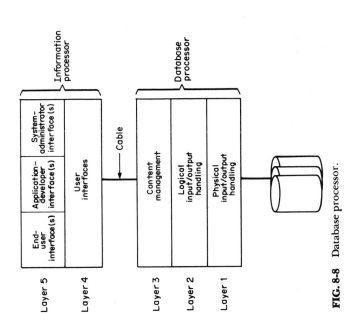

FIG. 8-8 Database processor.

9

IBM'S SYSTEMS NETWORK ARCHITECTURE—SNA

The announcement in September 1974 of the Systems Network Architecture (SNA) by International Business Machines Corporation (IBM) opened the current era of commercially available network and system architectures. This event was preceded by a number of years of research and experimental work, not only by IBM but by a number of other organizations.

The ARPANET is generally considered the precursor of all computer networks and packet-switching networks. It was probably not the first computer network, but because it was funded as a major research project by the U.S. Department of Defense (of which the Advanced Research Projects Agency—ARPA—is a part) and because of its broad scope, it received a great deal of publicity. Other experimental computer networks include the National Physics Laboratory (NPL) net in the United Kingdom and the Cyclades net in France. All these networks made use of the general concepts of functional layers and multilevel protocols described in Chapter 8.

By the time that SNA was announced, a considerable body of experience and expertise in computer networks existed in the computer research community. In the general computer-user community, however, there was no comparable body of expertise, even in the implementation of large terminal networks. While a good many networks had been implemented by late 1974, it is fair to say that many had been "brute-force" efforts. Such efforts often succeeded in spite of the state of the art, not because of it.

These factors had led to the proliferation of different network-processing (*teleprocessing* in IBM's terminology) software access methods and protocols. At the time of the SNA announcement, IBM sites were using over thirty different communications protocols and access methods. Each of these arose because of a particular requirement such as remote job entry, time sharing, transaction processing ("database/data communications"), and message switching. Each served a particular class of user or application well but proved difficult to extend when it was a question of gaining broader scope or increased generality.

These limitations caused some large leading-edge users to develop their own extensions and/or completely new capabilities. Some of these, such as the HASP (Houston automatic-spooling protocol) multileaving workstation interface for remote job entry (RJE), circulated within the IBM-user community and gained semistandard or even standard status. The result was a proliferation of different and inconsistent access methods and protocols.

The proliferation of incompatible access methods and protocols was not a major problem during the first half of the 1960s. Few users operated multidimensional systems. A computer used for database/data communications in an airline reservations system, for example, would typically be dedicated to that function alone. However, as the System 360 came into general use and multidimensional systems became the rule, the teleprocessing situation became more of a problem. Incompatible access methods and protocols often forced organizations to maintain separate terminals and separate links in order to support each different application. For example, an organization might have two similar terminals, side by side, at each remote location, each with its own telephone line to the central computer. One terminal might be used for order entry to one application and the other for database inquiry related to another application. If one terminal or link was down, the other could not be used for both purposes because of the software incompatibilities. The problem was only intensified by the introduction of larger computers such as the System 370.

Network protocols also suffered from inefficiency. When terminals were first attached to computers, telephone lines were expensive, applications were new, and it was usual to transmit only relatively small volumes of data. In addition, transmission speeds were slow, because carriers had little experience in balancing analog telephone lines for digital data transmission. (In 1964 one company spent several months establishing a successful 2400 bps link between the Pacific Northwest and the Midwest. That was considered quite "highspeed" transmission at the time.) As a result, protocol inefficiencies did not, at first, represent a serious difficulty. But as the volume of data to be transmitted grew, these inefficiencies inevitably became a real problem. Large users sometimes formulated their own solutions. For example, some extended the binary synchronous communications (BSC) methods to allow *full-duplex* (FDX) transmission, thus enabling them to send and receive at the same time on the same link. However, these were not general solutions available to all IBM users.

All of these factors made IBM vulnerable to vendors of intelligent front-end processors. COMTEN, Collins, and vendors of minicomputers, such as DEC provided front-end software geared to solve at least some of the IBM user's teleprocessing problems. In addition, IBM users tended to become locked-in to current equipment when running complex remote applications—sometimes with heavily modified system software. They found it hard to take advantage of new IBM offerings. This of course presented IBM with problems in managing the growth and evolution of its customer base.

These factors dictated that SNA must:

- Provide consistent network access methods, making network and terminal characteristics transparent to application programs.
- Allow one terminal to access more than one application in a given computer.
- Improve the efficiency of link protocols.
- Allow different types of terminals to share a single multipoint link.

Initially, SNA was structured with a host-centered, host-controlled philosophy, but it is gradually evolving toward a more flexible approach tailored to true distributed systems and meshed networks.

It is important to view SNA against this background, as the architecture and its initial product realizations grew out of the environment described. SNA and the associated products have evolved considerably since 1974; this chapter describes the currently announced SNA capabilities.

9-1. FUNCTIONAL STRUCTURE

It is possible to gain a general understanding of SNA through analysis of certain concepts which are basic to the architecture and through analysis of its functional and protocol layers. This unit provides an overview of both these topics.

Basic Concepts

In SNA an information network is viewed as a collection of network-addressable units (NAUs). An SNA network links NAUs together via the transmission subsystem—the data-communications network facilities—and provides an interface to each NAU in the form of a transmission subsystem interface (TSI). These SNA logical entities are shown graphically in Figure 9-1.

The network-addressable unit is a location to which data can be sent

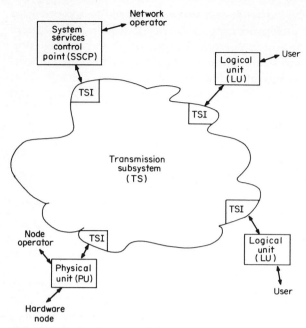

FIG. 9-1 Basic elements of Systems Network Architecture (SNA). Network-addressable units are LU, PU, and SSCP. TSI = transmission subsystem interface.

(that is, NAUs can be addressed). The function of the SNA transmission subsystem (TS) is to route and deliver messages between NAUs.

Each NAU is provided with a transmission subsystem interface. The TSI provides the necessary transparent interface so that the NAU is shielded from the details of the communications network.

The NAU is a general concept, which is realized in three logical entities: physical units, logical units, and the System Services Control Point.

Physical units (PUs) handle the device interface with the network for several types of hardware. These are:

- A terminal with one or more operator stations (keyboards, etc.)
- A terminal cluster controller handling multiple terminals and operator stations
- A communications controller (front-end processor or remote concentrator)
- A host computer

Logical units (LUs) are ports by which applications can communicate with other applications and/or obtain services provided by the network. The LU associated with an application allows that application to be an addressable end point in the SNA network.

The System Services Control Point (SSCP) provides a set of services necessary to the operation of the SNA network. The SSCP is involved, for example, in setting up logical connections between pairs of NAUs when data exchange is required. The SSCP is also responsible for certain error-handling functions. An SSCP is configured in each host processor, and at least one SSCP is necessary to the continued operation of an SNA network.

Logical connections between pairs of NAUs are represented by *sessions*. Before two entities—such as a terminal and an application program—can exchange data, a session must be established. The establishment of the session and its termination involve the SSCP.

The final basic concept described in this section is the idea of attaching multiple-level, or "*cascaded*," headers to data during movement through an SNA network. (This concept was introduced in Chapter 8 and illustrated in Figure 8-6.) As an increment of data passes through the SNA functional layers, each layer may attach another header, which will be stripped off by the comparable layer at the receiving location.

Layered Structure

SNA includes these three major sets of functional layers:

- Application
- Function management
- Transmission subsystem

The application layer includes all of the user-supplied functions as well as a number of vendor-supplied functions. For example, time-sharing services execute in the application layer. The function management layer provides the interface between applications and the transmission subsystem, allowing applications to ignore the details of the communications network and the physical terminal devices being used. The transmission subsystem controls the data-communications network, allowing the transfer of data between programs and devices which are not co-located.

The overall SNA layered structure is shown in Figure 9-2. Each of the sets of functional layers is described in the following paragraphs, starting at the bottom layer.

The transmission subsystem consists of three functional layers, each with associated protocols (see Section 9-2). In fact, SNA includes the same bottom layer—physical control—as all other architectures (see the explanation of CCITT X.25 in Chapter 8) but it is not explicitly defined as a separate layer in most SNA literature.

Data link control (DLC) is the lowest layer of the transmission subsystem. It manages point-to-point or multipoint links between major components of an SNA network. For example, data link control handles links from a host's communications controller to a terminal cluster controller, from the communications controller at the host to a remote communications controller used as a concentrator, or from the concentrator to a cluster controller.

The standard data-communications protocol supported by data-link control is synchronous data-link control (SDLC), described in Section 9-2. DLC also supports a System 370 channel interface protocol, permitting control of channel links to communications controllers and local cluster controllers. Older protocols, such as binary synchronous communications (BSC) and teleprinter, are supported by DLC in order to ease the transition from existing networks to SNA. However, terminals attached via older protocols do not have access to the full range of SNA features.

Path control, the next layer of the transmission subsystem, provides for analysis of destination addresses and selection of the correct route through the network. Path control includes the concept of a *virtual route,* which is a logical path between end points. The concept of virtual route eliminates the need to carry physical-path information with a transmission. Because the virtual route can be implemented across different physical routes as conditions change, it makes SNA less vulnerable to link failures than would otherwise be the case. In general, a standard routing table indicating the shortest paths to specified destinations is used. But the concept of virtual route also makes it possible to implement other, more complex, routing schemes.

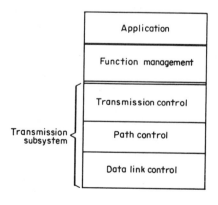

FIG. 9-2 Systems Network Architecture's layered structure.

Transmission control provides for the overall management of sessions between NAUs. The functions provided include the establishment of sessions, termination of sessions, and error management. When an NAU requires communication with another NAU, transmission control —via the SSCP—determines if the connection is allowed and then sets up the necessary control information and opens the session. During a session between two NAUs, transmission control provides the interface between the higher-level function management capabilities and the lower-level transmission-subsystem functions. Transmission control is also involved in closing out a session when communication between the NAUs has been completed.

Function management is the layer of SNA which deals with messages. (Lower-level functions, by contrast, transmit only bit strings.) The addressing of messages takes place in function management. In addition, function management includes the presentation-control facilities which provide a degree of device-independence from terminal characteristics.

The application is the layer in host or satellite processors which includes user- and system-supplied facilities for information processing. In intelligent terminals which support SNA, the application layer provides the necessary addressing function.

9-2. PROTOCOLS

As described in Chapter 8, protocols in SNA allow communication between the same functional layers resident in two different processors. Some of the protocols of SNA are fully visible to the user or, at least, to the application programmer. Others are basically transparent and invisible except to system-software personnel. The major protocol supported by the data link control layer of SNA is synchronous data link control (SDLC). SDLC is a bit-oriented protocol, capable of two-way simultaneous operation on suitable (i.e., 4-wire) transmission facilities.

There are a number of quite similar bit-oriented protocols now defined, and the differences among them can be quite confusing. IBM's work on the protocol which became SDLC triggered much of the interest in protocols of this type, and IBM was very active in the American and international standards activities which defined the ADCCP (advanced data communications control procedure) and high-level data link control (HDLC) protocols. ADCCP, defined by the American National Standards Institute (ANSI), and HDLC, defined by the International Standards Organization (ISO), are both quite similar to SDLC in overall structure and capabilities. But because at a certain point IBM did not adjust its implementations of SDLC to conform to evolving standards, SDLC is similar to but not identical with the ANSI and ISO standards.

SDLC eliminates all the major deficiencies of earlier communications protocols:

• SDLC is bit-oriented, not character-oriented. It is therefore not code-sensitive and can be used to transmit any type of code. It can also be used to transmit pure bit strings (for example, binary data used for downline loading). Older protocols require complex programming to ensure that random bit strings do not duplicate control characters and cause undesired results.

• SDLC can be used in two-way simultaneous (TWS) mode as well as in two-way alternate (TWA) mode. This allows simultaneous transmission and receipt of data on a single circuit (with suitable physical characteristics). Older protocols, designed when unintelligent terminals were incapable of TWS operation, are generally two-way alternate. Today, transmission is increasingly between two intelligent entities, and TWA mode, which wastes much of the potential capacity of the link, is a great handicap.

• SDLC transmission does not require an immediate acknowledgment and as a result can accommodate long transmission delays (provided that the devices have adequate buffering). In general, at least 7 frames (transmission increments) can be sent before an acknowledgment response (ACK) must be returned. With sufficient buffering as many as 127 frames can be sent before an ACK is returned. Older protocols usually require that an ACK be received before the next transmission occurs.

• SDLC separates the control of the data link from higher levels of control such as the management of message sequencing, etc. Many older protocols include combinations of data-link control and higher-level control functions, making it very difficult to evolve them in an orderly manner.

SDLC supports not only point-to-point links and multidrop links, but loop multipoint links as well (see Figure 17-1 in Chapter 17). Loop configurations are especially suited to the economical management of a number of terminals in a relatively confined area. For example, teller terminals in a bank branch or factory-data-collection terminals in a specific area of a factory form ideal configurations for linkage via loop to the communications controller.

These features make SDLC a very attractive protocol, especially for use with intelligent terminals or between communications controllers (e.g., host-to-host communication). However, conversion to SDLC does require new communications interface hardware and often additional cost. These factors led to the need for continued support in SNA products of binary synchronous communications (BSC) in order to provide a reasonable period of transition to the new SDLC environment.

SNA was not designed originally for use with public data networks (PDNs), but was oriented mainly toward private single-user networks. In addition, it was designed prior to the time that CCITT began work on the X.25 and similar recommendations for interface to shared or public networks. As a result, interfaces such as X.25 are not a basic part of SNA. However, IBM has provided X.25 interface capabilities in SNA to its customers in Canada, for use on the Datapac network, and to its customers in France, for use on the Transpac network. While these interfaces do not provide full X.25 capabilities, they do allow SNA-compatible equipment to be connected to the X.25 public nets. It would appear that as pressure for X.25 interconnection grows, both in countries with government-controlled public data networks and in the U.S. because of value-added networks, IBM will evolve to provide better support for X.25 and similar network interfaces.

9-3. PRODUCT SUPPORT

IBM's focus on SNA makes it clear that all new products are, and will be, SNA-compliant. There are still a large number of pre-SNA products and systems in use, but these will be gradually phased out as users convert to the SNA environment. Because SNA, like other architectures for systems or networks, relies heavily on software, the main emphasis in this section is on the software systems which provide the SNA features.

The products which fit within the SNA framework include the following host information processors:

> System 370
>
> System 303x
>
> System 43xx

These computers operate under one of the following systems:

> DOS/VS or DOS/VSE
>
> OS VS1, SVS, or MVS
>
> VM/370 with at least one of the above

Remote information processors in SNA can include the following:

> 8100 distributed processing system
>
> System 32, 34, 38
>
> Series/1

The ways in which these can be interconnected are described in Unit 9-4. The two key elements of SNA are:

1. Host-resident access method, which can be either of the following:
   a. VTAM (Virtual Telecommunications Access Method)
   b. TCAM (Telecommunications Access Method)
2. 3705 communications controller with NCP/VS (Network Control Program/Virtual Storage) software

In the host system, the telecommunications access method software provides the major SNA functions. When SNA was first announced, the new access method VTAM was the only software provided. However, user pressure forced a retrofit of SNA capabilities into TCAM software because this was in wide use and was felt by many to be more efficient than VTAM. SNA support continues to be provided in both TCAM and VTAM; full SNA features, however, are available only through the use of VTAM.

VTAM implements the main functions described in Section 9-1, ranging from the function management services for applications to the control of sessions and part of the routing logic.

NCP/VS, in the 3705 communications controller which serves as a front-end to the host, provides the lower-level SNA functions of data-link control and local routing. The 3705 can operate in both SNA mode and pre-SNA emulation mode, but only SNA mode is supported when VTAM is used in the host.

A 3704 or 3705 communications controller can also operate as a remote concentrator, but this is an optional SNA function. The front-end communications control functions are required in SNA.

TCAM provides generally the same functions as VTAM and allows both SNA mode and pre-SNA emulation mode interfaces to the communications controller. Terminals operating through the emulation interface are not really SNA devices—but simply coexist on the same host as full SNA devices.

The System Services Control Point (SSCP), which resides in either VTAM or TCAM, retains control of sessions as well as providing the network operator interface for monitoring and control. Originally SNA supported only host-centered star networks, and this dependence on the SSCP severely restricted SNA flexibility. More recently, a software extension called *Advanced Communications Function* (ACF) has been provided for VTAM, TCAM, and NCP (Network Control Program). ACF supports multihost systems as well as peer interconnections among smaller processors such as the 8100 and 43xx.

In addition to these basic hardware and software products, IBM offers a continually expanding set of supporting software. For example, a Teleprocessing Network Simulator (TNS) is available to allow the performance of a network/system to be predicted. A Network Communications Control Facility (NCCF) provides for manual intervention into, and control of, a distributed system during operation. For example, a system administrator can directly access and analyze application programs, the operating system, or access methods. A Network Problem Determination Application (NPDA) is available with NCCF. The NPDA records and tabulates error occurrences and diagnoses the probable causes of those errors.

9-4. DISTRIBUTED SYSTEM STRUCTURES SUPPORTED

SNA was originally implemented for the support of host-centered networks using intelligent terminals of limited functionality. An example of a simple SNA configuration, representative of many existing systems, is shown in Figure 9-3. Both local channel-connected and remote terminals are included in this example.

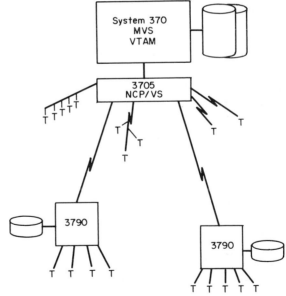

FIG. 9-3 Simple Systems Network Architecture system. MVS = Multiple Virtual System; VTAM = Virtual Telecommunications Access Method; NCP = Network Control Program; VS = Virtual Storage; T = terminal device.

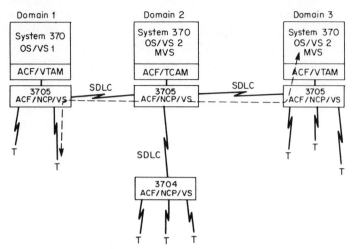

FIG. 9-4   Systems Network Architecture's multihost system. OS = operating system; VS = virtual system; MVS = Multiple Virtual System; SVS = Single Virtual System; ACF = Advanced Communications Function; VTAM = Virtual Telecommunications Access Method; NCP = Network Control Program; SDLC = synchronous data link control; T = terminal device.

The addition of ACF provides much greater flexibility. An example multihost system, including three hosts and both local and remote communications controllers, is shown in Figure 9-4.

This illustration includes three System 370 hosts, each defined with its local terminals as a *domain*. (A domain includes the NAUs for which a given SSCP is responsible.) A terminal attached to the Domain 1 host is allowed to access an application in the Domain 3 host. This type of connection is established through the coordination of the SSCPs involved (in this case in the Domain 1 and 3 hosts). Once the session is established, the communications controllers manage the data exchange without intervention by the Domain 1 and 2 hosts.

The announcement of the 8100 processing system, a more powerful replacement for the 3790 intelligent terminal, opened up significant new distributed processing capabilities within SNA. However, later announcement of the 43xx—especially the 4331—has led to some confusion as to the roles these two products are expected to play. Although there is some overlap of functionality, in general the 4331 and 8100 fit into SNA as follows. The 4331 (or 4341) serves as an exactly compatible smaller host, or intermediate processor, in cases where this compatibility is important and the ability to grow at a significant rate is needed. The 8100, on the other hand, is best suited to situations where large numbers of terminals and/or large numbers of remote sites are involved and exact host compatibility is less important.

An example of an SNA system using both of these elements is shown in Figure 9-5.

SNA has evolved significantly, and this evolution can be expected to continue. The most likely direction is toward further compatibility with industry standards such as CCITT X.25 as user pressure for this compatibility increases.

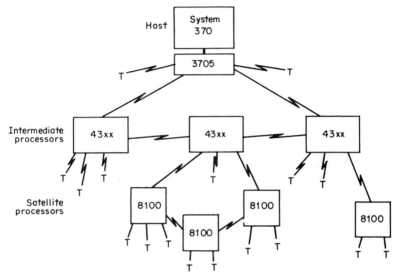

FIG. 9-5 Complex Systems Network Architecture (SNA) system. T = terminal device.

10

DIGITAL EQUIPMENT CORPORATION'S DECnet

In April 1975, soon after IBM's fall 1974 announcement of SNA, Digital Equipment Corporation announced DECnet, a network and distributed system capability. Because of the differences between the minicomputer and general-purpose computer businesses, DEC originally had quite different goals than did IBM.

General-purpose computer vendors such as IBM must manage the installed computer bases of their equipment. Users of large-scale data processing equipment look on computers as relatively long-term investments. They expect to be able to enlarge an existing computer installation as needed, and they also expect to be able to add more advanced functions as these become available. Because continuity is a basic consideration for users of general-purpose computers, it is also a basic consideration for the manufacturers of these computers. Thus, IBM had considerable incentive to provide methods for evolving users away from the existing multitude of teleprocessing access methods and onto a single set of compatible software so that users could more easily accept future IBM offerings.

DEC, on the other hand, had no comparable incentives. Minicomputers have until recently been treated almost as though they were "disposable." A mini was purchased and installed for use in a given application, and unless the initial implementation was unsuccessful, the hardware was seldom changed or enlarged. Mini manufacturers, such as DEC, were therefore under little pressure to provide continuing enhancements and upgrades. (Today the mini market is becoming more like the general-purpose computer market, but this is quite a recent development.) However, users of minicomputers have, in general, a greater need for resource sharing than users of larger computers. In order to lower system cost, it is very desirable to be able to configure a mini without peripherals for applications such as laboratory work. It is advantageous in such cases for the mini to have access to a larger mini configuration for program development and possibly for data-reduction operations. This type of resource sharing, relatively unusual in general-purpose computers, is much more important to users of minicomputers.

It was this situation which provided a major impetus for the development of DECnet.

With this in mind, it is easy to understand the differences in approach between DECnet and SNA. The focus in SNA was initially to improve the consistency of access methods in host-centered terminal networks. Only later did the focus switch to the support of true distributed systems. The focus in DECnet from the beginning was to support meshed networks of resource-sharing computers.

10-1.   FUNCTIONAL STRUCTURE

DECnet includes DEC's overall capabilities for networking and distributed-system resource sharing, all of which are built upon the Digital Network Architecture, DNA. DNA provides the message-movement capabilities which the other DECnet facilities use. DECnet, like IBM's SNA, has evolved considerably since its 1975 announcement. This chapter describes the current DECnet definition, sometimes called Phase III.

Basic Concepts

An understanding of DECnet and DNA requires an understanding of its underlying concepts. Some of the more basic of these concepts are as follows.

Distributed system resources are treated as *objects* in DNA. For example, a file or database is considered an object. A program or system module is also considered an object. This approach provides for consistency in the treatment of local and remote resources.

Objects are described by *global object-type descriptors,* which provide the necessary information about an object's attributes and location. These descriptors in effect form a distributed directory or catalog (see Unit 15-3 for a discussion of directories).

All nodes are treated identically within DNA, regardless of physical differences among products. This concept is valid at the architectural level, although product implementations may in fact involve subset or superset capabilities. A basic goal of DNA is to provide a generalized, location-independent means of communication between any two objects. In DNA this communication is termed a *dialogue.* A dialogue is logically equivalent to a session in SNA.

These concepts support the goal of allowing the configuration under DECnet of heterogeneous computers interconnected for a variety of reasons such as resource sharing, remote computing, and distributed processing. And, finally, a highly layered design is used in order to ensure system modularity and flexibility.

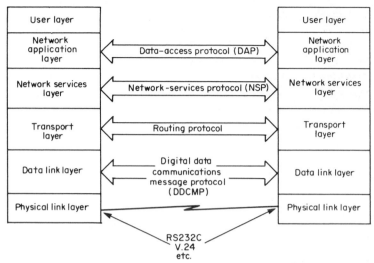

FIG. 10-1   Digital Equipment Corporation's Distributed Network Architecture (DNA) structure.

Layered Structure

The DNA layered structure of functions and protocols has evolved since 1975, expanding to add new capabilities. The DNA structure is shown in Figure 10-1.

In addition to the structure shown, an optional X.25 interface (to be described later) is supported. This option allows for bypassing several of the normal DNA layers. The basic structure, starting from the bottom, provides the following capabilities.

Physical link is the layer which determines the physical interconnection mode between the DTE and DCE devices. DNA supports EIA RS232, CCITT interfaces such as V.24, and in general accommodates all interfaces in common use at this level.

Data link is the layer which manages the data transmission on a communications link, including error detection and recovery. Unlike other major vendors, DEC chose not to use a bit-oriented protocol but to develop a unique character-oriented protocol, DDCMP (Digital data communications message protocol). This is considered the "standard" protocol in DNA and DECnet. Its characteristics are described in Unit 10-2.

Transport is the layer which provides the logic necessary to route messages, selecting the correct path through the data-communications network in each case. Different routing algorithms can be supported, including a table-driven fixed routing scheme and an adaptive routing scheme.

Network services is the layer which establishes and manages logical links, or dialogues, between pairs of objects such as application programs, terminals, etc. The facilities provided by the associated network services protocol (NSP) come in two forms: full and subset.

When full NSP capabilities are used, the system guarantees end-to-end message delivery and the correct sequencing of messages at the receiving location. Flow control is also supplied on the logical connection. This ensures that the receiver is not overloaded by incoming traffic. The subset mode of NSP supplies a lower level of service at lower overhead. No flow control is provided in the subset mode, and message delivery is not guaranteed. The user must supply any necessary end-to-end message control functions.

Network application is the layer which contains the highest system-supplied functions in DNA. This layer provides services such as remote file access, file transfer, and remote system load. The protocol used at this layer is the data-access protocol, or DAP. DAP provides a machine-independent format for the exchange of data among computers. It allows applications operating on one computer to access remote files essentially as if they were local. This capability is a key ingredient of resource sharing—the main focus of DECnet.

Functions provided by DAP include:

- Open a remote device or file
- Get (read) data
- Put (write) data
- Control the device or file (for example, set a record pointer in a file)
- Get device or file status
- Close device or file

The DAP protocol includes a negotiation process to determine whether or not the two systems involved in a data exchange use the same file format. If so, no data translation is needed. If not, one or both systems must convert to or from the defined network standard format.

In addition to the ability to access a remote file, a utility is provided which allows either data or command (job control language, procedure) files to be moved between nodes. For example, the content of a data file can be moved to another node. A file at a remote node can be deleted. A command file can be transmitted to a remote location and submitted for execution there. An existing command file at a remote node can be activated for execution.

The user layer includes all application code and user-supplied functions. Applications executing in this layer make use of the DNA services described through the DAP and NSP protocols.

The X.25 module is a recent addition to DNA. It provides for interface to public data networks which conform to the CCITT X.25 definition. DEC has reportedly installed an X.25 DECnet interface in Canada on the Datapac network. Since X.25 uses the HDLC bit-oriented protocol (see Unit 8-2), the standard DDCMP data-link layer of DNA is bypassed. The X.25 module, which includes the necessary HDLC protocol, is accessed directly from the transport layer. Optionally, the X.25 module can be accessed directly from the user layer.

Network and system control in DECnet is distributed, not centralized. This is in keeping with DNA's overall focus on resource-sharing systems. Functions such as downline load, control of the operational state of a node or a link, status monitoring, and the initiation of tests can be activated from any appropriate location within a DECnet system.

10-2. PROTOCOLS

DECnet and DNA support a number of protocols, including, for example, the DAP protocol described in the preceding section. The major protocols for interconnection of components in DECnet are described in this section.

The main link-control protocol used in DNA is the Digital data communications message protocol, DDCMP. Use of this protocol represents a major departure from the direction taken by most other vendors, who are implementing various forms of industry-standard bit-oriented protocols. DEC instead chose to develop its own unique (but nonproprietary) character-oriented protocol.

DDCMP differs from bit-oriented protocols such as SDLC and HDLC in the following ways:

- It does not use a unique bit pattern (*flag*) to delimit a transmission on the link.
- It includes a count field in each transmission to indicate the number of characters sent.
- It can operate on asynchronous as well as synchronous transmission facilities.
- It can handle parallel (e.g., TouchTone* input) as well as serial transmission.

DDCMP shares the following characteristics with the bit-oriented protocols:

- Two-way alternate (TWA) or two-way simultaneous (TWS) operation

*Registered trademark of the American Telephone and Telegraph Company.

- Code transparency
- Point-to-point or multipoint operation

The use of a count field, rather than a unique flag and bit stuffing as in the bit-oriented protocols, means that only software changes are needed to support DDCMP. Hardware changes are not necessary. This, plus the other features listed, make DDCMP quite attractive. However, given the frequent requirement for IBM connectability—today largely SDLC—and the strong movement toward CCITT recommendation X.25 (including HDLC) as a universal packet-network interface, lack of compatibility with these industry trends is quite a severe disadvantage. In order to overcome this disadvantage, DEC has moved to provide X.25 support. It has also moved to provide a number of coexistence protocols for interconnection of DECnet systems with other vendors' equipment.

Coexistence with other vendors' non-DNA systems—usually host computers—is achieved by emulation of existing remote job entry (RJE) workstation or interactive terminal protocols. The following protocols can be emulated by DEC products which can also operate within DECnet.

- *IBM 2780* emulation allows a PDP-11 to exchange data with a number of IBM RJE programs (and with other hosts which support the 2780 protocol).
- *HASP workstation* emulation extends the 2780 capabilities through multileaving of job streams. Connection is possible to IBM or other hosts which support the HASP protocols.
- *IBM 3271* emulation supports an interactive interface between an application running under DNA in a DEC computer and an application running under an IBM system such as CICS (Customer Information Control System). The IBM system uses a protocol interface consistent with a remote 3271 device.
- *Univac 1004* emulation allows jobs to be sent from a DECnet system to a Univac host—such as an 1100 Series computer—for processing.
- *MUX-200* emulation provides both an interactive and a batch interface from DECnet to a Control Data Corporation (CDC) system running under the Scope or Kronos executives.

An SNA gateway is also said to be under development for use as an addition to DECnet. The gateway is intended to allow a fuller mapping between DNA and SNA protocols and functions.

10-3. PRODUCT SUPPORT

The original focus of product support for DECnet was the PDP-11.

Today, for all practical purposes, all DEC products support DNA and can participate in DECnet systems. Hardware and operating-system software combinations which can be used are shown in Figure 10-2.

Hardware	Software
PDP-11	RT-11 RXS-11S RXS-11M IAS RSTS/E
VAX-11/780	VMS
DEC system-10	TOPS-10
DEC system-20	TOPS-20

FIG. 10-2   DECnet hardware and software support. DEC = Digital Equipment Corporation.

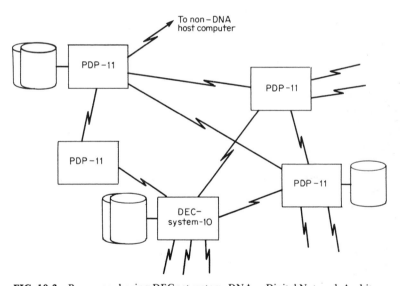

FIG. 10-3   Resource-sharing DECnet system. DNA = Digital Network Architecture.

10-4.   DISTRIBUTED SYSTEM STRUCTURES SUPPORTED

DNA and DECnet support a very wide range of distributed information-processing and network structures. The DECnet design is probably best described as horizontally distributed processing (see Unit 5-1) in a peer relationship, supported by a meshed network structure and used for resource sharing. An example minicomputer network of this type is shown in Figure 10-3.

The DECnet data access protocol (DAP) in this example system structure would allow computers without local databases to access remotely stored data. Applications on multiple computers could exchange data to coordinate their activities. Although not part of the DECnet system, an IBM, Univac, or CDC host could be linked as shown in the illustration in order to provide for data exchange.

Although they are clearly not its major focus, hierarchical processing structures can also be supported in DECnet. Effectively, there seems to be no reason why the DECnet architecture cannot support all possible combinations of processing and network structures. The resource-sharing approach is an extremely good base and provides more inherent flexibility than a hierarchical host-centered orientation.

11

HONEYWELL'S DISTRIBUTED SYSTEMS ENVIRONMENT—DSE

The third example architecture to be described is the Distributed Systems Environment, or DSE, provided by Honeywell Information Systems Inc. (a wholly owned subsidiary of Honeywell Inc.). The basic concepts of DSE were announced in January 1977. Additional architectural details have been announced more recently. The overall framework within which Honeywell presents its distributed systems capabilities is DSE; the architectural rules governing the implementation of these capabilites are known as the Distributed Systems Architecture, or DSA.

The focus of DSE lies somewhere between IBM's SNA and DEC's DECnet. As a mainframe supplier, Honeywell felt some of the same pressures as IBM to support host-centered networks. On the other hand, Honeywell's minicomputer business placed greater emphasis on networks of peer computers, similar to the networks for which DECnet was designed. The DSA architecture is therefore intended to support both of these structures, either independently or in hybrid combinations.

Honeywell Information Systems (HIS) and the associated French enterprise, Compagnie International pour l'Informatique Honeywell Bull (Cii HB), have also been in the process of unifying several computer lines which have been combined as a result of a series of mergers and acquisitions. The 1970 merger of the General Electric and Honeywell computer businesses formed HIS and left the new company with products from both original companies. The subsequent merger in Europe of Honeywell Bull with Compagnie Internationale pour l'Informatique (Cii), producing Cii HB, brought in the Cii product lines. Acquisition of the Xerox computer-user base in the United States by HIS added still other products. The long-term unification of these product lines has therefore been an important goal for Honeywell (*Honeywell* will be used for convenience to indicate the combination of HIS and Cii HB). The introduction of interconnection capabilities under DSE is one facet of this direction. Products which can be connected via data networks can be used together even when they are of somewhat different internal structures.

11-1. FUNCTIONAL STRUCTURE

The DSA architecture includes certain concepts which are part of its fundamental design. Like the other architectures discussed, DSA uses a layered structure of functions and protocols.

Basic Concepts

At the overview level of architectural description, there are four concepts basic to DSA—the activity, the process, the end point, and the session.

An activity represents a cluster of related tasks and the resources necessary to accomplish those tasks. In DSA an activity can be manual, automatic (computerized), or partially manual and partially automatic.

A secretary in an office with a typewriter, telephone, files, and operating procedures provides an example of a manual activity. In this case a person, the secretary, executes the procedures associated with the activity, using tools such as the telephone and typewriter and accessing files (perhaps stored in filing cabinets) as needed in order to obtain and/or store information.

In a distributed computer system under DSA, automatic activities consist of procedures (programs), computer resources to execute those procedures, and files or databases to be accessed and perhaps updated by those procedures. An installation could define an automatic activity to include only one procedure; for example, the program which handles order input in an order-entry system. In other cases, an activity could be defined to include several related procedures. This might be the case when complex input is processed in a hospital patient-monitoring system.

It is possible to view an activity, whether automatic or manual, as follows:

- The activity includes procedures which define the work to be done. In a manual activity, these procedures can take the form of an operating manual or, perhaps, simply word-of-mouth instructions about how to do the job. In an automatic activity, these procedures are programs.

- The activity provides for access to files, which can be consulted and/or updated. If it is appropriate, the files can be shared among a number of activities. In a manual activity, files can include any type of stored information: memos, pictures, a library, and so on. In an automatic activity, files consist of data stored—temporarily or semipermanently—on disk, diskette, tape, or similar media.

- The activity must have resources with which to execute its procedures.

In a manual activity, resources include one or more persons and, perhaps, tools such as a soldering iron, a typewriter, an adding machine, a wrench, or a stethoscope. In an automatic activity, resources include processor(s) and working storage.

The DSA concept of activities provides consistency, because manual and automatic, or computerized, procedures can be conceptualized in the same way. Procedures which are currently manual can, over a period of time, be automated if appropriate. Within an automated system, activities can conceptually be moved as the load shifts or as the system is reconfigured. This allows leveling of the total workload—either statically or dynamically. (The term *conceptually* is used to indicate that although these ideas are inherent in DSA, they may or may not be included in specific product implementations.)

Activities can also be *hybrid,* or partially manual and partially automated. For example, a person using a terminal to enter transactions can be considered part of a hybrid activity which includes the person and terminal plus the computerized procedures for processing input supplied by the person. A basic concept, therefore, of DSA is that a distributed system is a collection of activities, some manual, some automated, and some hybrid.

A process is an occurrence of the execution of a procedure. An automated activity can accomplish work only when a process associated with that activity is initiated. Depending on the specific implementation and set of options selected, an activity may have one or multiple processes in execution at any time.

End points are the addressable entities associated with the activities in a DSA system. Each end point has a unique name, which is used when activities need to address and communicate with one another. In fact, each activity must have one or more end-point names, since otherwise it would be impossible to send messages to that activity. If desired, an activity can have multiple end point names, each in effect forming a queue of different types of messages designated for that activity. For example, an activity designed to process order-entry transactions might have two end-point names, one associated with original orders and the other associated with changes in the original orders. This would allow the activity's process(es) to establish a priority sequence, handling all original orders prior to any order modifications. In addition, it is worth noting that since each terminal device is managed through a terminal activity, usually provided by the system, each device has one or more end-point names.

The end-point concept supports one of the major goals of DSA— transparency of the network configuration to terminal users and application programs. All entities which can be addressed (i.e., all entities to which messages can be sent) are known by logical end-point names. The system software associates these logical end-point names with the physical location and identity of the device or program to which the name belongs. The person or program which addressed the end point need not know where it is located or even what type of end point it is.

Sessions provide for the exchange of data between two activities. Before data can be transmitted, the process at the initiating activity must request a logical connection with the desired receiving end point and supply its own end-point name as well. Once this connection—the session—is established between the pair of end points, data can be transferred according to the rules of message exchange.

The establishment of a session does not require any centralized or host control; it is accomplished by the system software of the location(s) involved. For example, if a terminal initiates a connection to an application in a satellite processor, the operating system of the satellite does any necessary security-and-privacy and privilege checking and, if the requesting terminal (and associated user) is authorized, establishes the session. From a conceptual point of view, two terminals can establish a session without any other intervention, although whether or not this is actually possible depends upon the implementation of the specific terminal-management software. A session can also be established between two activities (with two end-point names) in the same location; for example, between two processes executing in the same host computer. The processes involved need not know whether they are co-located or remote; the system software makes this transparent.

It is important to emphasize that a session is always a *logical* connection. The physical path which connects the two activities can be quite complex, but it is controlled by system software and is transparent at the level of the session. Conceptually, the physical connection can change dynamically during the duration of the session. For example, if a communications link fails and is replaced by a dial-up link, the logical connection is not disturbed (although data exchange may be temporarily interrupted during the switch over). In a connection to a network (for example a public data network) with heuristic routing, the actual physical transmission paths may be altered dynamically and be different for each exchange of data. Again, the logical connection—the session—continues unaffected.

There are other concepts defined within DSA, but the concepts of activity, process, end point, and session are the most basic, and an understanding of them is sufficient for a general understanding of the architecture. The way in which these concepts combine within DSA is shown in Figure 11-1.

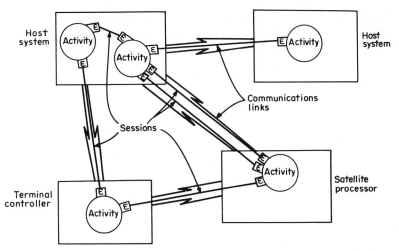

FIG. 11-1 Basic concepts of the Distributed Systems Architecture. E = end point.

Layered Structure

The layered structure of DSA follows the recommendations of the International Standards Organization (ISO) for a "provisional reference model of Open Systems Architecture" from Technical Committee 97, Subcommittee 16 (TC97/SC16). This reference model has been defined, and proposed for standardization, by ISO in coordination with national standards bodies such as ANSI. The intent of the Open Systems Architecture is to provide ways to design systems which are essentially "open" in that they can be of any interconnection structure, can assign tasks to any desired location, and can consist of any arbitrary combination of equipment as long as all elements obey the rules of the architecture.

DSA consists of seven functional layers as shown in Figure 11-2. These seven layers can be more conveniently thought of in three groups: the application layer, the message management layers, and the communications management layers.

The *communications management* layers, at the bottom, provide transport services using a data-communications network.

Physical link, the bottom layer, specifies the electrical connections between the data-terminal equipment (DTE) such as terminals and computers and the data-communications equipment (DCE) such as modems and links. DSA supports the commonly used standards such as RS232C and the V series of interfaces defined by CCITT. DSA also supports X.21.

Link control is the next layer. It manages data transmission over a link between two entities in a DSA network. For example, the link-control layer manages the data-communications circuit between a host's front-end network processor (FNP) and a satellite processor. The standard protocol for link control is high-level data link control (HDLC), as defined by ISO (see Unit 11-2). On the network links which interconnect intelligent entities such as host and satellite processors, HDLC is the only protocol supported for private networks. On links which connect local terminals to an FNP, satellite processor, terminal controller, or concentrator, other protocols can be used for compatibility with existing terminal devices. For example, the VIP (Visual Information Projection) protocol is supported for use with Honeywell display terminals which implement this protocol. Certain forms of binary synchronous protocols are supported for connection to IBM-compatible devices.

Network control, the next functional layer, provides routing logic when required. In a simple point-to-point network, or when DSA components are interconnected to a public data network which provides routing logic, this layer contains minimal functionality. In more complex networks which provide multiple possible paths between end points, the network control layer is required to select the appropriate path for each data transfer.

Transport control, the highest layer within the communications management group of layers, provides for end-to-end control during transmission and for handling overall data sequencing, acknowledgements, flow control (pacing), and so on. In simple networks, with only point-to-

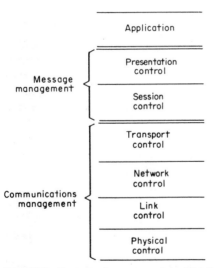

FIG. 11-2 Functional structure of the Distributed Systems Architecture.

point links between sources and destinations, the transport-control functions are unnecessary.

These communications management layers are concerned with data transmission, and in the case of medium-to-large scale hosts, they reside in the host's FNP (see Unit 11-3). Smaller systems also require these layers, but they form extensions to the operating system rather than residing in a separate processor.

The next two layers of DSA can be conveniently grouped under the heading *message management.* These layers are concerned with the control of logical message exchange, either across a communications network or between processes resident in the same computer. In the former case, message management interfaces with communications management to accomplish message transfer. In the latter case, all functions are provided by message management.

Session control forms the lower layer of the message-management group of layers. Session control handles the initiation of sessions (logical connections) between pairs of activities via their end-point names. This includes checking for access permissions, etc., when necessary. Session control also manages the message transfer while in process, through protocols which determine which location(s) can send at a given point in the session. Session control is also concerned with end-to-end message integrity, ensuring that all data sent are received correctly.

Presentation control, the other message management layer, will provide for a variety of reformatting possibilities, so that application processes can access terminals, devices, and other processes in a transparent, or virtual, mode. That is, the application can work with a preferred data format, called a *standard device protocol,* and presentation control (at one or both ends of the logical connection) will provide the necessary transformations to and from the characteristics of the real device. This terminal transparency is one of the major goals of DSA, but of course it is difficult to achieve because of existing application programs (which often include terminal-specific logic) and the differing characteristics of available terminal devices.

The Application is the layer of DSA which includes all other functions, such as application programs, many system-supplied facilities, and interfaces to functions such as database management.

11-2. PROTOCOLS

As in all layered structures, DSA supports protocols and interfaces at each level of the architecture. Those which are of major importance, in terms of connectability and functionality, are described here.

The protocols which accompany the communications-management functions determine what forms of connectability DSA provides. The main protocols supported are:

- High-level data link control (HDLC)
- X.25
- X.21

(Note that X.25 and X.21 are, technically, more properly defined as interfaces, but it is convenient to group them with protocols in the present discussion.)

High-level data link control (HDLC) is very similar in structure and capabilities to SDLC (see Unit 9-2). A major difference is that SDLC is an IBM-defined protocol which is similar to, but not identical with, any standard bit-oriented protocol. As explained in Chapter 8, HDLC was defined by ISO as a general-purpose bit-oriented protocol for interconnecting computer and intelligent terminal equipment in either a point-to-point or multipoint mode. The original ISO definition covers a wide range of options for the support of different forms of data exchange, such as two-way alternate, two-way simultaneous, balanced (two primary stations), unbalanced (one primary and one or more secondary stations) transfer, and others.

As part of the CCITT definition of recommendation X.25, a specific subset of HDLC was included as Level 2 of the X.25 interface (see Unit 8-2). DSA supports this HDLC subset, both for interface to X.25 networks and for use on private networks.

X.25 is also supported. One of the strengths of the Open Systems Architecture, and also of DSA, is the natural interface it provides to public data networks (including value-added networks in the U.S.) which use the CCITT X.25 or X.21 interface definitions.

Figure 11-3 shows how a DSA interface is provided to an X.25 network such as Transpac, the public data network in France. The transport control layer provides the X.25 Level 3 interface. Network control is unnecessary when interfacing to an X.25 network because routing is automatically supplied within the network and is transparent to the sending and receiving locations.

The higher-level protocols of DSA are required to handle the logical message exchange over the X.25 network.

X.21 interfaces to circuit-switched networks are also provided by DSA. The X.21 is a circuit-switched interface, not packet-switched, and requires a somewhat different interface. Connection from DSA to an X.21 network, such as the Nordic Public Data Network in the Scandinavian countries, is shown in Figure 11-4.

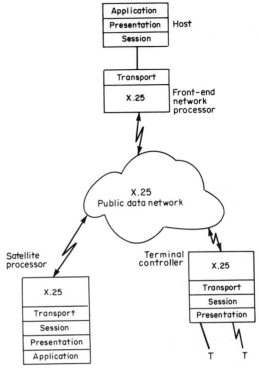

FIG. 11-3 X.25 interface. T = terminal device.

A number of application-level protocols are supported by DSA, including the following standard capabilities.

File transfer is provided among DSA-compatible components. Capabilities range from the ability to transfer basically undefined bit strings to the ability to transfer database segments between computers which support comparable data structures. Several options for file transfer exist, including transferring data from an existing file on one processor to an existing file on another processor (replacing the former file content), establishing a new file and transferring data to it, and appending transferred data to the end of an existing file. The file transfer protocols are used for database transmission, to send data accumulated during keyboard data entry to another location for processing, to downline load programs, and to upline dump memory content after a system problem or failure.

Remote job entry/output protocols are provided, allowing smaller systems (specifically Honeywell's minicomputer family) to act as remote job workstations for medium-scale and large-scale computers.

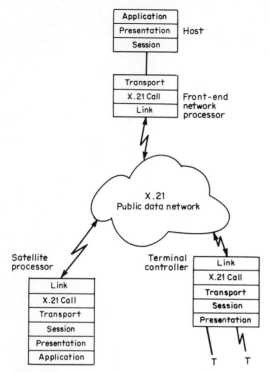

FIG. 11-4   X.21 interface. T = terminal device.

Interactive data entry protocols are also supported. These allow data to be entered via intelligent terminal controllers and processed interactively on a designated satellite or host processor.

11-3.   PRODUCT SUPPORT

The functional layers and protocols described are being phased into implementation on existing and new products supplied by Honeywell. Product support falls into two categories: products which provide basic interconnection capabilities using conventional protocols and products which provide a wider range of distributed system features via interconnection using the DSA protocols. Products in the former category are considered to be part of the Distributed Systems Environment (DSE), but they do not conform to the rules of DSA. Newer products are also part of DSE and in addition are compliant with DSA rules.

DSA facilities have been announced on Honeywell's minicomputer, the Level 6, its medium-scale 64/DPS and DPS 7 computers, and its large-scale DPS 8 and 66/DPS computers. The interconnection capabilities provided are shown, in summary form, in Figure 11-5.

On the larger systems, the four lower functional and protocol layers are implemented in front-end processors based upon the Level 6 minicomputer. This makes the front-end responsible for control of the communications network and/or the interface to a public data network. When the Level 6 is used as an information processor, it includes all of the DSA functions and protocols within the main processor. On the larger systems the upper layers—the message-management group—are included in the host of software.

The large-scale DPS 8 and 66/DPS systems operate as host processors or as exactly compatible co-host or intermediate processors. The 64/DPS and DPS 7 medium-scale systems can also operate as hosts. Medium-scale and large-scale processors use compatible front-ends, both based upon the Level 6. The Level 6, operating under the GCOS 6 software system, can operate as a satellite processor to a medium- or large-scale host.

An example distributed system in DSA, with a typical allocation of functions across components, is shown in Figure 11-6.

In this example system, the Level 6 satellite processor provides functions such as keyboard data entry, which allow data to be entered and batched, usually for later transmission to the host for processing but possibly also for later local processing. The Level 6 also supports remote job entry/output for the host, with the ability to multiplex (multileave)

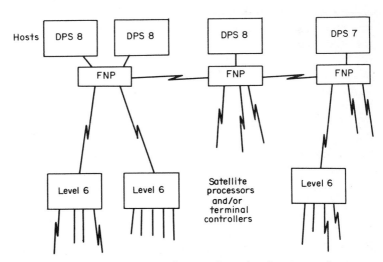

FIG. 11-5 Distributed Systems Environment's product-interconnections capabilities. FNP = front-end network processor.

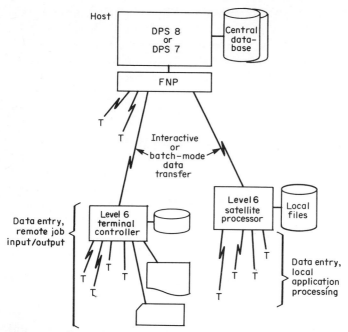

FIG. 11-6 Allocation of functions in a typical distributed systems environment. DPS = Distributed Processing System; FNP = front-end network processor.

job streams in and/or out over a single physical link. In addition, local application processing can take place at the Level 6. This processing may be related to the host processing, in which case data can be exchanged with the host via file transfer. In other cases the local processing may be for functions unique to the remote locations and unconnected with the host's functions.

As shown, the host system could be either a large-scale Distributed Processing System (DPS) 8 model or a medium-scale DPS 7 computer; the same relationship to the Level 6 satellite processor can exist and the same general set of functions can be used in either case.

Interconnection among the systems is via the DSA protocols. It is transparent to the specific physical mode of network interconnection and can be via point-to-point private network or via a public network.

Other Honeywell products can also cooperate in distributed systems. These include the Level 62 small business system and the 68/DPS large-scale computer which operates under the Multics (Multiplexed Information and Control System) software. Both Level 62 and 68/DPS can be connected to the Level 6 mini using protocols such as VIP and BSC.

Honeywell terminals, including hard-copy printer and keyboard devices and CRT-based devices, can be connected directly to an information processor or connected to a Level 6 used as a terminal controller/ concentrator. Control of the terminals is provided either by the local controller or by the front-end of the remote host.

11-4. DISTRIBUTED SYSTEM STRUCTURES SUPPORTED

The goal of DSE is to support a variety of systems structures, including those described earlier in this volume as hierarchical, horizontal, and hybrid.

DSE provides a wide variety of hierarchical system interconnection possibilities, including:

- DPS 8 or 66/DPS host, Level 6 satellite processors
- 64/DPS or DPS 7 host, Level 6 satellite processors
- DPS 8 or 66/DPS host, additional DPS 8 or 66/DPS co-hosts, and Level 6 satellite processors (three-level hierarchy)
- 68/DPS host, Level 6 satellite processors
- Level 62 host, Level 6 intelligent terminal controllers

Support for horizontal systems provides for data exchange between peer computer systems. DSE configurations of this type include:

- DPS 8 or 66/DPS with DPS 8 or 66/DPS
- 64/DPS or DPS 7 with 64/DPS or DPS 7
- Level 6 with Level 6
- DPS 8 or 66/DPS with 64/DPS or DPS 7

The large-scale DPS 8-class systems and the medium-scale DPS 7-class systems use the same Level 6-based DSA front-end network processor (FNP), and can be connected via FNP-to-FNP link. However, the systems are of different structures and support only a subset of the functionality available when like systems (e.g., DPS 8 and DPS 8) are linked.

There is no restriction on combining the above hierarchical and horizontal interconnection capabilities to create several different forms of hybrid system structures if appropriate.

12

OTHER VENDOR APPROACHES

It is impossible, in a volume of any reasonable size, to describe all of the system/network architecture approaches in use today. Two major, but different, approaches—SNA and DECnet—were described in Chapters 9 and 10. A third approach—DSE—falling somewhere between the other two in focus and objectives, was described in Chapter 11. This chapter provides a selected sampling of how other vendors support distributed systems.

12-1. UNIVAC'S DISTRIBUTED COMMUNICATIONS ARCHITECTURE— DCA

Support for networks and distributed systems by Univac, a Division of Sperry Rand Corporation, is embodied in the Distributed Communications Architecture, DCA. DCA was announced in November 1976 and has been supported by subsequent product announcements.

Functional Structure

DCA views a distributed system as consisting of these logical entities:

- Transport network
- Termination system
- Communications system
- Communications-system users
- End users

An overall view of how these entities fit into a system is shown in Figure 12-1.

The transport network includes all data-communications facilities— private links, switched links, public data network—and any communications processors needed to handle these facilities.

The termination system consists of the software facilities which provide network management features such as message fragmentation and

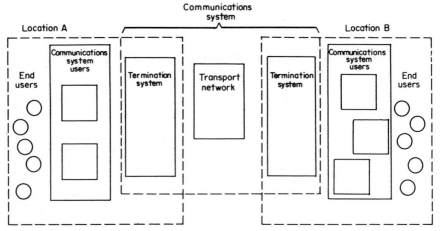

FIG. 12-1 Logical entities in Univac's Distributed Communications Architecture (DCA).

reassembly and flow control. This software also provides presentation services in the form of message formatting.

The communications system encompasses the transport network and the termination system, as shown in Figure 12-1.

Communications-system users are software packages which provide services to end users. Examples include the Query Language Processor and the Transaction Interface Package on the 1100 Series processors. These software systems interface the end users to the communications system and also to the processing services of the host computer.

End users include people at terminals and user-supplied application programs.

Protocols

DCA includes a bit-oriented protocol called universal data link control (UDLC). This is described as including all of the variations of ISO HDLC, ANSI ADCCP, and IBM's SDLC (except for the loop multipoint configurations handled by SDLC). In addition to this wide range, UDLC also provides four commands which are available to the user. These allow extension of the protocol to handle special conditions unique to the site or application. For example, these commands might be used to allow interconnection of a DCA network to a net using some other protocol.

Support for X.25 interfaces to public packet networks is also included in DCA. The X.25 support applies not only to the high-level transport network facilities, but also to circuits between a communications processor and associated terminals (assuming that the terminal controllers are X.25-compatible).

Product Support

Univac provides DCA support on effectively all of its current products. Two elements are key to DCA—the Distributed Communications Processor (DCP) and the associated software package, TELCON. Also required is an interface package between host and front end, CMS1100, when using an 1100 Series host. Additional support software is provided in both the 1100 and 90 Series processors. Univac also calls this entire combination of software, plus the DCP hardware, TELCON.

DCP can operate as a front-end processor, as a remote terminal concentrator, or as a free-standing nodal network processor. As a nodal processor it connects only to other DCPs (no terminals) and provides switching services in a private network.

TELCON software in the DCP is a disk-based operating system. It supports the standard UDLC protocol, as well as a variety of other asynchronous and synchronous protocols which enable it to coexist with older terminals and facilities. The logic for message routing and queuing is also provided by TELCON in the DCP. Both fixed and alternate routing are supported. Flow control is provided to avoid saturation of the transport network or of the communications-system users.

The host-resident software normally provides functions such as the establishment of sessions (logical connections) between entities which wish to exchange data. Data formatting is also provided by the host-resident TELCON.

An important attribute of DCA is that control of the network rests in the DCPs (via Network Management Services software), not in the host(s). NMS includes control of physical resources, network administration, security, maintenance, and session control. These functions can be distributed among multiple DCPs within a network or distributed system. If this is done, failure of a host or DCP disrupts only users being served by that host or connected to that DCP. Other users continue unaffected by the failure.

Series 90 systems and V77 minicomputers are also included within the DCA framework. These can be interfaced to a DCP as a termination system, but apparently they do not provide full host functionality (as the 1100 Series computers do).

ADAPT is a software package which enables many older Univac and non-Univac products to coexist with DCA. ADAPT is a specialized communications-system user which converts as needed between DCA and

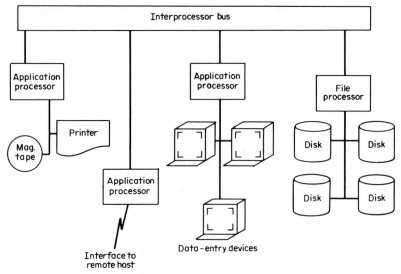

FIG. 12-2   Datapoint's Attached Resource Computer (ARC).

non-DCA hardware and software characteristics. Details concerning the support of non-Univac devices have not been supplied by Univac.

Distributed System Structures Supported

The DCA approach conceptually supports any network or distributed system structure ranging from simple star networks to multihost horizontal or hybrid systems connected by private meshed networks. Univac stresses the ability to support either X.25 public nets or private nets. Indications are, however, that many users will remain with relatively simple star networks for some time to come.

12-2. DATAPOINT'S ATTACHED RESOURCE COMPUTER SYSTEM

Datapoint Corporation, a vendor of highly intelligent terminal systems and small computers, announced the Attached Resource Computer (ARC*) system in late 1977. This provides the ability to configure a number of small computers all attached to a common bus for resource sharing.

An example ARC system configuration is shown in Figure 12-2.

ARC system processors are of two types: application processors and

*Trademark of the Datapoint Corporation.

file processors. The former execute application logic; the latter handle the database. Multiple processors of each type can be attached to the bus. This type of redundancy can provide for manually assisted fall-back capabilities. For example, if a file processor fails, its demountable devices can be moved to another processor. Since the application and file processors are basically interchangeable, storage devices could be transferred from a file processor to an application processor if necessary. The physical proximity of all system elements makes these procedures feasible.

Other processors can be effectively dedicated to local (cable-connected) and/or remote (communications-connected) terminal handling or to the control of local peripherals such as printers.

A communications interface can connect either to another remote ARC system or to a remote host computer—usually an IBM host. In addition, an interface is provided from the interprocessor bus to an I/O channel of an IBM System 360 or 370 family host. This effectively allows the IBM computer to act as an application processor within the ARC system.

Generally any Datapoint processor can be used as a component in an ARC system. The interprocessor bus provides the hardware and software logic necessary to interconnect these in the user-defined configurations.

The ARC system approach provides considerable flexibility in configuring resource-sharing processors exactly tailored to a user's requirements. The two forms—local and remote—of connection to a larger host make it possible to exchange data with the host as required. An ARC system is therefore ideal for relatively freestanding local processing functions, such as those of a specific department, with occasional data exchange with a central host.

12-3. NCR'S DISTRIBUTED NETWORK ARCHITECTURE—DNA

The Distributed Network Architecture (DNA) of NCR, announced in the summer of 1977, is intended to provide smooth evolution of their user base into more .complex capabilities. A three-phase evolution is envisioned, as follows:

1. Simple host-centered networks with data-communications functions handled by the host.

2. Addition of a communications processor (front-end) to offload communications-related tasks from the host.

3. Distributed systems consisting of multiple hosts and multiple terminal clusters interconnected via a network managed by multiple communications processors.

It is the intent that user application programs be insensitive to the particular phase of evolution and operate identically in every case.

Functional Structure

DNA uses a layered structure of functions and protocols, as shown in Figure 12-3.

Correspondent is used to describe applications and terminals—that is, entities which can communicate via DNA. The assumption is made that terminal control logic is available to handle the device end of the communication.

Telecommunications Access Method (TAM), a host-resident facility which provides interfaces to applications, provides correspondents with services. The main access method interface is oriented to ANSI COBOL '74, and uses the Message Control System interface defined in COBOL.

Communications system services (CSS) function, which provides the necessary fragmentation of messages into packets at the sending location and reassembly at the receiving location, receives messages passed from TAM. The protocol which allows two copies of CSS, at two different locations, to communicate is the end-to-end protocol.

Route management, the next functional layer, determines which path to use to send packets through the network. Route management in DNA

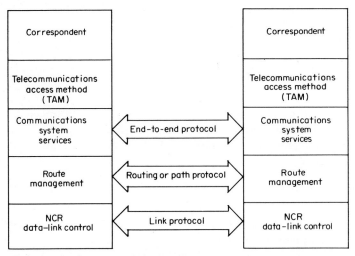

FIG. 12-3 Logical structure of NCR's Distributed Network Architecture (DNA).

can handle point-to-point, multipoint, or dial links as well as interfacing to X.25 packet nets. Two options are defined for packet delivery. In the unnumbered option, message size cannot exceed packet size, and end-to-end message control is the responsibility of the correspondents. The other option, the dialogue or numbered form, automatically splits messages into packets and guarantees correct sequencing of the packets upon receipt. Route management uses a routing or path protocol to accomplish these activities.

NCR/DLC (data link control), the lowest level defined in DNA, uses the link protocol to control data transfer.

Protocols

The standard NCR/DLC protocol is bit-oriented and based upon X.25. It also extends the basic X.25 and HDLC capabilities through the use of an extended address field (1 to n bytes) and an extended control field (1 or 2 bytes). These extensions provide additional addressing flexibility, as well as the option to transmit up to 127 frames before an acknowledgment is required. NCR/DLC can operate in the modes (similar to those in HDLC) of normal response (one primary and one or multiple secondary stations per link), asynchronous balanced (two primaries), and "NCR in-house" mode. Because of the basic DCA and NCR/DLC structure, X.25 compatibility is provided.

Product Support

The Telecommunications Access Method (TAM) software operates in the NCR Criterion computer systems. The NCR 721 communications processor is a major new element announced to support DNA. When used in larger or more complex networks, the communications processor provides the communications system services, route management, and data-link control functions. One new terminal, the NCR 214 electronic cash register, has been announced as a DNA product.

NCR has taken the approach of distributed network control. The data communications network is not dependent on a host processor, and in a multihost system, failure of one host or of a communications processor does not cause the entire system to fail (although specific users may be delayed or disconnected).

Distributed System Structures Supported

There are conceptually no restrictions on the system structures which DNA can support, although it is probable that many sites will continue to use simple host-centered networks. However, they should be able to move as desired to complex structures of the type shown in Figure 12-4.

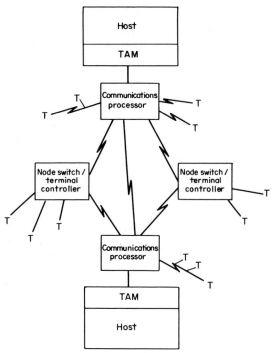

FIG. 12-4 Multihost NCR system with Distributed Network Architecture. TAM = Telecommunications Access Method; T = terminal device.

12-4. HEWLETT-PACKARD'S DISTRIBUTED SYSTEMS NETWORK—DSN

The Distributed Systems Network (DSN) of the Hewlett-Packard Company (HP) was announced in the fall of 1977. In fact, Hewlett-Packard had installed quite a few distributed systems for resource sharing before the DSN announcement. However, there was a need to formalize and modularize the system disciplines used. DSN provided that formalization.

As is the case with the other architectures described, DSN uses a layered functional structure. The functional layers which make up DSN are shown in Figure 12-5.

The Communication line control electrical interface is the layer which defines the modem interconnections supported. These include RS232 and the corresponding CCITT V.24.

Communication link protocol is the layer which handles data transfer and error control on a link. Asynchronous and binary synchronous connections to terminals are provided. Protocols for communication between computers, either pairs of HP computers or an HP computer and a larger host, are binary synchronous or modified binary synchronous.

Message-control protocol provides for the logical control of message transmission. This includes functions such as addressing. At this level, HP protocols are used when interfacing to HP terminals or computers. For connection to IBM or IBM-compatible hosts, emulation of the IBM 2780/3780, HASP II, and JES2 protocols is provided.

The Network manager, the next layer, maintains awareness of the network topology. It handles functions such as polling on multipoint links.

The Network access method is the layer which includes a variety of services for user-supplied application programs. The services provided include:

- Access to remote files or databases
- Remote command processing
- Access to remote devices
- Remote program management

DSN covers the Hewlett-Packard computers in the HP 3000 series, the HP 1000 series, and the HP 2026. These systems can be interconnected using data-communications links or via coaxial cable when distances are short (as in a factory-floor system). Connection to larger host

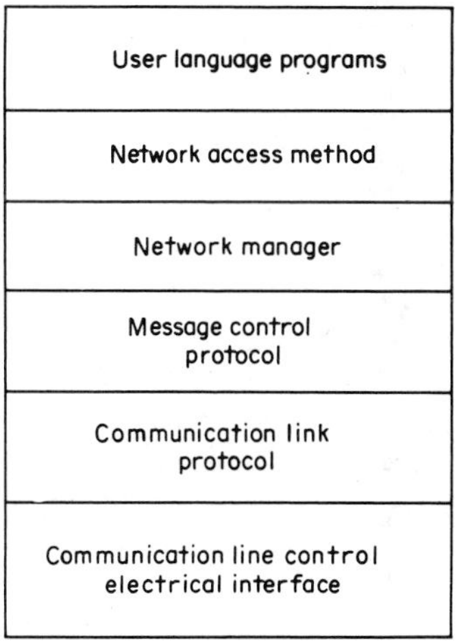

| User language programs |
| Network access method |
| Network manager |
| Message control protocol |
| Communication link protocol |
| Communication line control electrical interface |

FIG. 12-5 Functional layers of Hewlett-Packard's Distributed Systems Network (DSN).

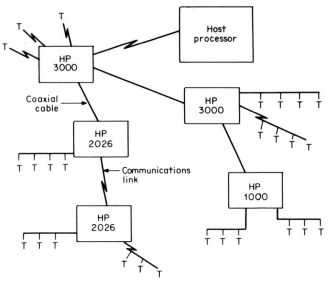

FIG. 12-6 Distributed Systems Network from Hewlett-Packard.
T = terminal device.

computers is via data communications using one of the emulation protocols listed above. An example DSN system configuration is shown in Figure 12-6.

As in the case of DECnet (see Chapter 10), the emphasis in DSN is on resource sharing. The services provided via the network access method allow programs on one computer to access files or databases on another, possibly remote, computer. Remote command processing allows a terminal user connected to one HP computer to initiate commands for execution at a remote HP computer. Program-to-program communication and file transfer facilities are also provided between HP systems. These facilities open up a wide range of possibilities for resource sharing within a distributed computer system.

According to an article* by Cort Van Rensselaer titled "Centralize? Decentralize? Distribute?" Hewlett-Packard clearly practices what it preaches. Van Rensselaer's article describes how Hewlett-Packard uses a very large network (110 nodes) to tie together distributed computer systems in H-P offices and factories in several countries. Hewlett-Packard's goal—an increasingly important one for many computer users—is to match the computer system to the organization it serves.

*_Datamation,_ Volume 25 Number 4, April 1979, pp. 88-97.

DESIGN CONSIDERATIONS

The design of a distributed information system is a complex process consisting of many iterative steps. This section discusses some of the more important points which the designer must consider.

The first step is to make a strategic decision about whether or not information-processing and/or database functions are to be distributed. Sometimes this strategic decision is made for business reasons, sometimes through technical trade-off studies; most often it involves a combination of business and technical analyses.

Technical considerations include trade-off studies which can be used to determine whether functional centralization or functional distribution is more advantageous in a particular situation. Trade-off studies are also useful for deciding which functions to distribute and which components should perform these functions. Chapter 13 discusses these fundamental strategic issues which affect the design of distributed systems.

Chapter 14 discusses how the various types of hardware components available on the market can best be used in distributed systems. The two generic classes of components—general-purpose computers and mini- and/or microcomputers—are each shown to have a specific set of strengths and weaknesses. These strengths and weaknesses dictate which functions the component can best perform and which role(s) it can best play within a distributed system.

In Chapter 15 a method for designing the information-processing functions is presented. The method is organized around the two major problems—workload allocation (where to do the processing) and resource sharing. Each of these can be approached either statically or dynamically. For practical purposes today, static workload allocation and resource management are most common, but the more complex dynamic methods are also discussed. The discussion includes descriptions of some of the technical problems which make these methods difficult to apply.

Database design in distributed systems is presented in Chapter 16. In this chapter emphasis is also placed on approaches which are well within the present state of the art.

The problems of data-communications network design are touched on briefly in Chapter 17. Emphasis is placed on basic cost considerations and on developing trends in public and private networks in the United States and Europe. A completely detailed explanation of how to configure a communications network would be far too extensive to include here, and in any case other sources of this information already exist. Several references are provided in the bibliography for those who need to pursue network design in detail.

Chapter 18 summarizes the global aspects of designing a distributed information system. A methodology organized around formulating and evaluating trial designs is presented. Although the design of any large information system remains somewhat more a matter of art than science, this chapter provides an orderly way to approach the problem.

13

STRATEGIES FOR FUNCTIONAL DISTRIBUTION

Certain basic strategic decisions must be made during the design of an information system. One of these is whether to centralize all functions or to consider some degree of functional distribution. Because it strongly affects the remainder of the design process, this decision must be made early in that process.

There are no hard-and-fast rules or formulas for deciding between centralization and some degree of functional distribution, largely because of the lack of widespread and generalized experience. In addition, the factors to be considered are complex, and as a result the decision is somewhat different for each application and/or for each enterprise. This chapter provides guidelines for analyzing the problem. The question addressed is not whether to distribute access via remote terminals, but whether or not information-processing and database functions should be distributed in order to form a distributed information system.

There are two reasons for considering the distribution of information-processing and database functions. These are:

- The application(s) cannot be implemented successfully in a centralized structure.
- The choice of a distributed structure rather than a centralized or decentralized structure provides advantages of cost, performance, survivability, response, flexibility, and/or control.

These reasons are discussed in Units 13-1 and 13-2, respectively.

13-1. FORCED DISTRIBUTION

The first case, in which the application must be distributed because of its size, is the simplest. It is also easy to recognize when it exists. Any on-line system which includes thousands of terminals (or possibly even hundreds of terminals) falls into this category. Also in this category are most high-volume transaction-processing systems which must process more than 100 transactions per second.

As a minimum, these very large systems require the distribution of network processing functions. Quite often they require the distribution of at least some of the information-processing functions as well. As the size of the application grows, the need to distribute additional functions also grows.

Functional distribution of some type is in effect forced for very large systems. No information processor built today—or likely to be built in the immediate future—can directly handle several thousand terminals, particularly if transactions are generated rapidly at each terminal. Equally important, the high availability and survivability needed in a system of this size would be difficult to provide in a single information processor.

Application systems which are so large as to force functional distribution are relatively easy to recognize. Any application which cannot be handled by a single information processor (perhaps using a multiprocessor or multicomputer configuration) while retaining adequate room for growth within that configuration, falls into this class.

Until recently, very large applications have usually been implemented in decentralized configurations, perhaps with some data exchange via magnetic tape or disk-pack transfer. Today, these applications are more often candidates for implementation in a distributed system.

13-2.   OPTIONAL DISTRIBUTION

The bulk of all information-system applications fall into a second category. In the case of the information-system applications in this category, it may or may not be advantageous to distribute functionality. Design decisions concerning functional distribution therefore become quite complex. This section provides broad guidelines for making these complex decisions. Each of the following sections discusses one of the potential reasons for selecting a distributed system structure rather than a centralized or decentralized structure.

On-line versus Batch Applications

If the application in question is best implemented in batch mode, that is, without interactive terminal interfaces and without rapid response requirements, it is not a good candidate for functional distribution. Such an application might be a candidate for decentralized processing; that is, implementation in a stand-alone information processor separate from, and unconnected to, other processors operated by the same enterprise.

Wide Geographic Dispersion

An on-line application which interfaces with terminals located in widely scattered geographical areas is a good candidate for functional distribution. The impetus for distribution in this case is to lower data-communications transmission volume and thereby cost. If this cost saving is greater than the added cost of functional distribution, the distributed alternative is attractive.

An information system of this type is shown, in "Before" and "After" configurations, in Figure 13-1.

In the "Before" example, a centralized host serves six to twenty terminals in each of seven cities remote from the host location. A significant cost is involved in the dedicated-link connections from the host to each of these terminals. This cost will vary, depending on whether the terminals are on single-station or multidrop links and upon the specific tariff(s) involved. But in any case the cost will be an important factor.

The "After" configuration shows a terminal controller/concentrator

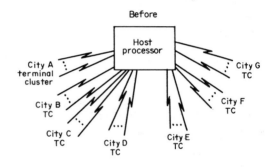

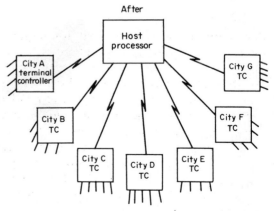

FIG. 13-1   Functional distribution for link cost savings.

in each of seven cities. Only one link now connects each of these cities to the central host. (There are probably dial facilities available in case the dedicated link fails.) Network-processing—concentration and terminal/ link control—functions and possibly some information-processing functions such as forms management and input/output editing have been removed from the host and distributed to these remote locations.

The cost trade-off here is quite straightforward. If the concentrators plus transmission facilities in the "After" configuration cost less than the transmission facilities in the "Before" configuration, a cost saving exists. A potential added benefit is the off-loading of the host; this may provide a cushion of added capacity which can be used to avoid upgrading the host, for a time, if the workload increases.

Of course it is possible, in the Figure 13-1 example, to move more of the functionality to the remote cities. A satellite processor, with a local database, could be installed in each city. Data transfer to and from the host might be still lower in volume than if only terminal controllers were used remotely. However, the satellite processor costs would be higher than those for terminal controllers. Again, cost trade-offs will either prove favorable or unfavorable to the proposed distribution of functions.

Application Independence

A major new or reimplemented application which is logically independent of the other applications of the enterprise may be a good choice for distribution. If the application is completely independent of all others, it is a candidate for stand-alone decentralized implementation. For example, a separately funded major research project in a university might best be supported by its own minicomputer.

An application is best distributed when it is independent in the sense that there are no requirements for high-volume data and/or process interchange with other applications, while at the same time there is a need for control interfaces. For example, factory-control applications are often either decentralized or distributed. Real-time process control is a complex operation which can accept relatively small amounts of input, such as data for schedules and goals, and produce relatively small amounts of output describing production status. The bulk of the processing, however, is "local" to the factory application.

To generalize on this principle, one potential distributed system structure therefore groups related, but semi-independent, applications into a multiple-hierarchy system in which each hierarchy handles one application. An example of this type of structure is shown in Figure 13-2.

In the example system each hierarchy handles one application quite

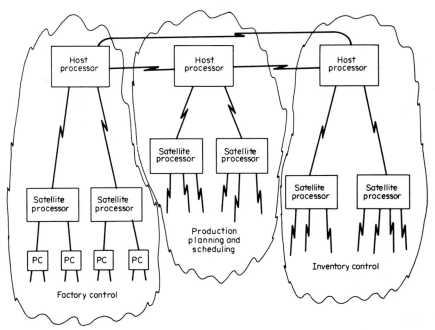

FIG. 13-2   Specialized interconnected hierarchies. PC = production-control equipment.

independently, but when information interchange is necessary, the linkages among the hierarchies allow this.

The same rationale can be applied to organizational-entity independence. Major subdivisions of an enterprise may each use a processing hierarchy, with linkages between the hierarchies as necessary. These subdivisions can be categorized functionally—e.g., personnel, finance, engineering, manufacturing—or by major divisions or departments of the organizational structure.

This system structure is only appropriate, however, if the organizational structure of the enterprise makes its subdivisions quite independent of one another. This is often the case in large companies whose management philosophy favors decentralization or in companies whose subdivisions were once separate companies acquired through merger or purchase. In a more integrated enterprise organization subdivisions have closer ties, exchange more data, and may not be adequately served by the system structure shown in the Figure 13-2 example.

Fast-Response Requirements

Many on-line applications which support business, educational, or governmental activities require fast response. An on-line teaching system, for example, is useful only if it interacts at the student's pace; if the student must wait two minutes for a trivial response, he or she will usually abandon the terminal. Similarly, a retail point-of-sale system should speed up the sales clerk's activities; if response is inadequate, it may slow them down instead.

The extreme example of fast response is, of course, a real-time application such as missile-tracking or oil-refinery control. Response must not only be fast, it must be consistent, as unrecoverable real-time data may otherwise be lost.

It is difficult to achieve consistently fast response to a large number of end points using a centralized general-purpose system, especially if that system is handling other tasks (such as batch processing) concurrently. For this reason, fast-response systems have usually been decentralized onto dedicated computer systems. Sometimes these are large-scale processors, as in airline reservation systems; sometimes these are minicomputers, as in many process-control applications.

A distributed system structure can be used to meet fast-response requirements by moving functions into dedicated components close to the end users or real-time devices. These components are then interconnected, usually in a hierarchical structure and usually with a host processor to provide supporting functions and a focal point for consolidated report preparation.

Deciding whether or not fast-response requirements dictate a distributed system structure is relatively simple. First, if real-time response is required, a dedicated computer will be needed to service each group of real-time devices. If the application is completely independent, these dedicated computers can be left in a decentralized (unconnected) structure. If it is not, a distributed system is called for. Second, if response requirements are rapid but not real-time, a cost/performance trade-off study should be made. A trial centralized system design should be formulated and the cost estimated. An alternative distributed system design, or perhaps multiple alternatives in the case of a very large or complex system, should also be formulated and estimated.

Examination of this trial design may lead to the conclusion that the system belongs in the class of systems which are really too large to be handled in a centralized structure. If the system is so large that desired response cannot be guaranteed with a reasonable cushion of reserve power for expansion and/or unexpected peaks, the choice of a distributed structure is dictated. In other cases, both the centralized and distributed trial designs may be workable. Costs should then be compared, both in terms of initial cost and in terms of the cost of expanding capacity of the system and/or modifying it later as requirements change. The cost of extending and/or modifying the system may bias the decision toward a distributed structure, as it is often easier and less expensive to expand or change a distributed system than a centralized one, because of the greater modularity of the distributed structure.

High-Availability Requirements

Another possible reason for choosing a distributed system structure is to meet high availability requirements. On-line systems generally need both fast response and high availability to meet their users' needs.

Availability factors can be analyzed by means of trial designs, just as fast-response trade-offs can. The expected availability of a centralized design can be computed using mean time between failures (MTBF) and mean time to repair (MTTR) figures for the components involved. The result can then be adjusted to take into account automatic-restart, reconfiguration, and other capabilities which may exist to mask and/or recover from failures. The result of this study will be an estimated probability of the availability of the information system when needed by a user. It may be necessary to repeat this process with several different trial designs, each providing a different degree of equipment redundancy. The system cost for each trial design must also be computed.

This same process is then applied to one or more distributed system trial designs. The result in each case will be an estimated probability of the system's availability when needed by users together with an estimated cost for implementing the trial design. Trade-offs can then be made among the candidate designs.

One factor which must be kept in mind is that availability is improved when the number of components required to function simultaneously is reduced. Functional interdependence, in contrast, usually decreases availability. This dictates the avoidance of designs for distributed systems having series of components which must all operate in order for work to be accomplished. This principle is illustrated in Figure 13-3.

In this example system, a user is located at terminal A. In one case, the system design might require that the terminal device, the terminal controller (TC), its link to the satellite, the satellite processor and its database, its link to the host, and the host with its database (and of course modems or other coupling devices are associated with each link) must all be operational to fulfill a user request.

As the number of components required increases, the probability that all will be operational when needed inevitably decreases. The rate of decrease depends on the specific failure characteristics of each component. These are summed to determine collective failure probability.

Availability is improved in the Figure 13-3 example if most or all of the user's needs are met by the satellite processor. This eliminates the host link, the host, and the host's database from this user's availability

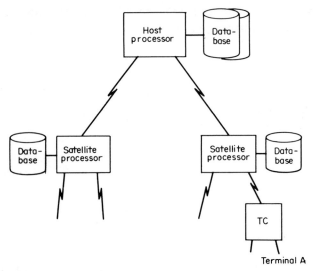

FIG. 13-3 Component independence for availability. TC = terminal controller.

considerations. Similarly, if some of the user's requirements can be met by the terminal controller (TC), the system availability from this user's viewpoint increases still more. For example, the TC might be able to accept and store input even when isolated from the satellite. This would require that a diskette or disk storage device be attached to the TC, reducing its availability somewhat. But this may be a good trade-off for increased independence from the satellite processor and satellite link.

The rule, therefore, is that high availability can be more easily and more economically achieved if the number of components needed to meet the user's normal requirements are minimized.

Distributed system availability, as illustrated in the preceding discussion, must really be addressed from the user's viewpoint. To each user, system availability is gauged by whether or not a needed service can be obtained *when needed*. It is pointless, therefore, to perform reliability or availability calculations on the system as a whole. These calculations must instead reflect the availability of the system as seen by the user. This may mean that multiple availability calculations are required, because different classes of users may experience different availability characteristics.

Administrative Control

Another reason for considering a distributed system is to distribute administrative control of the information-processing facilities. Whether or not this is a consideration depends on the managerial and operational philosophies of the enterprise.

Centralized administrative control can of course be combined with a distributed system structure. A regionalized airline reservation processing system would be under tight central control; the application and system structure are so integrated that "local options" cannot be allowed. Other applications, however, offer wide choice. For example, each bank branch manager might be given a satellite minicomputer with the ability to specify and implement reports best suited to local needs. The satellite processor's other functions, including teller-terminal control, might be standardized across all branches. This would occur, of course, only in an enterprise with a philosophy of assigning functional responsibility to local management. If, instead, the enterprise believes in totally centralized responsibility, the branch manager's mini will probably be programmed centrally, with no local modification allowed.

Still more local control might be allowed. For example, in a paper company, each mill manager might be permitted to acquire computer equipment freely, within local budget constraints. The only restriction might be the requirement to accumulate certain data needed by headquarters and to transmit these data at specified times, using a company-standard set of data-transfer protocols.

All of these combinations of centralized and distributed control with centralized and distributed functionality are feasible within the distributed system concept. The selection of a specific combination will generally reflect the managerial philosophy of the enterprise. (Chapter 19 discusses managerial control in more depth.)

Cost Trade-offs

Lower total cost may be a reason to consider a distributed system structure. The key is *total;* hardware, software, personnel, supplies, facilities, data communications, and any other costs must all be included. While cost is a strategic consideration, it is also an important element in the detailed trade-offs made later in the design process. Cost considerations and trade-offs are discussed in Chapter 17 and 18.

Summary

This section lists a variety of reasons for considering the selection of a distributed, rather than a centralized or decentralized, system structure. Of course, none of these reasons can be considered in isolation from the others.

For example, fast-response requirements may dictate a distributed system structure even though management philosophy is in favor of centralization. The availability trade-off study may show that a centralized structure is more cost-effective, while geographic dispersion results in cost savings in data-communications facilities if the system is distributed. Each of these aspects must therefore be considered and weighed in making the strategic decision in favor of distribution, centralization, or decentralization. Calling this a *strategic decision* emphasizes the fact that it is generally made on the basis of management goals and philosophies, as well as on the basis of technical considerations.

Chapters 14 through 18 provide further guidelines for the tactical aspects of information-system design when the strategic decision is in favor of distribution.

14

SELECTING DISTRIBUTED SYSTEM COMPONENTS

Distributed information systems are configured using a variety of processor and terminal components; the most frequently used are medium- or large-scale general-purpose computers, minicomputers, and components built around microprocessors for terminal and/or device control and for the control of real-time processes.

In some cases there is no question which type of component is best able to perform a particular set of functions. Surprisingly often, however, it is not clear when and/or how a general-purpose computer, a mini, or a micro should be used. This chapter discusses the roles and functions for which each type of processor is best suited. It also discusses how each type of processor can be used most advantageously in distributed systems.

14-1. GENERAL-PURPOSE COMPUTERS VERSUS MINIS AND MICROS

The roles best played by general-purpose computers, by minis, and by micros—and the functions which each can best perform—are sometimes contrasted. And, it is plain that the most appropriate roles and functions for each type of component are determined by that component's strengths and weaknesses. It is important to understand the basic differences between a general-purpose computer and a minicomputer. To some degree, the distinction is a matter of arbitrary terminology. However, there are also some real differences. These differences are particularly apparent when large-scale general-purpose computers are compared to minis.

First, minis and micros can operate in a semihostile or hostile environment. They can operate without raised flooring, special power supplies and safeguards against heat and humidity. Generally, any office or factory environment in which people can work in reasonable comfort is also suitable for a mini—as well as for the low-end general-purpose computers. Even this distinction between general-purpose computers and minicomputers, however, cannot be taken for granted. As minis evolve into satellite processors, with larger and larger disk devices and magnetic-tape handlers attached, they may need temperature humidity, and dust control just as larger systems do.

Minis are sometimes offered in special-purpose heavy-duty packaging. This type of packaging, known as *ruggedizing,* enables the mini to withstand shocks, vibration, electrical fluctuations, electromagnetic interference, and extremes of temperature, altitude, and humidity. Ruggedizing usually protects only the main processor and memory; the peripherals are still vulnerable to environmental effects. Nevertheless, it remains true that the environmental requirements of a mini or micro are usually less stringent than those of a general-purpose computer, especially a very large computer.

Second, differences between the amount and type of software provided for general-purpose computers and that provided for minicomputers are also typical. General-purpose computers provide a wide variety of languages, data management, and application software; minis may not. Until recently, in fact, most minis provided only FORTRAN or BASIC and assembly languages, no data management, and few if any applications.

Today, however, most minis support multiple languages, including COBOL and perhaps report program generator (RPG), as well as FOR-TRAN and an assembler. Most micros are programmed in programming language for micros (PLM), a subset of programming language 1 (PL1) specifically designed for microprocessors. Most minis provide basic data management sufficient to handle sequential and indexed-sequential files, and some provide true database management. Application programs are now available for minis, although usually not as wide a range of applications as for general-purpose computers. Software support is thus different in minis and micros than in general-purpose computers, but the differences are less than they were two or three years ago.

Finally, the internal bandwidth of minis, even very large minis such as the DEC VAX-11/780—"mega-minis"—differs from that of large-scale general-purpose computers. The bandwidth defines how fast data can be transferred internally, memory-to-memory and between memory and peripherals. Bandwidth becomes important in high-speed transfers to and from disk storage. Greater bandwidth is one of the reasons that very large, very active databases are best handled by large general-purpose computers rather than by minis. Because of their bus-centered structures, minis usually have no more than a 32-bit bandwidth and are able to transfer data in and out of memory 32 bits at a time (or 16 bits at a time on smaller minis). General-purpose systems usually access 2 or 4 words in memory at a time. Their bandwidths are 64 bits, 72 bits, 96 bits, or even more. These systems also typically provide more parallel data-transfer paths than the mini's single bus.

Adaptibility to semihostile environments, variety of languages, data management, and application software, and size of bandwidth are the three main differences between mini- and microcomputers, on the one hand, and general-purpose computers, on the other. The next sections discuss the contrasting strengths, weaknesses, and overlapping capabilities of general-purpose and mini- and microcomputers.

Strengths and Weaknesses

A basic strength of general-purpose computers, not surprisingly, is generality. Most general-purpose systems have hardware and software designed to handle a wide range of tasks. This is, of course, more true of large-scale information processors than the smaller ones. Minis and micros, in contrast, are better suited to specialization for a particular task (micro) or small number of predefined tasks (mini). In fact, one of the significant strengths of minicomputers—simplicity—is sacrificed by trying to achieve the same generality on a mini as on a large-scale general-purpose computer. Each type of component should be used in ways which emphasize its strengths and avoid its weaknesses.

Medium-to-large-scale general-purpose IPs are usually designed for concurrent processing of several different tasks, often of different types; they can handle transaction processing, time sharing, and local and remote batch operation concurrently. Smaller general-purpose systems and minis are better suited to concentrate on one or two of these modes, with correspondingly lower overhead because of specialization. Micros are really only capable of one mode of operation at a time.

The power and capacity of large-scale processors provide very high throughput and support very large databases. Minis do not have this power, but instead offer attractively low cost; although the price performance curves of minis and general-purpose computers are moving closer together. The power of micros is even lower—at correspondingly lower cost.

To build upon these different strengths, a large-scale general-purpose processor often acts as the host which occupies the apex of a hierarchically distributed system. Because of its power, capacity, and flexibility, a large-scale information processor can provide services needed to support the less powerful minis and/or micros which occupy the lower levels of the hierarchy.

A smaller version of the general-purpose processor may act as an intermediate or satellite processor in the hierarchy, providing a high degree of compatibility with the larger host.

The mini can be used in several ways in a hierarchically structured system. It may serve as a satellite processor, as a real-time or semi-real-time process controller, as a terminal controller, as a network processor, or it may perform limited combinations of these functions. In these hierarchical systems minis are generally given the simple, repetitive, normal processing tasks, while the general-purpose processor host is assigned the complex, nonroutine tasks. For example, satellite-processor minis may handle all normal transactions and produce all regular reports used locally where the minis are installed (bank branches, warehouses, factories, etc.), leaving the handling of complex transactions and the preparation of complex and/or unplanned reports to the large-scale host processor. To provide these services each mini may support a moderate-sized local database. The host processor, in contrast, often supports a very large database, possibly utilizing complex logical structures.

The micro's roles are very similar to those of the mini: process controller, terminal controller, network processor. However, a micro is poorly suited to act as a satellite processor, and in the other roles the micro usually performs a more limited set of functions—with less flexibility—than the mini when playing that role.

The large-scale host can provide flexible end-user facilities. These include ad hoc inquiry and/or reporting capabilities, which allow unplanned requests for data to be formulated and responded to rapidly. Such capabilities are not usually available on minis, which more often carry out only regular, preplanned functions. (Note, however, that in hierarchical systems the large-scale host must be able to access database partitions or copies stored at the minis to fully meet end-user inquiry and reporting requirements.)

A large-scale host generally operates in a multidimensional mode, providing concurrent batch, transaction processing, and time-sharing services. Because of this flexibility, new functions can usually be added quite easily. But changing existing functions in the complex host environment can be complex. Because of its simpler set of functions, the mini may be able to change more easily and rapidly than the host.

At the lowest levels of a hierarchically distributed system, components are often specialized for functions such as terminal control, the control of real-time processes, or the control of data-communications-network facilities. Where the functions are well-defined and reasonably unchanging, a micro is the better choice; if greater flexibility and/or more combinations of functions are required a mini is the better choice.

An example of semispecialized allocation of functions is shown in Figure 14-1, the production-control system also used as an illustration in Chapters 3 and 6.

The large-scale host in this system performs production scheduling

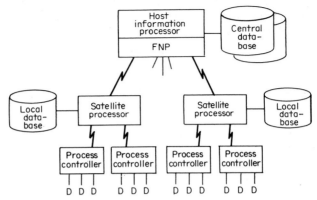

FIG. 14-1 Functional specialization in a production-control system. FNP = front-end network processor; D = device.

for the entire factory. This is a batch-mode operation which involves high-volume computations and the use of a large database containing bill-of-material information, production goals, factory loading and capacity information, and so on. The host interacts with the satellite-processor minis on a periodic basis, updating each satellite's schedule as necessary for the next period of operation.

Each satellite mini is responsible for short-term scheduling and for the (indirect) control of a certain number of factory devices. The minis handle normal conditions falling within predefined limits and can call for assistance from a human production scheduler if unusual situations arise. The minis interact with the process controllers every few minutes in order to receive device status information and to pass new commands to the micro controllers.

The micros which act as process controllers operate in real-time mode, interacting directly with the production devices and/or with factory-data-collection terminals.

The pattern of functional allocation is very clear in this example system. Each lower level of the hierarchy has a smaller, simpler set of functions to perform and acts on a shorter time scale. At the top of the hierarchy, the time scale is long and the functions performed are complex. This is a fairly typical pattern in hierarchically structured information systems.

Overlapping Capabilities

Although the functions described represent the primary uses of the general-purpose and mini- or microprocessors in distributed systems, other alternatives certainly exist. In some cases, roles and functions can be interchanged to meet the requirements of a specific system more exactly. This is true of the minicomputer and microcomputer. These components can play many of the same roles and perform many of the same functions. The choice of a micro or mini is therefore usually based on the range of functionality and degree of flexibility needed.

Interchangeability is also possible, sometimes in a limited form, between the general-purpose IP and the mini. For example, a large-scale IP can perform some of the functions normally assigned to a mini, such as terminal, device, or network control. In fact, in a centralized system, a large-scale IP often performs these functions. However, large-scale IPs perform these tasks as a sideline to their major functions, while micros and minis perform them as dedicated functions.

Large-scale and mini processors can also be interchanged when they play the roles of satellite or host processor. Although a large-scale system most often acts as a host, it can also act as a satellite. Or, a smaller but compatible general-purpose processor can be used as a satellite. Similarly, while the mini most often acts as a satellite, it can also play the host role. It is perfectly feasible to configure a distributed system made up entirely of minis or entirely of general-purpose processors (plus terminals).

Choices of components for the various roles and functions are extremely application-dependent and can only be evaluated fully in the context of a specific distributed system whose desired functionality, performance, and availability have been defined.

14-2.   COMPATIBILITY CONSIDERATIONS

When selecting the components to be used in a distributed system, compatibility is one of the most important considerations. A specific large-scale computer and a specific mini might each provide very good price, performance, and functionality. However, if each supports totally different languages, data management, and network protocols, it may be very difficult to use them together effectively.

Compatibility must be analyzed in four functional areas:

- Languages
- Data management
- Network protocols
- System architectures

Languages

The language most used for commercial or business data processing is COBOL; PL1 and RPG are runners-up. For a distributed system which uses different kinds of components—general-purpose computers, minis —COBOL is probably the best choice. Few minis support PL1, and RPG is too limited for use as the major system implementation language. PASCAL is receiving much attention at present, but it is not widely used for business data processing.

It is important to look beyond labels, however, in order to determine exactly what variety or range of COBOL is supported. The COBOL language was originally defined by the Conference on Data Systems Languages (CODASYL) committee, which also defines proposed language extensions. This is an industry standardization group, made up of representatives from computer users and computer vendors. Each extension is documented in the CODASYL *Journal of Development* (JOD), and then generally accepted as a standard by the American National Standards Institute (ANSI).

The CODASYL- and ANSI-standard definitions of the COBOL language undergo a major revision every few years, and vendors who wish to bid on U.S. federal government procurements are under some pressure to update their COBOL compilers to match each revision of the standard.

The standard defines COBOL as a nucleus plus a series of modules (e.g., table handling, sequential I/O, sort/merge, etc.). The nucleus, which provides the generic COBOL capabilities, has two levels. The low level provides for basic internal operations; the high level provides more extensive options. Most of the other COBOL language modules also have two levels.

To determine the level of compatibility between two COBOL compilers, therefore, it is necessary to determine:

- The revision date of the ANSI standard implemented
- Which modules have been implemented
- Which level of each module has been implemented
- Whether any nonstandard extensions have been implemented

Other languages, such as FORTRAN, PL1, BASIC, RPG, have either formal or de facto industry-standard forms. The general type of analysis described above is, in each case, necessary to determine the compatibility between compilers.

Of course, the fact that the two types of components to be linked for distributed processing do not support identical languages does not mean that they cannot be used together. However, care must be taken to document the differences and take them into account during design and implementation. Most important, if some part(s) of the application logic are to execute on both types of components—either continually or in fallback situations—a compatible language subset must be defined. All application logic which executes on both types of components must then be implemented using only the defined subset.

Data Management

Compatibility considerations similar to those described above for languages also apply to data management.

Attempts to standardize database management have not been as thorough as attempts to standardize languages. Formal standards exist only in the area of CODASYL definitions of data-management techniques. These include a data definition language (DDL) for describing database structures. The first DDL "spec" (published in the JOD) was completed in 1969 and has subsequently been updated. In addition, a COBOL-based data manipulation language (DML) was also defined by CODASYL and subsequently included in the ANSI-standard COBOL language definition. The COBOL language standard also includes modules for handling indexed (indexed-sequential) and relative (random) I/O. These can be viewed as a DML for access to files or databases using those structures. A FORTRAN-based DML is also being defined by CODASYL, with the goal of formal standardization.

The CODASYL-defined DDL and COBOL DML have been implemented by a number of vendors (most notable omission: IBM), including some minicomputer vendors. In consequence, true integrated databases can be created on at least some minis. Software supplied by independent vendors such as CINCOM allows another approach to data-management compatibility. Their TOTAL database software is available for operation on all IBM general-purpose computers, on other large-scale systems, and on several minicomputers.

Finally, as in the case of languages, it may be unnecessary to achieve true compatibility between components. For example, a complex integrated (CODASYL) or hierarchical database might be used on a large host processor. Satellite minis might maintain local data in an indexed-sequential structure or perhaps in a random structure. Although this approach does not allow the same application logic to execute on the host and on the satellites, this is unnecessary in many distributed systems. Also, if this approach is taken, data must be moved back and forth between the host and satellite processors by means of structure-inde-

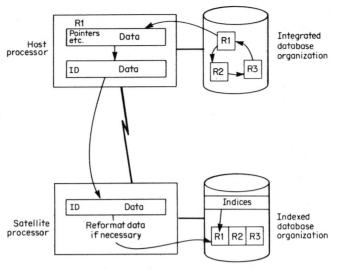

FIG. 14-2   Flat-file data transfer.

pendent techniques. This is sometimes called a *flat-file* technique. It is shown graphically in Figure 14-2.

Structure-specific information such as linkage pointers is stripped from each record in the host processor in the Figure 14-2 example. If necessary, record ID information is appended, and the record is then transmitted to the satellite processor. At the satellite, the record identifier is used to determine where to store the record. In addition, if record formats are not identical, the data are reformatted as necessary. Although this could also have been done at the host location and although the host may have more processing power available to do reformatting, such an approach makes the host vulnerable to any change in satellite database structure. So reformatting, if needed, is best performed at the satellite. The flat-file approach can be used to translate between any types of data structures, whenever completely identical structures are not used.

Network Protocols

Components which interface via communications facilities (or even via channel connections) must share a common network protocol. Otherwise, data transmission is impossible. Here, again, several formally standardized protocols exist. So do many more widely used industry-standard protocols. The latter become de facto standards because of extremely wide usage. One example is the teleprinter protocol used for most low-speed keyboard terminals; another is the binary synchronous communications (BSC) protocol originally defined by IBM.

The protocols that are most formally defined are the new bit-oriented procedures such as HDLC discussed in Unit 4). In fact, the current trend, internationally, toward shared circuit- or packet-switched networks has intensified the push toward formal protocol standardization. As more and more networks of this type come into operation, more and more vendors of computer or communications equipment and software can be expected to support the new standard protocols. Some form of the X.25 recommendation of CCITT shows promise of developing into a truly international network interface.

As in languages, network protocols must be carefully analyzed to determine what level of compatibility exists. For example, BSC is often referred to simply as "a protocol," but in fact it is a basic transmission protocol with a wide variety of optional features. 2780 BSC, for example, consists of a set of options suitable for the 2780 remote-job-entry device. Even at this level, however, the protocol has two "ends," so to speak. A device can support 2780 BSC by emulating a 2780 device or by acting as a host able to interface with a 2780 (or 2780-like) device.

When in doubt about network protocol compatibility, it is best—if at all feasible—to find an installation at which the components being considered have been successfully interconnected. Lacking this type of demonstration, a certain amount of faith, and risk, are usually involved.

Architectures

Now that a number of computer vendors have announced network architectures, as discussed in Unit 4, it is germane to ask: Do you really need an architecture to install a distributed system? Clearly the answer is no.

An architecture provides standard interconnectability between the products (generally new products only) supplied by that vendor under the architecture. It also provides modularity and flexibility for future change within that environment. Most (not all) architectures, however, have the characteristic of providing only limited interfaces to products not supplied by the vendor who defined the architecture. All architectures, for example, support teleprinter terminals, because these are so widely used. However, an architecture usually supports more complex intelligent terminals only if they are supplied by the vendor of the architecture or if detailed emulation of that vendor's terminals is provided. Flexibility in acquiring components from different vendors may therefore be lessened when a system architecture is used.

Many distributed systems which exist today, including some very complex ones, were implemented without any overriding architecture. It is perfectly possible to find a set of network or system protocols which are quite widely supported and to use these as the basis for interconnecting unlike components.

For example, the 2780 BSC protocol for remote batch input/output is often used to link non-IBM remotes to an IBM-supplied or IBM-compatible host. So many "real" 2780s are in use that this interface is unlikely to be changed. It is therefore a stable base which can be used with minimum risk.

The device interfacing to the host via the 2780 BSC protocol might in fact be a large-scale non-IBM host—this has been done more than once. So the remote device might perform very complex information processing and database management, using the BSC link to exchange data with the IBM system as necessary.

A good rule to follow is: Use the simplest approach which will meet the stated objectives. If a very complex system structure is required and the needed components are supplied by a single vendor, then that vendor's architecture (if any) should be used. If the system needs can be met with a simple structure and components from multiple vendors provide attractive benefits, use of an architecture is probably unnecessary.

Of course, this situation will change as vendors' product lines evolve to support only a specific architecture. It is to be hoped that "gateway" approaches and/or the evolution of international-standard protocols (see Chapter 8) will provide for interconnection of equipment from different vendors. Otherwise the choices open to computer users may be unnecessarily restricted.

15

DESIGNING INFORMATION-PROCESSING FUNCTIONS

The distributed-processing structures described in Chapter 5 can be used in a variety of ways in order to meet a variety of application objectives. This chapter describes the different ways in which information-processing functions can be allocated within a distributed system.

The discussion in this chapter and in Chapter 16 (Designing Database Management), is concerned with broad system-level design questions. It does not describe how to design specific application programs which will perform functions allocated to a distributed-system component: there are other sources of information for guidance on that level of system design. The emphasis here is on how to choose the best overall structure.

The most fundamental decision in the design of distributed system is how to allocate the total workload among the components of the system. The topic is discussed in Unit 15-1. A second important aspect of some distributed systems is resource sharing. Resource sharing is a matter of providing access to unique resources—databases, programs, peripherals —for users at other locations. Unit 15-2 discusses this topic. Finally, some distributed systems require systemwide (or global) catalogs or directories by which objects such as database partitions, programs, or terminal end points can be located. Methods of creating and using global directories, when needed, are described in Unit 15-3.

15-1. WORKLOAD ALLOCATION

The problem of workload allocation in distributed systems is the problem of assigning the total workload to the components—hosts, satellite processors, controllers—of the system. This allocation is usually performed during system design and then remains static during system operation. That is, a specific set of functions is assigned to each system component and that component always executes the same functions. Alternatively, in some systems, some basic preassignment of functions is made, and then during system operation, the workload is dynamically reallocated. This mode is often called *dynamic load leveling*. It is also possible, in some systems, to combine static and dynamic workload allocation.

Static Workload Allocation

The method most often chosen is static, predefined workload allocation, in accordance with the principles defined in Chapter 14—assigning functions to emphasize the strengths and minimize the weaknesses of each type of component used. A good example of a static workload allocation environment is the complex banking system used as an illustration in Chapter 3 and repeated in Figure 15-1. Static workload allocation is generally used in hierarchically distributed systems formed of unlike components; e.g., large-scale information processors, minicomputers, terminal or device controllers, and microcomputers. This is largely due to the extreme difficulty of accomplishing dynamic load leveling in such a heterogeneous environment.

In this banking application, the total set of information-processing functions was first defined and then distributed across the available components during system design. (Database elements were similarly assigned statically to the host and satellite processors.) Each type of component was then implemented to perform its assigned subset of the application. A short discussion of the specific functions assigned to each component illustrates how this was done.

The terminal controllers handle all input/output for the banking-terminal devices and for back-office printers used for local output in the bank branches. Application-specific editing is performed on each input transaction in order to ensure that it is as nearly correct as possible before it is passed to the closest satellite processor.

Each satellite processor handles what are considered the normal transaction types. For example, deposits and withdrawals can be handled by the satellite, using its resident application programs, provided that the customer's home branch is within the satellite processor's local area. These normal transactions account for better than 80 percent of the volume of transactions which originate at the bank-branch terminals.

Conditions which the satellite cannot handle include complex transactions such as account-history queries and credit card applications. These complex transactions are sent up to the nearest large-scale host, which has a more complex set of application programs and maintains a much larger database than the satellites do. Satellite processors are also unable to handle situations occurring when a customer enters a remote branch which does not maintain that customer's account balance and requests a withdrawal. (Approximately 3 percent to 5 percent of all transactions

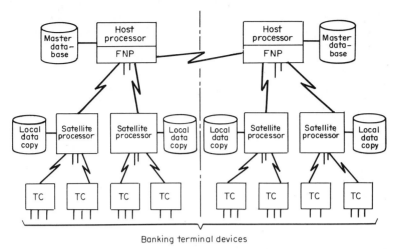

Banking terminal devices

FIG. 15-1   Banking system with static workload allocation. TC = terminal controller.

handled by this bank are of this type.) This type of withdrawal transaction is passed on by the satellite processor where the transaction was entered and travels up the hierarchy to the nearest host. From there it is forwarded, via the other host if necessary, to the satellite which handles the customer's home branch. The withdrawal is processed normally by that satellite, using the account record on its local database, and the response is returned to the original satellite and to the terminal at which the transaction was entered.

This banking system is a good illustration of how to distribute both application-related functions and database information as close as is feasible to the point where transactions originate. It also illustrates the principle of centralizing the handling of small numbers of complex transactions which cannot economically be handled by each of the satellite processors.

Database design often makes use of the so-called 80-20 rule; that is, 80 percent of database accesses are concentrated against active records which make up only 20 percent of the database. Many applications also exhibit an 80-20 relationship in the sense that 80 percent of the transactions (by number) fall into a simple or normal processing category, while the remaining 20 percent fall into a complex or exception category. This pattern is apparent in the banking system in Figure 15-1. When a logical pattern of this type can be discovered, it is a good basis for allocating processing functions within a distributed system.

Static workload allocation, like dynamic load leveling, is intended to spread the total information-system workload advantageously over the existing components. Unlike in dynamic workload allocation, in static workload allocation the system designer must attempt to foresee all possible uses of the distributed system and to preallocate functions so that all of these uses can be handled satisfactorily.

Such preplanning is very advantageous, because it avoids the use of dynamic decision-making logic which can impose a large overhead burden during system operation. In fact, the logic which must be executed during operation for workload allocation is minimal. The specialization of functions which often results from this mode of operation may, however, make procedures to handle failure situations very complex. A static load-allocation system tends to be much more *tightly coupled* than a system in which dynamic load leveling is used; that is, the components are closely interrelated and are more likely to be affected by each other's failures than in the dynamic load-leveling environment.

Tight coupling may also mean that the system is somewhat inflexible. It can handle circumstances which have been foreseen and planned for in detail, but if a new situation arises, the system may be unable to react appropriately. In contrast, a well-designed system with dynamic load leveling is potentially, at least, more responsive to unforeseen conditions.

Dynamic Workload Allocation

In dynamic workload allocation, also called *dynamic load leveling*, the information-processing load—and sometimes the database elements and the database-access load—are moved among the available information processors dynamically. Methods of moving the processing load are discussed in this chapter, leaving the implications for database access and data movement for Chapter 16.

The goal of dynamic load leveling is to make optimum use of the available computing resources. This is particularly important when temporary overloads occur at specific locations while other locations have unused capacity. For example, many organizations provide computer services nationwide within the United States, either on a service-bureau basis or as an in-house corporate service. Computer use typically peaks between 10 in the morning and 12 noon and between 2 P.M. and 4 in the afternoon, local time. Because of the three-hour time difference between the East Coast and the West Coast, these peaks do not occur simultaneously. It is therefore possible to make better use of computer resources if they are shared than if the computers serving each time zone are used only for local processing. With sharing, fewer total resources may be needed than if each computer center were required to handle all peak loads unassisted.

The environment within which dynamic load leveling is most often found is a horizontally distributed system. A good example of this type of system is a service bureau which operates three very large computer service centers. This is shown in very simplified form in Figure 15-2.

In this example distributed system, all of the host processing centers are "identical," in the sense that the hosts are made up of the same type of hardware (although not necessarily with exactly the same set of peripheral devices) and run under control of the same version of the same operating-system software. This commonality considerably simplifies load leveling.

If any one of the host processors shown in Figure 15-2 becomes overloaded—in other words, is receiving more work than it can handle within stated turnaround and response requirements—it can pass off some of its work, either to another host within the same center or to a host in one of the other service centers.

Certain types of work can be easily moved in this example system. For instance, a batch job which includes its program and data files in the input job stream can be handled by any host. Compilations can be run at any location. Time-sharing users who are building new programs and/or data files can be serviced by any host. Other types of work are less amenable to movement. For example, jobs or transactions which require access to an existing database present a problem, even in this environment. If a terminal user wishes to access data elements which are part of the Region C database in the Figure 15-2 example, then at least some of the processing will be required at one of the City C regional host processors. Methods of overcoming these difficulties are described in Chapter 16, where a discussion of how to use distributed databases is presented.

In some cases, however, difficulties arising from database access can-

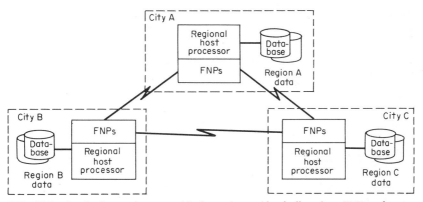

FIG. 15-2 Service-bureau system with dynamic workload allocation. FNP = front-end network processor.

not realistically be resolved. For example, a long-running job which requires high-volume access to a large database must be processed at the site where the database is located. It is impractical to move the entire database. It is also impractical to run the job at another location, obtaining remote access to the database as needed. Such database movement is realistic only when small-volume database access is involved. A large job of this type is therefore not a candidate for load leveling. If many jobs of this kind exist, the possibilities for dynamic load leveling are limited.

Difficulties also arise when load leveling is attempted in a nonhomogeneous environment. The Figure 15-2 example, in which all hosts include the same type of hardware and software, is the optimum situation. More often, the hosts are different. Sometimes they are different hardware models, perhaps from different vendors, and sometimes the hosts use different types of software.

Load leveling can sometimes be performed even between unlike information processors, although usually in a limited way. If the hosts all support standard languages, such as COBOL and FORTRAN, for which documented standards exist, it may be possible to run compilations anywhere. In many cases "compile-and-go" test runs can also be made anywhere. Jobs which use stored data present a more complex problem, but even these may be sharable if the hosts all support a common database-management method. However, in all these cases relatively minor differences—code sets, arithmetic precision, and so on—may cause confusing results when the same job is executed on different hosts at different times.

In general, the greater the differences among the information processors involved, the smaller the set of tasks which can be moved for load-leveling purposes. Also, considerable manual preplanning is required, and this often leads to the use of static workload allocation instead of the dynamic form.

In cases where dynamic load leveling is feasible, its control may be automatic and may be embodied in the system software in each of the host processors. In this case, each host must contain logic for determining:

• When it is overloaded
• Whether another host has the capacity available to handle the overload
• How to select work to be shared with another host

The question of whether a host is overloaded is sometimes difficult to answer. The host software may be able to determine, for example, that it has a queue consisting of fifty input transactions and twelve batch jobs, with twenty-five active time-sharing users. However, it is difficult to predict what this means in terms of system load. Very good predictions can be made, in some cases, of transaction-processing resources needed, but the load imposed by batch jobs and by time-sharing users is much more difficult to predict with any accuracy.

A simple algorithm for determining overload might be dynamic measurement by the host of its ability to meet response and/or throughput goals. Any failure to do so might be considered to indicate an overload. Another approach might simply be to assume that any queue length and/or number of users over predefined limits represents an overload. The drawback to simple algorithms is that they may or may not accurately determine the condition of the host. If an overload is sensed when none in fact exists, complex load-leveling procedures will be called into play unnecessarily. On the other hand, failure to detect an existing overload may allow the system's performance to degrade without corrective action being taken.

Once a host determines that it is overloaded, equally complex problems are encountered in deciding how to handle the situation. The host must first find out if another host can assume part or all of the overload, and if so, which part. This can lead to a complex negotiation procedure between the hosts, with one host "bargaining" to offload the tasks it finds most onerous and the other "bargaining" to pick up only those tasks most suitable to its current capabilities. As in bargaining between humans, many difficulties can arise.

It can readily be seen that automatically controlled dynamic load-leveling logic is very complex. In fact, there is a real possibility that this logic may create so much processing overhead that it outweighs any advantages to be gained through the dynamic reallocation of the workload. In many cases, in fact, it may be more realistic to embody the dynamic load-leveling logic in system administrative personnel. The status of a large distributed system must be continually monitored, usually from a central location (see Chapter 20). If overload conditions arise, administrative personnel may be best able to judge how the work can be redistributed across the available processors. Commands must then be available which these administrators can use to cause the processors affected to take the necessary action.

Dynamic load leveling, whether automatic or manually controlled, may cause response time to degrade for interactive-mode end users. If data and/or processes are moved dynamically, response must inevitably be lengthened and can easily become too long to be practical. Since interactive operations cannot accept the slow response which moving tasks and/or jobs between locations will probably cause, dynamic load leveling may therefore, in practice, be limited to moving batch-mode jobs.

Both dynamic and static workload allocation have a place in the spectrum of distributed information systems. At present, more examples of the static mode exist than of the dynamic mode. This is because the dynamic workload allocation is more complex, has more significant limitations, and is generally understood less well.

15-2. RESOURCE SHARING

Resource sharing is the ability to make resources available to users who need them, regardless of where the users and the resources are located. Workload allocation, as discussed in Unit 15-1, is of course one form of resource sharing. In this section, resource sharing is discussed in terms of the problem of allowing users to access unique resources not available locally.

This discussion will cover only part of the total spectrum of resource sharing. In practice, resource sharing is needed most often in connection with database access. Techniques for providing access to remote database elements are covered in Chapter 16 (Unit 16-2).

Resource sharing can apply to any resource which is not available at every location within a distributed system. For example, if a distributed system includes three host processors, one of which is a very fast scientific processor (a CRAY-1, for example), that processor represents a unique resource. Users at other locations may wish to access the scientific processor for specific types of work while running their normal workload on the local general-purpose hosts. A distributed system which includes a host which supports extensive graphics capabilities supplies a second example of the problems of resource sharing. Users anywhere within the system may wish to access those capabilities. Indeed, it is crucial to repeat that any unique resource—a program, a library, a file or database, a peripheral—may create the need for resource sharing. Procedures for resource sharing, like those for workload allocation, can be either completely predefined and static, or they can be dynamic.

Static Resource Sharing

Static resource sharing is preplanned when the system is designed. This is by far the simplest approach, and should be chosen whenever possible. In the example system in Figure 15-3, Host 3 may have a very high-speed output printer. Jobs run on Host 1 or Host 2 which produce very large-volume output may direct that output to Host 3 for printing.

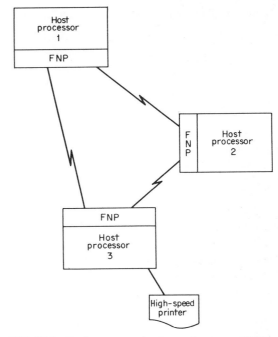

FIG. 15-3   Static resource-sharing environment. FNP = front-end network processor.

This example is static because the printer is fixed at Host 3 and the applications which produce output for that printer must have built-in logic to cause their output to be sent there. Because some operating systems and/or system architectures do not support this mode readily, this type of resource sharing may not be easy to implement. DEC's DECnet (see Chapter 10) is designed for this type of resource sharing, but many other systems are not.

To overcome these problems, it may be necessary to design a pair of cooperating processes to transmit and receive the output data. The receiving program can then pass the data on for printing in the normal way. The concept of cooperating processes is basic to distributed systems (since it is most often used to manage access within a distributed database, it is discussed in Unit 16-2).

Static resource sharing can be applied to any type of resource, in any distributed system structure. It is the most straightforward approach and requires little control overhead. However, if the resources to be shared are likely to move, the static approach will cause system- and/or application-software changes each time a move occurs.

Dynamic Resource Sharing

The advantages and disadvantages of dynamic resource sharing are just the reverse of the advantages and disadvantages of static resource sharing. The dynamic mode involves complex software and the overhead inherent in complexity. On the other hand, dynamic resource sharing provides flexibility for change, since resources can be relocated without affecting system users or applications.

The Advanced Research Projects Agency computer network (AR-PANET) supplies a good example of dynamic resource sharing. An extremely simplified schematic of part of the ARPANET is shown in Figure 15-4.

ARPANET includes a large number of host processors (over 100 in 1979) which communicate via the "communications sub-network." This subnet is controlled by more than sixty mini-based interface message processors (IMPs) linked together in a meshed network of broadband transmission facilities. Packet switching is the transmission method used; indeed, ARPANET was the prototype for all contemporary packet-switched networks.

The main purpose of ARPANET is resource sharing, allowing research workers at multiple locations (mostly universities) to exchange information, make use of each other's unique computer resources, and generally develop synergy by means of the network. Since there is no way to foresee what a specific researcher will need in order to advance new or current projects, resource sharing in ARPANET is dynamic. The control of resource sharing is therefore applied manually, by the users. Figure 15-4 illustrates this by showing a user at a terminal attached to

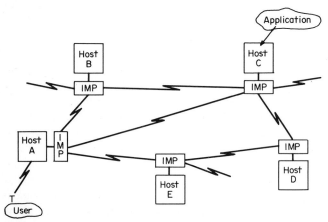

FIG. 15-4 ARPANET dynamic resource sharing. IMP = interface message processor; T = terminal device.

Host *A* and an application program available at Host *C*. This user can access that remote application via the network, just as though the terminal being used were connected to Host *C* rather than Host *A*. To accomplish this, however, the user must determine where the application is located—either through the use of on-line directories (see Unit 15-3) which may contain this information or by asking other ARPANET users who may know where the required capability exists. In addition, the user may have to contact the system administrator at Host *C* to obtain a valid user identification and usage permission(s). Whether this is necessary depends on the security measures taken at each host location. Since the various organizations whose hosts are attached to ARPANET are all independent entities, associated only because all perform government-funded research, they have different approaches to security control. In a resource-sharing network belonging to one organization, the security-protection requirements would more likely be uniform at all hosts.

ARPANET also provides some dynamic load leveling, under user control. Although some resources attached to the network are unique, others exist at more than one host. For example, there are a number of DEC PDP-10s on the network which are extensively used for time sharing. If a user finds one PDP-10 too busy to provide quick response, it is possible to access another nearly identical system and try there.

ARPANET also makes it possible to take advantage of the particular strengths of the different hosts. A number of users access the Multics host at the Massachusetts Institute of Technology (MIT) to do program development because of its superior text editors and interactive compilers and debug aids. The debugged program, perhaps in PL1, may then be sent to a large IBM host for final compilation and execution in batch mode.

Although ARPANET provides extremely sophisticated capabilities for workload and resource sharing, it is important to place this network in perspective. ARPANET's users are largely research-oriented and many are in fact engaged in computer-related research. The focus of the network is to enhance the productivity of these researchers, who are after all extremely sophisticated computer users. In contrast, most distributed systems focus on enhancing the productivity, in a production environment, of very unsophisticated (in terms of computer-related knowledge) users. Complex terminal-use procedures taken for granted in ARPANET would be completely impractical in a retail point-of-sale system or in a production-control system. So, although consideration of ARPANET provides many interesting insights into distributed processing and networking, ARPANET can seldom be used as an exact pattern from which other systems can be built.

15-3. CATALOG AND DIRECTORY STRATEGIES

When designing the information-processing functions of a distributed system, it may be necessary to provide global catalogs or directories which indicate the location of resources. All centralized systems maintain directories of local resources, especially on-line (and sometimes off-line) files or data sets. A directory (the term directory is used here inter-changeably with *catalog*) cross-references a resource name, such as a file name, to a physical location where that resource is stored. The directory allows application developers to write programs without concern for physical storage strategies. (In the 1950s and early 1960s, programmers *did* have to worry about physical locations, both on-line and off-line, making programming much more difficult than it is today.)

There is a similar need to know where resources are located when dealing with distributed systems. And, the situation is more complex in distributed than in centralized systems. In a centralized system a peripheral, for example, is either attached to the central computer or does not exist. In a distributed system, the desired peripheral may exist at some remote location.

Today many distributed systems have the directories built into the application logic flow. This is feasible if workload allocation and resource sharing are both static. For example, a hierarchical structure is shown in Figure 15-5. In this type of system, it is typical for incoming transactions to be handled by a common transaction editor in the satellite processor. Transaction types which are invalid are rejected to the terminal user for correction. Types which can be handled by the satellite cause the related application program to be called into execution. All other transaction types are sent up to the host for processing there.

In this illustration, the transaction editor includes a table of transaction types which is really a directory indicating where specific application routines are located (local, host-resident, or possibly resident at another satellite processor). If the design of the system is reasonably stable and the needed directories are reasonably small and can be isolated in one or a few application programs, this is a very satisfactory way to handle the problem. However, if either dynamic load leveling or dynamic resource sharing is required, it is necessary to consider whether to implement global directories. These directories may be provided in system software, achieved through changes to system software, or included in application logic, depending entirely upon the equipment and software being used. Whatever specific methods of implementing global directories are employed, the following remarks remain valid.

A global directory can be easily thought of as an extension to existing

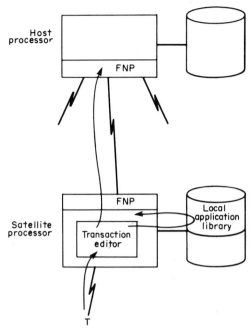

FIG. 15-5 Application-embedded directory logic. FNP = front-end network processor; T = terminal device.

local directories. Figure 15-6 shows a file directory with a hierarchical structure for maintaining location and access-permission information. The illustration shows how easily a structure of this type can be extended to include remote files.

In the example, User A might be a system administrator responsible for a distributed personnel application. The "Pay" file of payroll data is stored locally, on the specific disk volume indicated. The "Exp" file of work experience points to Host C, indicating that it is stored there. The directory at Host C would then indicate exactly where the file was physically stored.

This directory structure includes access permissions because it is usually necessary to validate each access in order to ensure that only authorized usage is allowed. In a global directory, the access permissions might be null in all locations except the one where the data are stored, minimizing the problems of updating these permissions at multiple locations. Generally speaking, indeed, resources can be separated into two categories: those which are accessed only locally and those which are

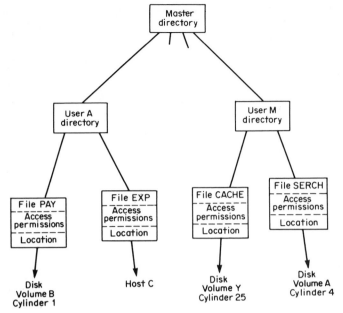

FIG. 15-6   Global directory structure.

accessed from one or more remote locations. Only the latter need be included in the global directory.

There are three strategies for creating and maintaining global directories. These are:

- One copy
- Copies at selected locations
- Copies at all locations

One copy of the global directory minimizes the difficulty of keeping the directory up to date. It also makes it possible to concentrate integrity and security protection for the directory at one location, increasing the ease with which full protection can be provided. On the other hand, a single copy of the global directory forces all remote resource requests to be sent to the directory location. This can cause a considerable transmission volume in the communications network and also delay access to the resource. Perhaps more important, a single copy makes the distributed system vulnerable. If the site which maintains the directory is not operational, no access to remote resources is possible.

Copies at selected locations remove the worst disadvantages associated with the one-copy approach to the global directory. It is more likely that a copy of the directory will be local, avoiding transmission overhead and delay. It is less likely that all copies will be unavailable, so remote access is assured. However, if multiple copies are used any update to the directory must be made to all copies, preferably simultaneously. This causes some added overhead and, more important, creates problems if all updates cannot be applied. For example, if one host which maintains a copy of the global directory is off-line when a directory update is made, the update must be retained and made later. Because the logic to account automatically for all possible conditions is too complex to be practical this must usually be accomplished by a system administrator.

Copies at all locations reduce overhead and vulnerability to the minimum. However, the problem of updating all copies may be intensified as the number of copies increases.

Trade-offs must be made between the advantages and disadvantages of these strategies. Some references to published papers on this topic are provided in the bibliography. The following summarizes (and simplifies) the conclusions of researchers in this area concerning the best strategic choices for creating and maintaining global directories.

In a production-mode system updates to the global directory will be made relatively infrequently. But when access to a remote resource is required, fast response is important. This combination calls for copies of the global directory at all locations. Fast response is provided, vulnerability is very low, and updates to the directory seldom cause problems because they occur infrequently.

In a distributed system shared by a number of researchers or students, new additions to the global directory will be made frequently as users create new files, etc., available for shared use. This environment does not require the fast response of the preceding example. This combination of frequent changes together with little pressure for a fast response time calls for a single copy, or at most two copies, of the global directory. Updates occur frequently, and are very likely to cause synchronization problems. Vulnerability is less important in this environment and can be handled through journal backup to the directory, and/ or through manual methods of locating remote resources (as in ARPANET, discussed earlier).

A specific distributed system may fall somewhere between the extremes of these two examples. In each case an appropriate trade-off must be made, based on the specific environment and requirements of the planned system.

16

DESIGNING DATABASE
MANAGEMENT

When using any of the forms of distributed database—partitioned, replicated, or combination partitioned/replicated—described in Chapter 6, application programs must be able to obtain the data elements which they require. Ideally, a distributed database should be a virtual (or transparent) filing system, in which any element can be accessed and/or updated with equal ease and speed from any processing location. Unfortunately, a general implementation of such a capability is currently beyond the state of the art, and the following discussion considers only techniques which are feasible for use today. One technique for ensuring that application programs will be able to obtain the data elements they require, even when information-processing functions are distributed, is to leave the database centralized. This approach is discussed in Unit 16-1. Unit 16-2 discusses the task of designing a distributed database and the methods usable for providing remote access to that database.

16-1. DATABASE CENTRALIZATION

Distributed-database technology and experience are less advanced than those for networking and distributed processing. In some cases, therefore, it may be more advantageous to retain or create a centralized database rather than distributing the data. For example, a distributed system may evolve from an existing centralized system through the addition of intelligent terminal controllers. If the host processor supports a large database and can provide adequate access and response to system users, the best choice is to leave the database centralized. Implementing a distributed database simply to have done so, after all, is an expensive and pointless exercise. However, if the distributed system being described did not provide adequate response to users accessing the database, distribution of the database should be considered.

One difficulty in making these decisions is that database-related problems are often very complex, and hard to evaluate. For example, if response to database inquiries is too slow, it may be difficult to determine exactly why this is the case. Are the channels to the disk devices saturated with access requests? Is the central processor too overloaded to make optimum use of the disk devices? Is the front-end processor a bottleneck for remote traffic? Is the speed of the communications links too slow to handle the traffic? Is it some combination of one or more of these problems?

Generally speaking, if database distribution is being considered because a centralized database is performing inadequately, it is important to understand the cause(s) of this inadequate performance. Indeed, before seriously considering distribution, it is necessary to determine if the problem can be resolved in the centralized environment, and if the problem can be resolved by use of a centralized database it is necessary then to consider how difficult and/or how expensive it will be to resolve it. Only when these answers are known can an informed decision be made about whether to distribute or centralize the database.

An important reason for database centralization is that it is sometimes hard to segment an existing or planned database. Figure 16-1 illustrates this problem, as applied to a parts-explosion database. This type of structure is accessed in different ways, such as for bill-of-material processing and for "where-used" processing. Generally speaking, it is impossible to break apart this type of structure.

This difficulty might be thought to apply only to the partitioned form of distributed database, but in fact it applies to the replicated form as well. A replicated database typically involves copies of database segments, not the entire database. If the data cannot easily be segmented, neither partitioning nor replication is practical.

The two major reasons for considering a centralized database in a distributed system are therefore:

1. A centralized database exists, or can be implemented, in order to adequately serve system users.

2. It is impractical to segment the data which must be maintained.

If neither of these reasons applies, the techniques described in Unit 16-2 should be considered.

16-2. DATABASE DISTRIBUTION

Finding natural database-access patterns, as discussed in Chapter 6, is the key to creating a distributed-database design. When a design has been created, methods for providing access must also be supplied.

The ways in which access can be provided to the segments of a distributed database can be summarized in terms of the following choices:

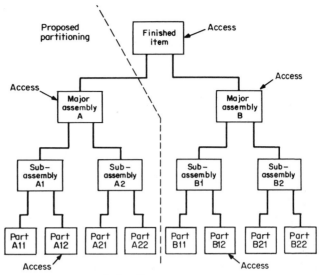

FIG. 16-1   Parts-explosion data structure.

- Move the program or process to the data.
- Move the data to the process.
- Combine these two methods.

In a specific system it may be most advantageous to move the program or process, to move the database information, or to take some combination of these actions.

The term *program* is used here to indicate a procedure which has not yet been placed in execution, while *process* refers to a program which is in the execution state. In the following discussion, the term *process* will generally be used, since the distinction between execution and nonexecution status is not usually significant.

In defining distributed-database-use techniques, it is also necessary to choose whether or not processes and/or data are moved dynamically. Dynamic movement involves deciding during system operation that moving a process or some data increment to another location is appropriate. An alternative solution, often simpler, is to make these decisions statically, during system design. (This corresponds to the choice between dynamic and static workload allocation and resource sharing discussed in Chapter 15.) The "movement" then becomes the preassignment of processes and data elements to various locations, placing them there at least semipermanently. Dynamic and static allocation of processes and data elements can also be combined: some preassignment can be made statically and some dynamic movement can occur during system operation.

Finally, there is a choice as to how much "visibility" database distribution will have. In the virtual filing system mentioned in the introduction to this chapter, database distribution would be "invisible" to end users and application developers; they would be able to obtain data without any knowledge of the location(s) involved, perhaps even without knowing that the database has been distributed. Other implementation approaches make database distribution known to the application developer and sometimes even to the end user.

The following sections cover all of these alternatives. They are organized in terms of the three major design choices: to move the process, the data, or some combination of process and data.

Moving the Process to the Data

When a distributed database exists, a process or user at one location may need access to data stored at another location. (In this section the discussion is kept relatively simple by assuming that only one remote location is involved. A later section explores a situation which involves data stored at more than two locations within a distributed system.)

One alternative in this case is to move the process to the data, which is most often the case in batch-oriented environments. A batch job typically accesses a large number of database elements, and database size is large (in comparison to the size of the program). It is therefore more economical to transmit the process—in this case a job or a subdivision of a job—and its input transaction and report output than to transmit the database information. The movement of the process may be either user-initiated or under system software control. It can, in other words, be either user-visible or transparent to the user.

User-controlled process movement requires that the end user or application developer know that the database partition to which access is required is located remotely and exactly where it is located. Once this knowledge is obtained, the job can be prefixed with an address indicating that it is to be sent to a specific processing location.

This approach simplifies the distributed system software implementation, but places the burden of coping with database distribution on the user. An example of this mode of operation is shown in Figure 16-2.

In the Figure 16-2 example system, User *A* at Information Processor 1 maintains programs in local storage. When Program *A* is run, however, it requires access to the database at IP 2. In this case the user enters a process-activation request (by means of JCL commands) specifying that Program *A* is to be transmitted to Information Processor 2, accompanied by any necessary input data, and activated there. Process *A* then

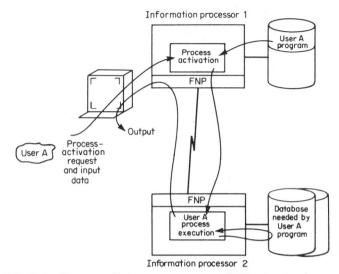

FIG. 16-2   User-controlled process movement. FNP = front-end network processor.

executes at IP 2, accessing the database without any special handling because of the distributed database relationship. Output produced by the process is addressed to User *A* and is transmitted back to that user's terminal—probably when the process has successfully completed execution.

In this mode, database distribution is fully visible, in the sense that the user must know where needed data are located and must be aware of any change in the location(s) involved. However, the distributed system must provide the basic process- and data-movement capabilities necessary to support this mode of operation. Some systems today do not provide this support. It may be more practical for a user in these circumstances to maintain programs at the same processor where the required data are stored; if data at multiple locations must be accessed, at different times, it may be necessary to maintain a copy of the program at each location. At all times the design of the distributed system must be consistent with the supporting software capabilities available.

System-controlled process movement is only possible if the information processors of the distributed system maintain global database directories. When a global database directory is available, each information processor can analyze the database requirements of each process. Any process which requires access to remote database elements can be automatically transmitted there for execution. This mode of operation is shown in Figure 16-3.

In this example the Job *A* job-control language (JCL) indicates that

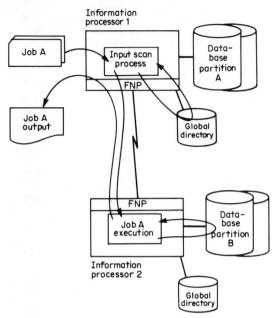

FIG. 16-3   System-controlled process movement, FNP
= front-end network processor.

the job will access Database Partition *B*. The input-scan process at IP 1
looks this up in the global directory and discovers that Database Partition
B is attached to IP 2 and therefore transmits Job *A* to IP 2. Execution of
Job *A* takes place at IP 2, with normal access to Database Partition *B*. Job
A's output must be directed back to IP 1, where the job initiator is
located.

Moving the Data to the Process

In some cases it is appropriate to move the needed data to the location
where the process is in execution rather than to move the process to
where the data are stored. This approach is most often chosen in the
time-sharing or transaction-processing environment.

In transaction processing, in contrast to batch processing, usually only
a small part of the database is accessed. It is therefore feasible to consider transmitting the data to the process, returning only updated elements (if any) to the location where the data are stored. In this case the
process, consisting of its program and status information, may be considerably larger than the data involved. As in dynamic workload allocation
(Unit 15-1), data movement may seriously degrade response to interactive users; this must be considered in deciding whether or not dynamic
movement is feasible.

Data movement may either be under control of the application or may be controlled by system software. As in the case of process movement, data movement can also be viewed in terms of the amount of visibility—ranging from complete user visibility and total system transparency to total user transparency and complete system visibility.

User-controlled data movement is shown in Figure 16-4, which is an example of data movement under application-program control.

In this case the executing process requests access to remote data by sending a message, indicating the data element(s) required, to the IP at which the data are stored. This message is transmitted to the location (address) indicated and is handled there by a so-called remote access utility process. The remote access utility attempts to obtain the requested data elements from the local database and return them to the requestor. If the data do not exist or are locked for access by another process, the utility returns a denial status code instead.

The major advantage of this mode is its flexibility. The use of a remote access utility makes it possible to map between different database structures and to convert data formats as necessary. For example, in the system illustrated in Figure 16-4, the two information processors might be of different types and the two database partitions might be of different structures and formats. Database Partition A might be an indexed-sequential structure maintained in the extended binary-coded decimal-interchange code (EBCDIC), while Database Partition B might be an integrated (linked) structure maintained in the American standard code for information interchange (ASCII). The remote access process in Processor 2 could accept an access request formatted for an indexed-sequential structure and fulfill it, using some conversion formula to locate

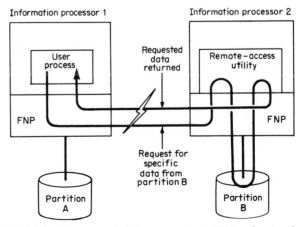

FIG. 16-4 User-controlled data movement. FNP = front-end network processor.

the necessary record(s), then convert the retrieved data to EBCDIC for return to the requesting process. The difference in structure and code set between the two database partitions would therefore be transparent to the user process; the distribution of the database, on the other hand, would be visible. There are, however, practical limits to how much transparency can be achieved in this way. Mapping between complex structures—for example, from a network database to a relational database—is very difficult, and may be only partially successful.

Another advantage of data movement under application-program control is that it can be provided without major modifications to the operating systems of the information processors involved. These operating systems must provide only a general transmission capability; they need not be aware of the database distribution. The remote access utility can generally be implemented as a user process, avoiding changes or extensions of the operating system. One possibility is to implement the remote access utility as a transaction-processing routine. Requests for database access would be formatted as transactions and easily handled by the normal transaction monitor or executive.

A major disadvantage of this mode of access is that the developers of the requesting application programs must be aware of how the database is distributed and thus must also be aware of any change in the location of elements within the database. Any change in the distribution of data will cause corresponding changes in all accessing programs.

Integrity problems also arise in this mode of access. For example, if the remote access process in Processor 2 (in Figure 16-4) fails while handling a request from Processor 1, some recovery action may be necessary at both locations. Similarly, access refusals because of conflicting concurrent access requests may require special handling at both locations.

System-controlled data movement is an alternative method of providing access to remote data. An example is shown in Figure 16-5. In this case the requesting process simply asks for a specified increment of data; it need not know where the required data are stored.

In this example the user-process request for database access is analyzed by the software of the database manager (DBM). Using a global database directory, the DBM determines where the requested data are stored. If they are stored locally, they are retrieved directly and returned to the requestor. If the data are remote, the DBM initiates a remote access request and transmits it to the DBM at the appropriate remote location. The remote DBM either fills the request or returns a denial status, which is passed back to the requesting user process.

The advantage of this method is that the location of any data element, and even the existence of a distributed database, need not be known to

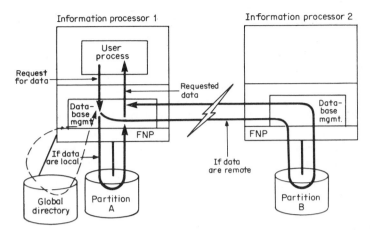

FIG. 16-5   System-controlled data movement. FNP = front-end network processor.

users or to application processes. The database can be reorganized and elements moved as appropriate; applications are unaffected and only the global directory requires update so that current data locations are known to all processors within the system.

This method of access involves the same integrity problems discussed in connection with user-controlled data movement. It also requires significant and complex software implementation. In practice, cooperating database managers are most easily implemented in homogeneous equipment; i.e., identical computers using identical database structures. This will support one class of user requirements, but it will not solve the problem of interfacing unlike processors. That situation is currently best handled by means of the remote access utility approach described earlier.

Combination Strategies

Large complex procedures may best be handled by some combination of process movement and data movement. Complex situations are most often caused by the need to access data stored at more than two locations. For example, an enterprise which operates a distributed system with a partitioned database may periodically require a report which consolidates input from all of the database partitions. In some cases the reporting program may also involve database updates. This type of report cannot be prepared using only the techniques of process movement. Nor can it be prepared using only the data-movement techniques. One method of preparing a multisite report, in a system which includes three processing locations, is shown in Figure 16-6. This method can be called *process chaining.*

In this example, the report-preparation procedure, which updates multiple database partitions at multiple locations, has been partitioned to form a series of processes chained together by means of a process-activation scheme. Each process in the chain can update only the data at one location. As each process completes, it activates the next process in the chain, in a different information processor at a different location. This method requires that the application developer be aware of the exact data distribution; i.e., this method is completely user-visible. Note that the placement of processes at the various locations represents a case of so-called static process movement and contrasts to the dynamic form of process movement discussed earlier.

In the Figure 16-6 example, the first process accesses Partition *A* at Processor 1, updating it and extracting data for reporting purposes. These data are then included in a message which also includes a process-activation request for Process 2. This message is directed to Processor 2, where Process 2 is activated and updates Partitions *B* and *C*, then consolidates the information obtained during both updates. A new process is activated in Processor 3, and so on. This sequence could be continued as many times as necessary to access all of the required data.

The last process in the chain completes any required reports, and sends them to the originator and/or to other desired location(s). If high-volume reports are to be printed, the final process can create and activate a reporting process in the IP closest to the originator, making the report available for local printing there.

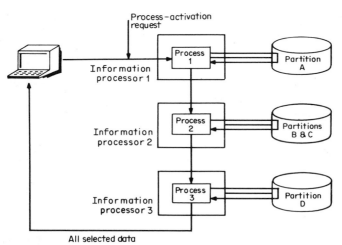

FIG. 16-6 Process chaining.

If this technique of process chaining is used, any type of access to the data at each location can be allowed. Since each process execution at each location is independent of the others, except for the passing of control, problems of database interference and delay across processors do not arise. Thus, the advantage of using process chaining to obtain access to data at multiple processors is that it provides great flexibility without causing any interference with other update users. And, from the operating system's point of view, it is extremely simple, since all complex control logic becomes the user's problem.

However, this approach has several disadvantages. First, the application developers must be aware of database distribution and must take this into account in system design. Second, when each process in a chain is in execution, it is independent of its predecessors. If an abnormal termination occurs, breaking the chain, it may be difficult or impossible to remove the effects of preceding processes. If, for example, a multiple-location update requires a chain of four processes, and the third process terminates abnormally, the updates performed by the first two processes will remain in effect unless complex procedures are implemented to reverse them. (Alternatively, any termination notice resulting from a chained process could be sent to the originator or to a system administrator, who could then take appropriate action manually. This type of process chain requires very careful design, so that the chain can be reinitiated at any point if an abnormal condition occurs.)

There is also no easy way to present an unchanging picture of database status if the process-chaining technique is used. The data retrieved by each process represent that part of the database at a point in time different from the point in time represented by the data retrieved by the other process. In contrast, a process running in a single host with exclusive access to the database can obtain a completely static picture of the entire database. Indeed, the only way to achieve this same result in a distributed database is to implement a global locking capability. This would simultaneously lock all partitions required, at their respective locations, and prevent any update-mode access until the reporting process(es) completed execution. In some cases this may be feasible; for example, if multisite updates and reports are run during periods when no on-line users are active. Although in other cases prolonged locking of the entire distributed database would be impractical, it may well be that problems associated with global locking are theoretical rather than practical. Many applications provide slack periods (nights, weekends) in which global database locks can be easily applied.

In contrast, applications which involve continual access—hospital patient monitoring, airline reservations—do not allow global database locks. But a static view of the contents of any of these databases would be meaningless. A report on airline reservations summarizes transactions run against the database rather than the status of the active database. Similarly, reporting from a hospital information system is concerned with number of beds occupied, patient account status, and so on, not the minute-to-minute status of a particular patient. So if reports are to be run from a distributed database, it will probably be possible to choose a slack time and lock the entire database during report operation.

Situations requiring data access at more than two locations, and/or which require a combination of data and process movement, should be avoided in system design if possible. This is because of the complexity and potential problems involved.

16-3. DATA SYNCHRONIZATION

One of the most complex problems in managing a distributed database is the question of how to synchronize the data in its various parts. In a replicated database, copies of some data elements exist at two or more locations. Although it is not usually necessary to keep the copies identical at all times, it must be possible to reconcile differences which arise and to bring the copies back into agreement. In a partitioned database, elements in one partition may relate to elements in one or more other partitions. Changes which affect these relationships must be made in all partitions; otherwise, the relationships will no longer be correct. Although space does not permit a complete, detailed discussion of data synchronization, there are some basic rules which, if followed during distributed database design, can avoid the most serious problems of data synchronization.

Rule 1: Do not attempt to build a "hot-standby" distributed database. This rule applies to replicated databases and states that it is impractical to keep two (or more) copies of the same data exactly in synchronization in real time. There are very few operational "hot-standby" systems (the computers which support U.S. manned space flights form one exception). This is because it is extremely difficult, technically, as well as extremely expensive, to keep two or more computers exactly in synch. At least two large commercial information-processing systems foundered while attempting to implement geographically separate "hot-standby systems." It is pointless to get caught up in an attempt such as this; more important, it is almost never really necessary.

Rule 2: Design a replicated database so that a given data element is updated at only one location during each defined period of time. The complex banking system used as an example in Chapter 3 (Figure 3-8) design embodies Rule 2. Data elements copied at the satellite processors are mainly current balances, which are updated on-line at the satellite. During the banking day, while these updates are going on, the current balances are never updated in the master database at the host locations. After the bank branches close, balances are updated during batch processing against the master database; during this time the satellite processors are idle. On completion of batch processing, updated balances are transmitted from the host to the satellite locations, forcing synchronization of all data.

This approach, which is fairly typical of the way a replicated database is most often managed, does not attempt to keep the copies continuously in synchronization. However, it establishes a pattern of alternate updating of the copies and the master, so that at any point in time the relationship between them can be determined exactly. This general approach avoids the complexities and expense of keeping data copies exactly in synch, but it meets application requirements fully.

Rule 3: Do not split close data relationships when partitioning a database. In CODASYL database terms, this means that a set relationship should not be split across partitions on different computers. For example, an order-entry database might include customer identity, customer orders made up of order-line items and line-item status, and inventory status for stocked items. Since the two are very closely related, it would be impractical to split order-line item information from line-item status. It might be possible to store customer identity in one partition and the remaining elements in another, because customer data probably change infrequently and if necessary could be updated in both partitions. Line-item status and inventory probably cannot be split, as these are often tied together.

Two problems can arise when data partitioning is improperly done: performance may be poor, and system errors/failures can damage database integrity. If line items and inventory were in different partitions in the above example, each new order would be entered in one partition, but for each line item at least one access to the other partition would be required. Assuming that this involves the transmission of at least two messages over data-communications facilities, order entry might be rather slow. This provides an example of the way in which improper partitioning may lead to poor performance.

An example of integrity problems may be provided by the order/inventory split hypothesized. If a customer has canceled an order, those items ought to be returned to inventory. However, if network or equipment problems made it impossible to update inventory immediately, the two partitions could be out of synch. Or the inventory update might be partially completed but then be interrupted by a hardware or software problem. Even very complex recovery methods might not always ensure perfect synchronization of the database partitions.

In summary, potential problems in the management of a distributed database can be avoided by following these three rules. The result will be a database—whether partitioned or replicated—whose parts are relatively loosely coupled and in which it is always possible to determine precisely the degree of synchronization which exists.

17

DESIGNING THE NETWORK

Chapters 15 and 16 discuss two of the three function sets required in a distributed system, information processing and database management. This chapter covers the third and final function set, network processing.

As in the preceding two chapters, the intent here is not to present an in-depth plan for network design, but rather to provide an overview of the important points to be considered. In fact, the topic of data-communications-network design is already well represented in the literature. References are provided in the bibliography for those who need more detailed knowledge.

Two major topics covered in this chapter: approaches to network design for maximization of system economies and emerging trends in public and private networks. These overviews provide a background against which more detailed information can be put in perspective.

17-1. BASIC COST CONSIDERATIONS

Achieving a cost-effective network design is the most difficult part of selecting data-communications elements and facilities. However, cost considerations must not outweigh the requirement that each network design must:

- Handle the projected transmission volume
- Provide the desired speed of response
- Supply the needed level of availability

The goal of maximizing economy in network design, therefore, is to achieve a configuration which meets the above goals at minimum cost. This goal would not be so difficult to achieve if there were fewer types of transmission services available. The fact that many alternatives exist often leads to an embarrassment of riches which makes specific choices difficult. In the United States choices are made still more difficult because of the wide variety of competitive offerings now available and planned for the next several years. Rather than attempt to provide a comprehensive list of transmission facilities and services—a list which would no doubt be obsolete before publication of this volume—this chapter describes the types of offerings that are available and/or planned.

Cost-Optimization Techniques

The methods which are used to minimize the cost of data communications can be grouped as follows:

- Selecting among alternate services
- Configuring the network for lowest mileage
- Multiplexing
- Concentration
- Functional distribution

Selecting a service can be time-consuming, as so many different ones exist. These can, however, be grouped as follows:

1. Speed of service
   a. Low-speed, ≤300 bits per second (bps)
   b. Voice-grade, 600 bps to 10.8 kbps
   c. Broadband, 19.2 kbps and up
2. Type of service
   a. Dial (switched)
   b. Dedicated (private)
   c. Value-added or public data network

The speed of a communications link is determined by its bandwidth. A given service has a range of potential speeds and the couplers used determine the actual transmission speed. Voice-grade facilities, for example, have a nominal capacity of 2000 bps (dial) or 2400 bps (dedicated), but can operate much more slowly—at teleprinter rates—or much more rapidly—above 10 kbps—with appropriate coupling devices.

Speed equates directly to capacity and somewhat indirectly to response. A 300 bps rate of transmission usually equates to ten characters (or bytes) per second (600 characters per minute). If, therefore, the system design requires 1000 characters per minute to be handled at all times, or even only at peak times, a low-speed link is not adequate.

In addition, transmission overhead and pauses between transmissions must be allowed for. The latter are particularly important for interactive traffic. The practical carrying capacity of any link is therefore well below the theoretical capacity. Guidelines for determining true link capacity are given in some of the references provided in the bibliography.

Low-speed links are seldom used today, because they are not so widely available as voice-grade links are. More important, the cost differential which once made low-speed links much more cost-effective than voice-grade links for low-speed traffic no longer exists.

Generally, the higher the inherent speed of a link the higher the cost. On the other hand, the relationships between cost and speed are neither simple nor linear. For example, if a dedicated voice-grade link is considered to have a basic capacity of 2.4 kbps, it might be assumed that a broadband link capable of 19.2 kbps would be eight times as expensive. This is rarely the case; usually the cost of the higher-speed link is a much lower multiple of the lower-speed link cost than is the speed.

Dial links are generally less expensive than dedicated links. However, they are not necessarily available whenever needed, and the transmission quality may be low, resulting in a high error rate. Dedicated links are always there, and the quality can usually be adjusted by the carrier to provide high reliability.

Just as low-speed links have lost their initial price advantages over voice-grade links, so, the price differential between the formerly much-less-expensive dial service and dedicated links is less significant today. Depending upon the specific tariffs involved, crossover usage points can be plotted at which a dedicated link becomes more cost-effective than dial service.

Value-added services (often called VAN, or *value-added network*) provide "something added" besides a transmission link. Most often the added value consists of error detection and correction, redundant facilities for high availability, and cost sharing with other users. The predominant trends in value-added and public data networks (PDNs) are covered in Unit 17-2.

Configuring for lowest mileage also reduces cost. The cost of a dedicated link generally depends upon its length, although this dependency tends to take the form of a step function rather than a linear scale. Dial-call rates are also distance sensitive. (Only value-added services—and only some of these—are distance-insensitive; usually the charge is based upon volume of transmission rather than distance of transmission.) The locations of host and satellite processors are usually fixed because only certain suitable physical facilities exist. The locations of terminal devices are generally also fixed, because they are determined by where transactions originate and/or where end users are located. Thus, the key to configuring for low mileage is the determination of the best way to connect processors and terminals. The most straightforward way—connecting each terminal to a host or satellite processor using a separate link —is usually the most costly. Some terminals do need dedicated links, but these are usually high-volume remote-job-entry (RJE) terminals. Interactive terminals, which cannot exceed the speed of the user, generally waste link capacity. Multipoint links, as shown in Figure 17-1, can be used to minimize link costs by connecting several terminals to one link.

In a *multidrop configuration,* a link runs from the processor to the most distant terminal. Each intermediate terminal location is served by a "drop" connecting that location to the link.

In a *loop multipoint configuration,* the link runs from the processor past all of the terminal locations and returns to the processor, forming a loop. Loop configurations are best suited to terminal clusters within a limited area, as in the case of a number of teller terminals in a bank branch. Nonloop multipoint links are most often used when the terminal end points are geographically dispersed. Both forms of multipoint usage reduce link costs, but at the cost of some processor overhead to provide the polling and selection needed to manage the link. Usually this is a very viable trade-off.

Multiplexing allows the traffic from several lower-speed links to be combined on one higher-speed link. Like the use of multidrop links, multiplexing takes advantage of typical tariff patterns—one 4800 bps

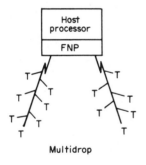

Multidrop

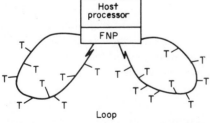

Loop

FIG. 17-1 Multipoint configuration. FNP = front-end network processor; T = terminal device.

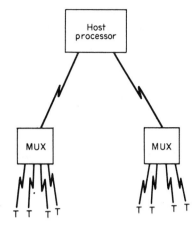

FIG. 17-2 Multiplexing. MUX = multiplexor. T = terminal device.

link is generally less expensive than an equivalent number of lower-speed links. Figure 17-2 shows a typical use of multiplexing.

There are two types of multiplexors (MUXs): time-division multiplexors (TDMs) and frequency-division multiplexors (FDMs). Use of a TDM requires that the terminals to be multiplexed be clustered geographically, with a logical point where the TDM can be installed. For example, all terminals in a remote sales office could be connected to a TDM for interface to a host processor via one link. When FDMs are used, the multiplexor can either be placed in the "center" of the terminal cluster or distributed in order to form a configuration very much like a multidrop link. A distributed FDM requires some of the multiplexing logic to be provided at each terminal location, allowing each terminal to use a unique part of the total link bandwidth. A distributed FDM configuration is shown in Figure 17-3.

FDMs are most cost-effective for small numbers of terminals, usually less than sixteen. TDMs are most cost-effective for larger numbers of terminals.

FDMs are transparent to host or satellite processor software, since they simply split up the link bandwidth and use it more efficiently. TDMs, in contrast, use time slicing on the link. A pair of TDMs is often used, one at the remote terminal cluster location and one at the processor location; the second demultiplexes the traffic so that it appears to come from many links. If the second TDM is not used, the host or front-end software must demultiplex incoming traffic and multiplex outbound traffic to match the remote TDM.

Multiplexors, until recently, were hard-wired "dumb" devices. Today, however, "smart" MUXs—sometimes called *statistical multiplexors*—are

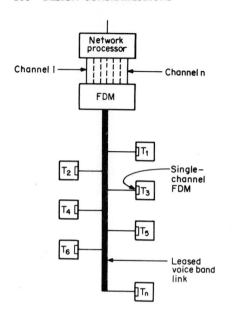

FIG. 17-3 Distributed frequency-division multiplexing. FDM = frequency-division multiplexor; T = terminal device.

available. These devices include a microprocessor, which allows them to provide error detection as well as to perform data compression based upon the statistical frequency of data patterns transmitted. Sometimes modems for use on high-speed links include built-in multiplexing and demultiplexing capabilities.

Concentration is functionally equivalent to multiplexing, except that a concentrator is typically a programmable device—a mini- or microcomputer. It can therefore perform other functions as well as multiplexing. For example, a concentrator can handle multipoint links, providing poll-and-select logic to manage the terminals on those links. It can also buffer traffic so that temporary overloads of input can be handled on the outbound link(s). Multiplexors, in contrast, must be configured to avoid overloads—the outbound links must be fast enough to handle the maximum simultaneous flow of all inbound links

Functional distribution is also a way to cut transmission costs. Moving processing and databases close to end users often cuts transmission volume substantially. This can result in lower data-communications costs. This aspect of cost reduction is discussed in more detail in Chapter 18.

In summary, there are many ways to cut communications costs. The best method to use in a specific system will depend upon the geographic areas and distribution, the application type(s), the response requirements, the transmission services available in the areas, and many other factors. While cost is important, and every effort should be made to minimize costs, this requirement must not overshadow other important requirements. The network processing facilities must provide the response needed by terminal users, must be capable of handling total transmission volume, and must provide the level of availability necessary to support the on-line applications. A satisfactory communications-network design must meet all of these criteria, as well as being cost-optimized.

17-2.   PUBLIC NETWORKS

In planning ahead for the network-related aspects of a distributed system, it is appropriate to consider the transmission services which are likely to be available. This section briefly summarizes current trends in the United States and in several other countries. As usual, a note of caution is in order: changes occur very rapidly in the services proposed, and this section presents a snapshot at a specific point in time. The *general* trends indicated here are expected to continue; any *specific* statements about available or planned services are subject to change.

United States Trends

A wide variety of transmission services is available in the United States. These include a public voice-telephone network, which is provided by the American Telephone and Telegraph Company (AT&T), the Bell System operating companies, and a large number of independent telephone companies. Both dial and dedicated links are available from these common carriers, with local intrastate services provided by the operating companies and independents, and interstate services and overall coordination available via AT&T Long Lines.

Today the bulk of all data communications in the U.S. travels on the public voice network. However, a variety of other services is available, and the gradual trend in data-communications usage is toward these newer services.

Specialized common carriers provide a subset of the services available from the more generalized common carriers. For example, MCI (Microwave Communications, Inc.) provides microwave transmission facilities between certain pairs of cities. The international record carriers, ITT and RCA, provide interfaces between U.S. carrier facilities and postal telephone and telegraph (PTT) facilities overseas.

American Satellite provides satellite transmission services, as do RCA and Western Union. In each case the satellite launching and physical management of the "bird" are provided by COMSAT (Communications Satellite Corporation). Satellite Business Systems (SBS), a consortium of Aetna Life Insurance, COMSAT, and IBM, plans to provide satellite transmission services in the near future.

Each of these services covers a specific geographic area or areas and provides certain services, as approved by the Federal Communications Commission (FCC). Certain services, most important private voice-telephone service, have typically been restricted to a single carrier in any geographic area. Data-transmission services, in general, have been open to many different carriers providing competing services.

Value-added services provide something more than simply data transmission. Typically a specialized common carrier leases transmission facilities from AT&T, the Bell operating companies, and/or independent phone companies, adds some further "value," and resells the value-added service to customers. Value-added services typically provide error detection and correction on the carrier's links. They may also provide speed and/or code translation between sending and receiving equipment —terminals and processors. Another value added by specialized common carriers is *sharing*, which permits a given link in the network to be shared by a number of users. This usually lowers the cost to each user. Still another added value is the provision of alternate paths through the network, so that link failure does not isolate users of that link. Multiple paths are always provided between any two end points, minimizing the probability that link failures will be catastrophic.

Two large value-added networks (VANs) are not operational in the United States: Telenet and Tymnet. Telenet, operated by a subsidiary of General Telephone and Electronics (GTE), is a packet-switched network which makes extensive use of the techniques developed in ARPANET, enhanced through further experience. The network is managed by mini-based network processors, and some micros, which interface customer hosts and terminals to the network. Telenet provides both emulation interfaces to handle currently used protocols (such as teleprinter) and an X.25 higher-level protocol interface. Telenet personnel have been very active in the international standards work within CCITT on X.25.

Tymnet—the second large U.S. value-added network—was originally the network serving Tymshare's remote service bureau customers. It was later split off into an independent, regulated subsidiary, providing value-added services both to Tymshare users and to others. Tymnet is a circuit- and message-switched network, rather than a packet-switched network, but it provides services which are comparable to Telenet's. Tymnet can supply an emulation interface to host processors, allowing them to avoid having to make any changes in their software, or it can supply an X.25 interface, which is more efficient than the emulation interface.

Both Telenet and Tymnet serve a large number of U.S. cities, and each provides specific interfaces to PTT facilities in other countries. Each has been quite successful in expanding its customer base, which has in many cases been drawn from companies who find VAN service more cost-effective than an in-house network. In addition, value-added carriers provide network management, and this is particularly convenient for small or medium-sized organizations, which often find network management a significant problem.

Another proposed value-added service is AT&T's Advanced Communications Service (ACS). The services proposed for ACS will include code and speed conversion, terminal-control programming (in the network) by the customer, forms storage and management, and store-and-forward message transmission. ACS was announced by AT&T in the summer of 1978 and will not be available until approved by the FCC. When approved, ACS could have a significant impact on other value-added service. However, this impact will very likely be long-term, rather than immediate, as a lengthy period of startup, both technically and in the marketplace, will be required.

Both existing and planned value-added services are aimed at low-to-medium-speed traffic to and from interactive terminal devices. Because of the human interactive time involved, it is difficult to use a link effectively for interactive traffic (one technique to avoid this is to multidrop the terminals). By sharing links among many terminal users, from different organizations, link use becomes very cost-effective. However, high-speed bulk transfers, such as high-volume remote job entry and output or file transfers, are best handled on dedicated links rather than on shared links.

Trends in Other Countries

Communications facilities in most countries other than the United States are government-controlled. (The controlling agency is generically called the PTT, although specific countries use different agency titles.) Data-communications trends are therefore government-controlled, and there is less variety of services than in the U.S. Two general trends in new data networks are apparent. One is packet switching, the other is circuit switching.

Several packet networks are in various stages of implementation in different countries. Datapac is operational in Canada. Transpac came on line in France in 1979. The PTT packet networks are standardizing on the CCITT X.25 recommendation which is already in use in the U.S. by Telenet and Tymnet and which ACS will also use. Intelligent terminals and processors will use the X.25 interface, while unintelligent terminals can use the CCITT X.28/X.29 recommendations or interface via a "black box" which provides X.25.

On the other hand, some countries are choosing, at least initially, a circuit-switched approach for their public data networks. The Nordic Public Data Network, being implemented jointly by the Scandinavian countries, will use the CCITT X.21 interface and provide circuit switching. The German PTT is also planning an X.21 interface, with evolution to X.25 later.

At an international level, several of the European PTTs are associated in plans for Euronet, which will provide packet switching via X.25 interfaces. And, in the Far East, Japan is planning a packet-switched public network, while mainland China appears interested in an X.21 circuit-switching approach.

Generally, the X.25 interface is gaining wide acceptance and so far seems to be the most likely candidate for worldwide use in providing international data exchange. However, international data transmission involves not only technical considerations but also the regulatory concerns of the governments involved. It therefore requires careful planning, preferrably guided by experts in this complex area.

17-3. PRIVATE NETWORKS

In some cases, even when public network facilities are available, a private network is preferrable. Large organizations, especially in the United States, tend to favor private networks for several reasons:

1. Cost
2. Privacy
3. Control

Many small or medium-sized users find that it costs them less to participate in a shared public network than to acquire a private network. On the other hand, large organizations, with high transmission volumes, may find a private network more cost-effective. Whether a public or private network is the more suitable choice for a particular user can only be determined through evaluation of the various services available and cost trade-off studies.

Data privacy and security can be of great importance. As more and more data volume is transmitted, more and more elements are potentially sensitive. Business plans, pricing strategies, and shipment volumes must be protected from competitors. Personal data such as welfare payments, health status, and credit rating must be protected to preserve the individual's privacy. Some people doubt that adequate protection can be provided by public services. For example, in a value-added service, a minicomputer responsible for switching might be subverted to copy selected messages for later analysis. *Encryption* (or, encoding) of traffic can protect against most "eavesdropping," but the cost of encryption may be higher than the cost of using a private network with uncoded data traffic.

Finally, control of the network can be assured if the net is private. Of course, this may be a mixed blessing. For a small organization, which cannot affort the expert networking staff needed to control private data communications facilities, a public network is advantageous. A large organization, which has the necessary expertise available in-house, may find the increased control possible in a private network worthwhile.

If a private network is chosen, either packet-switching techniques or more conventional approaches can be used. One large bank has chosen to implement a packet-switched private network. The software for the mini network processors was obtained from Bolt, Beranek & Newman (BB&N). Software to interface the bank's computers to the network follows the protocols defined for ARPANET. Since the ARPA protocols assume heterogenous systems, this approach is particularly suitable when different kinds of computers must interface with one another via a network.

It was mentioned earlier that packet nets are most efficient and cost-effective for interactive traffic. In addition, the cost of the controlling minis makes a packet network initially more expensive than an "unintelligent" network. A reasonably high volume of data transmission is therefore necessary before the costs of this type of network can be justified.

A dedicated link or links is the best choice for high-volume traffic between any two points. Even if a packet-switched network is installed to handle interactive traffic, it is probably better to configure dedicated links between any locations which exchange a great deal of traffic.

Many alternatives exist, as outlined in Unit 17-1, for the configuragion of private networks. Chapter 18 discusses how network design is integrated with the other aspects of the total design of the distributed system.

18

TOTAL SYSTEM DESIGN

This chapter presents an overview of the design procedure for distributed systems. Space limitations dictate that this must be an overview; a detailed discussion of the design process would require an entire volume. However, much of the information needed in the design process has been presented in the preceding chapters.

It is impossible to do a "single-pass" design of a distributed system—or indeed of any complex computerized system. The design process is therefore an iterative one, which consists of the following steps:

1. Formulate a trial design.

2. Analyze that trial design in order to determine whether functionality, performance, and availability characteristics are adequate and whether costs are acceptable.

3. If all parameters are not satisfactory, modify the trial design and repeat Step 2.

4. If a given trial design cannot be modified satisfactorily, return to Step 1 and try a different trial design.

This iteration typically proceeds until a satisfactory design is found. It is impossible to determine, objectively, which is the best possible design, so it is necessary to settle for one which provides the desired characteristics—or an acceptable subset of them—at an affordable cost.

18-1. TRIAL DESIGN

The formulation of a trial design consists of the following steps:

1. Select an information-processing structure.

2. Select a database structure.

3. Select the types of components to be used for processing and database purposes.

4. Allocate information-processing functions to components.

5.   Allocate database elements.

6.   Select a structure and components for the interconnecting network.

It may be necessary to repeat some or all of these steps several times before proceeding to an evaluation of the trial design. Although each step is presented as independent, they are complexly interrelated. A decision made in a later step can therefore affect an earlier decision, perhaps resulting in reevaluation and change.

The information necessary to perform the six steps in formulating a trial design has been provided earlier; this section simply summarizes and presents an analysis of how the various aspects of design fit together.

Select an Information-Processing Structure

It is necessary to determine how to use the information-processing components of the system. A choice must be made about whether to use a hierarchical structure, a horizontal multihost structure, or a combined (hybrid) structure. All of these structures are described in detail in Chapter 5.

The hierarchical structure is most suitable if the distributed system builds upon and extends an existing host computer. Allocating new functions to intelligent terminals and/or satellite processors leads to the formation of a hierarchy. A hierarchical structure is also very well suited to applications which are "naturally distributed." Branch banking, for example, is performed at bank branches which are geographically separate and distinct entities. Placing intelligence at the distributed locations, while retaining a central focal point for common processing functions, leads naturally to a hierarchical structure.

A horizontal structure, in contrast, is most often appropriate to two specific situations: when the distributed system is formed by connecting previously independent host processors and when distribution is chosen simply to modularize an application which has no natural pattern of distribution. Home-office banking functions provide an example of the second sort of situation to which horizontal structures are appropriate. Unlike branch-banking functions, home-office banking functions are not distributed geographically in any natural way. However, they can be partitioned by function. For example, one processor might handle communications input and output, another might manage the database, and another might perform the main computations. This is the general pattern of the Bank of America distributed system (which the bank calls "distributive").

The combination or hybrid structure is most often chosen because two or more hierarchies must be linked. Each hierarchy may be performing a different application, but one related to the other application(s) performed by the other hierarchy (or hierarchies). Or, each hierarchy may be serving a separate geographic region or, the total processing at the central location may be too high in volume for one host; two or more hosts, each supporting a hierarchy, may be required. Finally, there may be a need to partition the central host-resident processing to reduce failure and/or security vulnerability, leading to the formation of multiple hierarchies.

Select a Database Structure

The second step in the definition of a trial design is to determine whether the database is to be distributed, and if it is to be distributed, in what way this will be best accomplished. These topics are covered in Chapter 6.

A centralized database is appropriate so long as it will provide adequate performance. And, a centralized database is a necessity if the logical database does not lend itself to partitioning. A distributed database—whether partitioned or replicated—cannot be constructed unless there is some way to split the data consistent with access patterns. If no way of splitting the data consistent with access patterns can be discovered, the choice between a centralized database and a distributed database is foreclosed: the database must be centralized.

If a pattern of database segmentation can be determined, a choice must be made between partitioning (nonredundant data elements) and replication (selective copying of data elements). Partitioning is the optimum strategy and should be chosen whenever feasible. However, partitioning does not provide as much built-in backup or fallback capability as replication. In addition, replication is more suitable if multiple read-only copies of the data are needed in different locations to provide rapid access. In this case, or when backup copies are of great importance, replication should be chosen.

Select Information-Processing Components

After choices of an information-processing structure and a database structure have been made, it is necessary to select the information-processing components to be used. If a totally new system is being designed the designer may have great flexibility. In such cases, the best approach is often to create a request-for-proposal (RFP) or request-for-bid (RFB) document, present it to several computer and/or software vendors, and then analyze the resulting bids. Each vendor will propose the optimum mix of equipment from a particular product line.

While this approach may seem simple, in practice it requires a great deal of effort to prepare an RFP, evaluate the resulting proposals, and select a vendor or vendors to provide the required hardware and software. This approach is used by the U.S. federal government for many procurements, and in spite of a great deal of experience in the process, the preparation of each RFP is said to require many "personyears" of effort. On the other hand, for a large, multimillion-dollar (or equivalent) procurement, this is probably the best way to ensure that all viable alternatives are considered.

In many cases, the system designer has far less freedom. The new distributed system is often an outgrowth, expansion, or evolution of an existing system or systems. For example, a central host computer may use unintelligent terminals as remote I/O devices. When a major new application is to be implemented, the system designer may be faced with a choice between enlarging the host system and increasing the number of terminals on the one hand, and installing intelligent remote minis or terminal controllers on the other. In either case, the new components must be able to work compatibly with the existing host. This still leaves the system designer with a fair number of choices, but they are fewer than those available to a designer who is planning a totally new system. Chapter 14 covers, in more depth, the topic of selecting components for a distributed system. The following discussion summarizes some of the more important factors to be considered.

If it appears advantageous, from a cost and/or response standpoint, to place components at point-of-transaction locations, then the equipment chosen must be able to operate in those locations. For example, in a factory environment, terminals and/or processors must be able to operate without extra air conditioning, without raised flooring, etc. In some cases they must be able to operate in a corrosive atmosphere or to sustain exposure to vibration. If processing power is required under these circumstances, a mini- or microcomputer rather than a general-purpose computer will be the appropriate choice. However, when processors and/or intelligent terminals are placed at the point-of-transaction locations, the designer must ensure that each component can operate in "unattended mode." It must be possible to load the processor or terminal program(s) remotely (or possibly by some means such as a removable floppy disk), to restart it automatically in case of failure, and to diagnose and correct the cause of failure from a remote location. And if the component is essential to continued operation, it must be able to recover rapidly from errors and failures and to do so without (or with only minimal) human intervention. Before placing intelligent remotes in locations such as factories, bank branches, supermarkets, etc., these factors must be fully evaluated.

Compatibility—discussed in Unit 14-2—is another important factor to be considered. If an existing system is being expanded by the addition of remote elements, the degree of compatibility among elements must be evaluated and determined to be adequate before the remote elements can be selected. If an entirely new system is being designed, it must be determined that all of the elements selected can work together compatibly.

This does not mean that all components must be obtained from the same vendor, or even that all must be fully compatible. Rather, it means that in each system design a specific level of compatibility is important. Usually this means that system elements must be able to exchange data over communications links, and mutually to understand the data sent/received. In tightly coupled system designs, in which each system element is very closely related to and works very closely with every other element, a higher level of compatibility is required than in more loosely coupled systems.

Allocate Processing Functions to Components

The next step in the design process is to allocate the total set of processing functions to the elements that have been selected. In practice, this step and the preceding one (as well as the following one, in which database elements are allocated) cannot be taken independently. If a minicomputer-based satellite processor for remote locations rather than an intelligent terminal controller has been selected, the system designer has already decided that a fairly broad range of functions will be allocated remotely.

Chapter 15 discusses choices between static and dynamic workload allocation and resource sharing. The state of the art today makes it far less risky to choose static approaches for workload allocation. Each component should be assigned a set of functions, which may change dynamically when the system operates in degraded mode, but which will not shift dynamically for reasons such as workload imbalance.

Dynamic resource sharing, on the other hand, does not involve significantly greater difficulties than static resource sharing. If, for example, a system includes two host processors, only one of which has a fast FORTRAN compiler, it is quite easy to send all FORTRAN compilations to that location. (Of course, whether this strategy is better than the strategy of installing the same compiler at both locations can only be analyzed in terms of a specific system's cost, performance, reliability, and responsiveness characteristics.)

In general, static approaches should be chosen unless it is clear that the system's objectives cannot be met without dynamic techniques, and it is reasonably clear that the risk involved is manageable. One approach to risk minimization in these cases is to prepare an RFP for a turn-key implementation. The turn-key vendor in this case would assume the risk, with penalty clauses for nonperformance.

Allocate Database Elements

If the database structure selected is distributed, then the partitions or the copies of the data must be allocated to system components. Chapter 16 discusses the various strategies available in deciding on optimal allocations. It is best to avoid designs which would involve the dynamic updating of a distributed database simultaneously at multiple locations. On the other hand, the techniques for management of a distributed database in which updating is confined to only one location per transaction are reasonably well understood. For example, a given transaction might update a database partition at one location and inquire for data from several other partitions. However, if the transaction requires updating in several partitions, then very complex technical problems arise. At present it is better to avoid these situations. Usually this can be done by a reorientation of the system design in the direction of a system in which the various updating tasks are decoupled from one another. If a very complex distributed database approach appears essential to the overall system design, it is advisable once again to consider a turn-key vendor implementation.

Select a Network Structure

The final step in formulating a trial design is to select the structure for the data-communications network. One option is to interconnect the various locations by means of a public data network (PDN). In this case, of course, the structure need not be designed; the network is the responsibility of the carrier or PTT authority which supplies the services. The major factor in considering whether remote locations are to be interconnected via a PDN is cost (which will be considered in Unit 18-2). On the other hand, if an appropriate public network is not available or if there are reasons such as privacy or security for using a private network, then a network structure must be selected. Chapter 7 covers the major categories of networks: star, hierarchical, and meshed.

Star and hierarchical networks offer the advantage of simplicity, and often they are available for lower initial cost. However, they have the disadvantage of not providing built-in backup (multiple alternate paths between points) and built-in load leveling. Meshed networks provide these two benefits at a higher initial cost and sometimes at a higher cost for network administration. In general, therefore, in a distributed system which is not involved in applications which require very high availability (e.g., airline reservations, refinery control, hospital patient monitoring), a star or hierarchical network is a good choice. Where high availability and reliability are important factors, a meshed network can more often be justified. In each case, the appropriate speed links, coupling devices, multiplexors, network processors, and/or concentrators must also be selected for use.

18-2.   COST ANALYSIS

A trial system design consists of a set of proposed hardware and software elements, interconnected via a proposed network structure, with each component executing a defined set of functions. If the system is a large and complex one which will involve a very substantial investment, the trial design should be done in considerable detail. For example, estimates of application size ("lines of code"), transmission volume over the network, numbers of personnel who will operate the equipment and act as terminal users, and maintenance and support (hardware and software) requirements should all be included. If the system is less complex, and less costly, then the effort involved to create such a detailed trial design cannot be justified. A much broader, overview plan is suitable. However, in each case the same methods can be used to evaluate the trial design and determine its workability.

The first of these evaluation steps is a cost analysis. While cost is, realistically, not the only important factor, and perhaps is not even the *most* important factor, it is the one which receives the most management attention. Cost justification of any information-processing system—and especially of a large and complex one—is therefore of great importance.

Network Costs

The cost of data-communications facilities must be evaluated, and this is a very complex area because of the wealth of available offerings and tariffs.

Data-communications costs are, most often, recurring costs, which must be considered over the entire life cycle of the proposed system. The cost of leasing transmission facilities can be expected to rise at roughly the rate of general inflation, except in cases where competition has an effect on costs. In order to make a realistic estimate of cost expectations for the life cycle of the system, costs must be plotted on a rising curve. There are also some initial costs, such as the cost of modems when these are purchased, the cost of network monitoring or switching facilities, and so on.

In making a first-pass evaluation of a trial design, it is possible to estimate initial costs and plot recurring costs on the basis of the most straightforward method of acquiring the leased and/or switched transmission facilities required. Methods of design reevaluation, and reiteration through the design process, are discussed in Unit 18-4. Reevaluation of the network structure, and therefore network cost, occurs very often in the course of progressively refining trial designs until a final design is selected.

Information-Processing and Database Hardware and Software Costs

Initial and recurring costs for information-processing and database hardware and software, including terminal devices, must be computed. Initial costs include equipment purchase prices (if the equipment is to be purchased rather than leased or rented). Recurring costs include maintenance and support costs and the costs of hardware and software leased or rented.

If the trial design assumes a specific set of hardware and software, then the cost evaluation can be quite accurate. As in the case of network costs, assumptions must be made about changes in recurring costs over the life of the system. Maintenance costs, which carry a heavy labor content, are generally rising with inflation, and this progressive rise should be included in the estimates. And, although equipment costs for new equipment are falling, the cost of installed equipment is generally fixed if the equipment has been purchased or less apt to change significantly if the equipment has been rented or leased. Software rental costs and support costs are generally rising.

If the trial design is not specific as to hardware and software products, then some bench mark must be chosen for cost evaluations. IBM prices are generally appropriate for use in evaluating general-purpose components; DEC prices are generally appropriate for use in evaluating minicomputer-based components. While use of bench marks will lead to less accurate cost estimations than would be made were specific components preselected, the overall error factor should remain within reasonable tolerances.

Personnel Costs

In evaluating personnel costs, the data-processing department staff costs must be estimated. If the system requires no new personnel, then a proportional allocation of costs can be used. In the case of a major new system, additional staffing will usually be required, and costs for this staffing must be estimated. The cost of recruiting and training these new staff members should also be estimated.

Operational requirements must be closely analyzed when a distributed system, or even a complex centralized on-line system, is being considered. (This topic is discussed in depth in Chapter 20.) It will probably be necessary to maintain a staff of system administrators to monitor operation of the system and to analyze problems and failures in order to recommend appropriate remedial action. Many centralized systems today do not require such staffs, and so this may be an incremental personnel cost. If a public or value-added network is used, system administration cost will be less, because the carrier will manage the data communications-aspects of the system. However, if remote elements such as satellite processors are used, the carrier will not handle problems and failures in those elements.

The most difficult aspect of personnel-cost evaluation is the question of end-user costs. If all terminal users are in the data-processing department and work full-time at operations such as data entry, their salary and overhead costs are easily determined and allocated to the system. However, today, this situation is less and less common.

When terminals are placed at point-of-transaction locations, the salaries of personnel using these terminals may be considered part of the information-system costs, included partially, or entirely excluded. For example, in a factory-automation system which requires that factory workers "punch in" and "punch out" of each task by entering an employee identity card and a task ID card, these operations take so little of the employees' time that the cost may be considered to be zero. On the other hand, in the case where a sales representative is given a terminal and asked to enter orders directly (rather than giving these to an order clerk or secretary for entry) a portion of the sales representative's time may be charged to the information system.

How end-user costs are allocated is often a question of policy and management philosophy. Since end-user savings are often an important aspect of system-cost justification, this area requires a great deal of attention.

Miscellaneous Costs

Every system includes other costs which do not fall into one of the above categories. These include supply costs for items such as printer paper, ribbons or cartridges, floppy disks (if these are used to distribute software changes to remote locations), and so on. Supplies for the point-of-transaction locations, such as printer paper and ribbons for remote hard-copy printers, must also be included. And, if the computer site and equipment are to be operated by an outside contractor, the facilities-management costs must be estimated.

If site preparation is required, either at one or more computer room locations and/or at the remote location(s), the costs for this preparation should be estimated. Site preparation for administrative control center(s) may also be required. When placing minicomputers in remote locations, for example, adequate power must be available. Although minis typically operate on normal house current, large configurations with disk storage may not. Also, power which fluctuates widely may be adequate for room lighting and electric typewriters, but inadequate to operate high uptime minis. These factors should be evaluated and included in the cost of the trial design.

Summary

After a trial design has been formulated and evaluated, it is important to obtain an estimate of what the system will cost that is as accurate as possible, both in terms of initial investment and in terms of recurring costs. Of course, if savings are expected these must be estimated as realistically as possible. But, the question of savings is an extremely complex and difficult one. A major focus of on-line systems aimed at end users is to increase user productivity and thus reduce total bottom-line costs. However, it is often difficult to evaluate productivity, and predictions prior to implementation of a system are often extremely suspect. Many systems, therefore, are better justified in terms of factors such as improved competitiveness and better customer service than in terms of hard cost savings. For example, many banks have installed automated-teller terminals (ATTs) which allow bank customers to obtain money and/or to make deposits without a teller in attendance. In fact, these terminals are usually available twenty-four hours a day, seven days a week. ATTs provide better service—the customer can obtain money outside of banking hours—and thus the bank can be more competitive than other banks which do not offer a comparable service.

In practice, many terminals of this type are used by customers during regular banking hours, as a convenient alternative to standing in line waiting for a human teller. So one can speculate that fewer tellers are required than if the ATTs had not been installed, but there is very likely no way to document this possible saving on personnel costs. The main focus remains the competitive advantage provided by better service to customers.

In any estimate of system costs, it is wise to be as accurate as possible, even if the resulting costs seem high and therefore likely to make it difficult to "sell" the system to upper management. Experience indicates that it is better to get these facts on the table early in the system development cycle, rather than to reveal them little by little later, in the form of unpleasant surprises. If management refuses to authorize the proposed system development, other trial designs should be explored, perhaps ones for systems with more modest objectives.

18-3. RESPONSE, AVAILABILITY, AND FLEXIBILITY

In addition to analyzing a trial design for cost, it is necessary to analyze it for responsiveness, availability, and flexibility. Unfortunately, these analyses are usually more complex than cost analyses. Unless they are performed, however, there is a serious risk of implementing an unworkable design.

Response-Time Calculations

The responsiveness of a trial design must be evaluated to determine how rapidly a terminal user will receive a reply when transactions are input. *Response time* is the amount of time it takes to send a transaction to the point of processing, process it, and to send back the reply. In a distributed system, this "circuit" may involve multiple transmission paths and/or multiple processing elements.

Figure 18-1 shows an example distributed system in which transactions are input by the users via cathode-ray tube (CRT) terminals. This system uses a key-word entry scheme: each item or set of items entered is preceded by a key-word, so that data can be entered in any convenient sequence. During entry of the items which make up a transaction (for example, customer identifier, order number, and item identifiers for ordered items) a dialogue takes place between the user and the terminal controller. The controller program edits each item—to the degree feasible without access to the main database—and flags errors immediately.

The calculation of response-time for the dialogue between user and terminal controller includes the time required to transmit each item over the link between the user's terminal and the terminal controller, which can be computed by using the number of characters transmitted (including overhead characters) and the link speed. Response also includes the time required by the terminal controller to edit the input and perform whatever processing is needed to determine whether it is invalid, and this may involve access to the diskette. Since the terminal controller is normally handling multiple inputs concurrently, the multiplexing among these must also be considered in evaluating the time required.

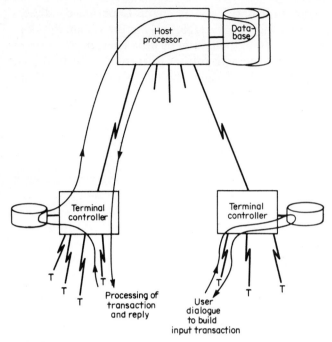

FIG. 18-1 Response-time calculations. T = terminal device.

Finally, the time needed to transmit the reply back to the terminal must be included. When the dialogue necessary to build a transaction has been completed, the data are transmitted to the host for processing against the central database and formulation of output for the user. To calculate the response time in the Figure 18-1 example distributed system the following must be determined:

1. Time needed for the terminal user's "Transmit" signal to reach the terminal controller.

2. Time needed for the terminal controller to obtain the complete transaction, possibly from diskette, and ready it for transmission to the host.

3. Transmission time to the host.

4. Processing time at the host, including database access and updating, preparation of a reply, and the effects of multiprogramming of multiple transactions concurrently (or simultaneously in a multiprocessor configuration).

5. Transmission time to the terminal controller.

6. Time required for any processing (such as formatting) by the terminal controller.

7. Time required to transmit the reply to the terminal for display to the user.

Response-time calculations are further complicated if transmission techniques such as concentration are used, since concentration may delay any given transmission in order to accumulate an appropriately sized block. If a packet network is used, average transit time must be determined, because actual time will often vary depending upon the specific route used.

It is possible to make an adequate calculation of response time for relatively simple systems by using only manual methods. While the calculation may not be absolutely accurate, conservative estimates will provide a reasonable degree of confidence in the results. And it is important to remember that even very complex response-time calculation methods are subject to error and must be considered only "range-of-accuracy" estimates.

More complex system designs cannot be evaluated accurately except by using mathematical models or simulations. If the necessary expertise is available in-house, it may be possible to develop a model which predicts the response-time characteristics of a trial design. In most cases, however, it will be easier to obtain these capabilities outside. Some computer vendors have sets of modeling and/or simulation tools to predict response and performance. Some consultants specialize in evaluations of performance and response time, especially for systems which use complex networks. Other consultants can develop specialized models or simulations for a specific system.

Availability Factors

Evaluation of the availability characteristics of a trial design is even more complex than the calculation of response time. In evaluating availability, it is necessary to determine how reliable the system will appear to its users and the effects of system failures.

An evaluation of availability can be broad-brush or extremely thorough, depending upon the objectives the system is being designed to meet. If extremely high availability is a main objective, a thorough analysis of availability is needed; if not, a less detailed approach can be used.

In a detailed evaluation of availability each possible failure should be listed, and its effects should be analyzed. For example, in the Figure 18-1 distributed system, items to be analyzed would be:

1. Terminal hardware failure

2. Failure of the link between a terminal and the terminal controller

3. Hardware failure which causes the terminal controller to cease operation

4. Failure of the diskette device at the terminal controller

5. Software (or firmware) failure at the terminal controller

6. Failure of the link between a terminal controller and the host processor

7. Hardware failure which causes the host processor to cease operation

8. Failure of one or more disk devices on which the host's database is stored

9. Operating-system failure at the host processor

10. Application-program failure at the host processor

(These items could be further refined; for example, link failure could be broken into a transmission-facility problem or a modem problem.)

It is necessary to determine: (a) the effect of each type of failure on the users of the system, (b) the probability of each type of failure, (c) potential methods of minimizing the effects of each type of failure, and (d) the cost of minimizing the effect of failure in each case.

While this appears to be a very time-consuming and tedious task, availability analysis is key to designing an acceptable distributed system. If any part of the system is prone to failure, and these failures are visible to system users, the system may be unworkable. Equally important, so-called brute-force methods of avoiding failure effects—such as dualing components—are often too expensive to be practical.

Most often the approach used to minimize failure effects is either to take advantage of natural pooling and/or to minimize vulnerability by minimizing the number of components which must be operational at all times. For example, there are usually multiple terminal devices in a pool at a point-of-transaction location. In a bank branch, there are almost always multiple tellers, each with a teller terminal if the branch is auto-mated. If one terminal fails it may be necessary to close that teller window, but the branch is still operational. Customers may have to wait a little longer, but essential operations are not threatened. In this case, it would not be economically justifiable to install extra terminals to ensure that all will be continually operational.

Returning again to the Figure 18-1 example system, if a terminal controller fails, all of the connected terminal users will be unable to use the system. However, the distributed system includes multiple terminal controllers, all probably with identical hardware and software. It may be possible to have the terminal users automatically or manually recon-nected to another terminal controller (or controllers) in order to con-tinue operation. This would be preferable to duplication of the ter-minal controllers at all locations. On the other hand, if an analysis of hardware characteristics indicates that the diskette device associated with a specific type of terminal controller fails relatively often, it may be appropriate to install two diskette devices at each location to ensure against failure for that reason. (Another alternative, of course, might be to select a different type of terminal controller.)

Minimizing vulnerability to failure by minimizing the number of components required to process meaningful work is very basic to distributed system design—and, indeed, to the design of any information system. The more components required, the higher the inherent probability that one will fail. The Figure 18-1 example illustrates a system in which a large number of components—the terminal, terminal controller, the host processor, plus all of the links and modems connecting a given user to the terminal controller and host—must all function in order to complete a transaction. The system design would be less vulnerable if more of the processing could be done at the terminal controller: perhaps a database subset there could allow local processing of all but exception transactions.

In any evaluation of various design strategies for increased availability, complex trade-offs arise. In the preceding example, if the terminal controllers are upgraded to satellite processors, system availability may be improved. On the other hand, system cost may also be increased. Whether or not this is a viable trade-off depends very heavily upon the specific availability requirements and cost constraints of the system being designed.

Other factors often enter into these calculations. For example, in a system which monitors patients under intensive care, all components are typically dualed, because failure could endanger the lives of the patients. One cannot assign a monetary value to this aspect of the system design. On the other hand, a system which schedules production equipment and labor power for a large manufacturer may be under stringent availability requirements, because if the system fails and is not restarted rapidly factory workers must be sent home (because of union contract provisions). In a case such as this, it is possible to assign a specific cost to the occurrence of a failure and, therefore, possible to evaluate the monetary value of availability safeguards quite accurately.

In any analysis of failure possibilities, it is important to consider not only the information-system hardware and software elements and data-transmission facilities, but external factors as well. Power outages, for example, may be frequent in specific areas and/or seasons, and should be taken into account. If certain areas are heavily unionized and vulnerable to strike action, this should be considered in evaluating availability. Natural disasters such as floods in certain areas must also be considered. People often laugh off consideration of such threats as unrealistic, but in a high-availability on-line system, one cannot afford to laugh them off unless they can be proven to be nonexistent or minimal.

Flexibility Evaluation

In evaluating a trial design for a distributed system, the flexibility of the system must also be considered. Such questions as how vulnerable is the system to change, how capable is it of accommodating various types of changes, must be answered.

Flexibility, like availability, is best evaluated in terms of a series of "What if?" questions. Following are some examples—rather than an exhaustive list—of the questions which ought to be asked.

1. What happens if transaction volume changes:
   * up 20 percent?
   * down 30 percent?
   * up 90 percent?
   (Analysts most often worry about increased transaction volume, because of the potential stress on the system. However, a dramatically decreased transaction volume could very well make the system ineffective from a cost standpoint.)

2. What happens if transaction profiles change:
   * more of transaction type A, less of transaction type B?
   * many more of transaction type C, many less of type D?

3. What happens if end-user profiles change:
   * end users are relocated among locations?
   * end-user profiles of transaction use change?
   * end users are less experienced, and use "help" systems more frequently?

4. What happens if the number of end users:
   * increases by 50 percent with a corresponding increase in transaction volume—or without one?
   * decreases by 20 percent with the same transaction volume?

In evaluating the vulnerability of the system to change, it is extremely important to have as much information as possible about likely business and organizational changes. For example, in a government organization, the legislature might be considering—or might be thought likely to consider—new legislation which could significantly increase the size of the database required in a new application. What effect would this have? In considering a system designed for a business application, the relevant questions might include ones concerning the historical patterns of processing growth and organization change, the likelihood of acquisitions or mergers which would increase volume and/or cause the planned system to interface with other systems for data exchange, the likelihood of changes in the business climate requiring overall expansion or contraction, and the likelihood that new applications will be required. It is not easy to obtain the kind of information needed to answer such questions, nor is it easy to judge the accuracy of the information obtained. However, every designer must remember that systems are becoming increasingly integrated into the organizations they serve, and as a result, information systems must be able to change as rapidly as their organizations change and/or the business and social climate and conditions change. This is an enormous challenge to all system designers, but it is a challenge that must be met if the promise of on-line information systems, and especially distributed systems, is to be realized.

18-4. TRADE-OFFS

At this point the trial design for the distributed system has been formulated, evaluated in terms of cost, response time, level of availability, and degree of flexibility. It is unlikely that any "first-cut" trial design for a complex system will survive these analyses intact. Instead, a series of trade-offs must usually be made to arrive at a satisfactory design.

The criteria for a satisfactory design are reflected in the following questions:

1. Does the trial design provide the required functions?

2. Will it handle the required volume, with adequate capabilities for expansion?

3. Will it meet the response-time requirements of users?

4. Will it provide the minimum required level of availability?

5. Can the cost of the system be justified (or is it within prestated limits)?

If a trial design receives positive answers to the five questions above, it meets the criteria of acceptability, but that does not mean that it is the best possible design. For example, it might be possible to reduce cost without negative impact on any of the other criteria, which would result in a better design. In general, however, once the criteria have been met design effort moves to detailed design and implementation rather than back to iteration to produce a better high-level design.

If the trial design does not meet all criteria, then alternatives must be evaluated until an acceptable one is found.

Response Time Alternatives

If evaluation of the design indicates that response times will be too slow to satisfy system users, several alternatives may be considered. The easiest of these is to increase the speed (capacity) of the data communications links, so that data can be sent more rapidly. For example, if a terminal is connected via a 300-bps link only 30 characters per second can be transmitted. The same terminal connected via a 2400-bps link can send 240 characters per second. Increased link speed can have a significant effect; often it makes the difference between a responsive system and an unresponsive one. As usual, there is a trade-off with cost considerations. Higher-capacity links are more expensive than slower-speed links. In some cases this trade-off may be an acceptable one; in others it may not.

If the database is the response-time bottleneck because too many users are trying to access the same data simultaneously, there are many alternatives to choose among in revising the design to meet response-time requirements. The database can be spread over more disk-file devices, and/or more disk-access channels can be added, so that more simultaneous accesses to the same data are possible. If this proves ineffective, it may be necessary to partition the database and distribute its parts in order to increase responsiveness.

Response time is, of course, also affected by processing power at the terminal controller(s), satellite processor(s), and/or host processor(s) and inadequate power may account for inadequate responsiveness. In this case, the system design can be modified in order to upgrade the processor(s) and/or more processors can be used.

A different distribution of functions can also help alleviate anticipated response-time problems. For example, if the satellite processor seems unresponsive, perhaps certain functions can be moved to the host processor(s) in order to reduce the satellite load. On the other hand, if the host processor seems underpowered, perhaps more functions can be moved to satellite processors and/or terminal controllers. Or the host processing load might be partitioned onto two or more hosts, leaving the rest of the distributed system's functionality unchanged.

Any of these alternatives, or combinations of them, may solve the response-time problem. In almost every case—except perhaps the redistribution of functions across components—the result will be higher cost than in the original trial design. This trade-off must be evaluated for acceptability. In some cases, it will be apparent that increased cost is necessary to meet system objectives—particularly responsiveness or availability—and if this is not acceptable to management, the system design must be considered technically unfeasible.

Volume Alternatives

If the trial design does not handle the required volume, generally or only in certain cases, the alternatives are usually the same as those used to improve responsiveness. The design can be changed so that link speeds are increased, more links are included, or processor power can be increased through upgrades and/or the use of more processors, or data storage can be increased. In some cases it may be possible to modify the design in order to redistribute functions to handle the required volume without increasing the speed or power of any component. These alternatives will generally increase the bottom-line cost of the trial design system.

Availability Alternatives

The availability analysis may indicate that certain failures cause unacceptable results. In that case, alternative designs must be formulated. The simplest way to increase availability is to dual system components selectively. For example, if a satellite processor's load cannot easily be picked up by another satellite or by a host processor, and continued operation at that location is vital, it may be appropriate to modify the design to include a dual redundant processor. If a high volume of vital data must be transmitted between two locations reliably, a modified design may include either two links or provision for using dial-up facilities in the case of dedicated-link failures. If the design includes a host which must operate continuously, dual processors (tightly or loosely coupled) can be configured.

If the use of dual components does not provide the needed availability, or proves too costly, then a further redesign of the system may be necessary. For example, if the system is vulnerable to failures because too many components "in a series" must operate to process important transactions, the design can be altered so that fewer components are required to process these specific transactions. This may or may not increase the cost.

With respect to availability, a distributed system usually provides more alternatives than a centralized system, which is often an all-or-nothing situation in terms of dualing. It is important to determine which transactions, locations, reports, etc., really imply high availability needs, so that the necessary level can be provided there, and only there. Less specific approaches may be simpler, but these are always more costly, and often much harder to justify. For example, in a factory-control system, factory data-entry terminals and their controllers do not usually require extremely high availability. There are almost always multiple places where a worker can enter the necessary data (the pool approach), so dualing is unnecessary. On the other hand, if process-control equipment is running automated portions of the factory, any interruption of operation of this equipment will interrupt factory work. In this case dualed processors can be easily justified.

Cost Alternatives

A trial design may not meet the predefined cost objectives. There are many ways to reduce cost, often without severely affecting the overall system design. One of the first areas to consider is redesign of the data communications network. Methods such as the use of multidrop links, multiplexing, rerouting of links to achieve lower tariffs, and changing link speeds can significantly reduce costs from a first-cut network design. (Chapter 17 describes methods for network cost reduction.)

Another possibility is to redesign in order to require the use of less expensive components. For example, there are a number of different types of intelligent terminals on the market, and terminal cost varies based on the specific features provided and the vendor's market share. Features which are "nice to have" but nonessential can be omitted to reduce cost, especially if these are options which could be provided later when, and if, their use can be cost-justified.

The cost of detailed design, implementation, and installation of the system can in some cases be reduced by looking for a turn-key vendor to assume the entire responsibility, rather than doing the work in-house. This has the added advantage of shifting the major risk of failure, and responsibility for success, to the turn-key vendor. It has the disadvantage of lack of in-depth knowledge in-house about the system, and this may lead to serious difficulties. However, use of a turn-key is certainly an alternative which should be considered when evaluating how to minimize costs. (It is also an alternative which should be considered when it is difficult—or impossibly expensive—to acquire the necessary in-house expertise.)

Costs associated with operating the equipment after the system is implemented may be lower if a facilities-management approach is used. Vendors who provide facilities-management contracts can sometimes do so at less cost than comparable in-house staffs can. As in the case of turn-key developments, this has the added advantage of shifting some of the responsibility and risk associated with the system to the outside vendor.

As a final possibility for cost reduction, it may be possible to reduce bottom-line costs by providing additional features to improve end-user productivity. For example, if by automating an additional major function the system could take over the work of a number of clerical personnel (who could then be assigned to other tasks), the cost of the salaries of those personnel could be considered to be system cost savings. Of course, this would be offset by the additional development costs for the new function and possibly, also, additional equipment costs, so the savings would have to be significant to justify this approach. If upper-level management is receptive to investing in productivity aids, this might be the key to success for an information system which could not otherwise be justified.

18-5. Summary

This very brief description of the system design process for a distributed system should make it clear that system design is a complex procedure. However, to keep this complexity in perspective, it should be recognized that a large on-line system with centralized processing is not significantly less complex. In both cases, the key is to analyze the entire system, including end-user aspects and costs, fully rather than simply concentrating on data-processing hardware and software elements.

Typically the design of a complex information system begins with a trial design arrived at in a way more intuitive than rational. That trial design is then evaluated—sometimes thoroughly, sometimes less than thoroughly. If the design proves inadequate, as is usually the case with the first effort regardless of how professional the design process used, then various alternatives must be considered. Each major alternative produces, in effect, a new trial design, which is then evaluated. This cycle generally continues until one of two situations develops:

1. A design is generated which meets all evaluation criteria.
2. The system designers are exhausted.

Unfortunately, with unorganized methods of system design, the second precedes (and precludes) the first. One of the goals of this book is to ensure that organized design approaches are used, so that a satisfactory design is attained before the design team gives up.

OPERATIONAL
CONSIDERATIONS

Although the design and implementation of a distributed system represent major challenges, it is important to remember that the operation of such a system is also complex. In fact, how the system will be operated and—this is especially important—controlled, must be considered throughout the design phase. The aspects to be considered are presented in this section. Chapter 19 covers the question of managerial control. Functions may be distributed in today's information systems, but managerial control generally remains centralized. The factors which enter into the allocation of control are presented, as are the implications of different control philosophies on system implementation. In Chapter 20, the operational-control aspects of these systems are described. System complexity and the geographical dispersion which usually exists make it mandatory that monitoring and administrative methods be carefully worked out. Although these methods will vary widely from system to system, this discussion outlines the range of possible choices.

19

MANAGERIAL CONTROL

Because the flexibility of distributed systems opens up a whole new spectrum of management options not available with centralized information systems, distributed systems have important affects on managerial philosophies and styles. Centralized computing implies centralized managerial control. No individual user group is free to choose its own hardware, operating system, and supporting software, nor can any single group operate the computer system. These functions must be performed by a centralized information-processing staff, which leaves to end-user groups or their representatives only the definition of application programs. In contrast, distributed information systems of the types described in this volume offer many different alternatives for managerial control. This chapter discusses the options for "static" control; how equipment will be selected, applications and databases designed and established, and how control will be exercised as changes occur in these aspects of the system. Chapter 20 discusses the more dynamic aspects of control: those forms of control which must be exercised as the system is operating.

19-1. EQUIPMENT SELECTION

The acquisition of hardware and software is an important aspect of control in both centralized and distributed systems. Selection and acquisition often involve a competitive process in which multiple vendors' offerings are analyzed for adequate functionality, reliability, and cost. The selection process may be very formal or quite informal, but in either case it results in the selection of one or more vendors to supply the needed equipment. The selected hardware and software are then leased or purchased.

This selection function can be either centralized or distributed. Many organizations today require central, high-level approval for computer equipment procurements above a specified cost, leaving items below that cutoff to local discretion. This is one of the reasons for the current popularity of minis and micros, which can often be purchased without authorization from the central information-processing management.

A new dimension is opened up by designs for distributed systems in equipment selection. Local equipment, hardware and software, must be interfaced to other local and/or central equipment. Compatibility problems which are minimal with local free-standing processors become important with interconnected processors. Although centralized managerial control aimed at minimizing compatibility problems can best be achieved by centralizing all information-system equipment selection and acquisition, such centralization may conflict with existing expenditure policies of the organization. Policies may have to be changed in order to achieve full control.

By centralizing the process, and setting guidelines for selection which ensure compatibility, the potential for acquisition of incompatible hardware and/or software is very small. Some organizations adopt a "single vendor" policy to avoid this problem. However, as Chapters 9 through 12 pointed out, choosing equipment from a single vendor does not ensure compatibility. In addition, many desirable features and capabilities may be unattainable in a rigid one-vendor approach. Regardless of how the guidelines are established, centralized equipment selection provides the highest level of managerial control.

Most organizations choose somewhat less tight control, requiring central approval of acquisitions above a specified value, with local control of other purchases. This approach has proven workable in many organizations, but in general the locally procured equipment has been intended for free-standing use. If, instead, it is to be part of a distributed system, compatibility becomes an important issue. Again, many organizations have handled this situation by setting overall guidelines, even for computer-equipment acquisitions not subject to central approval. For example, the guidelines might specify that all equipment to be used for business-data processing must support an ANSI-standard version of COBOL or that equipment for scientific processing must provide a standard FORTRAN compiler.

Today, it is most important that guidelines of this type specify which communications protocol(s) each component must support. Since distributed system components normally interface via data-communications facilities, a common protocol must be supported. Without this level of interface compatibility, higher-level standards such as languages and data management have no exchange medium.

As Unit 19-3 points out, the approach to managerial control in a distributed system is affected by many things. One of these is how tightly integrated the design of the system is. In an application such as branch banking, which is designed as a tightly integrated whole, local equipment acquisition is impractical. All equipment must be fully compatible, specified and selected centrally. In more loosely coupled systems, where relatively independent local applications exchange data, there is more freedom for local control within overall guidelines. It is important to establish guidelines before the fact in situations of this type. This will ensure that distributed-system elements having the required level of compatibility are procured. If this is not done, and the independently acquired components must later be connected, interface protocols must be established at that time. This is very likely to require software changes and, possibly, hardware changes also. Advanced planning, to avoid changes of this type, is vastly preferable.

19-2. APPLICATION DEVELOPMENT

The fact that whoever develops a system's application programs effectively controls the system is sometimes overlooked. In fact, this is the most important and far-reaching aspect of managerial control. The control of application development today ranges from centralized to distributed even in centralized systems. Some organizations have chosen to maintain a single centralized analysis and programming staff which develops all application programs in consultation with the user groups. Other organizations have chosen to support an analysis and programming staff in each major functional area (e.g., personnel, production control, order entry), with necessary coordination provided by the central computing staff. Each of these patterns has proven successful in many installations.

These same choices exist in distributed systems. The major new factor is that application development can apply to multiple host and satellite information processors and/or intelligent terminal/device controllers in several locations.

A typical hierarchically distributed system (also used as an example in Chapter 6) is shown in Figure 19-1. The central host processor serves as a focal point for consolidated reporting and for headquarters-level activities such as budgeting. Each of the satellite processors serves a different division of the organization, performing local processing functions.

In this type of system, some organizations may choose to centralize all application development at the headquarters level. This is most easily accomplished if satellite programs can be developed and tested on the host processor. For example, a cross-compiler is used to prepare satellite applications on the host, and a simulator is used to test satellite programs, in simulated execution, on the host. Object-form satellite programs are downline loaded over a communications link from the host to

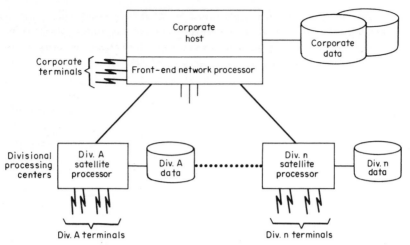

FIG. 19-1 Typical hierarchically distributed system.

the satellite, and satellite failure is handled by upline dump of memory content to the host location for analysis. If the satellite processors are of the same type as the host, then the host's native application-development facilities can be used. Such centralized application development is chosen when management wishes to consolidate control and/or minimize cost.

Savings often result from the centralization of the development and support staff. For example, a senior analyst, expert in an operating system or other complex software, may command a high salary. A centralized staff may require only one such expert; when a decentralized approach is taken, one expert per location may be needed. Or, an application-development staff may reside at each host and satellite location, with responsibility for the programs to be used locally. This may be more costly in staffing, but may make the system more responsive to local needs and in that way have the effect of minimizing local end-user costs. In this case, cross-compilers, simulators, and so on are not usually required.

Distributed application development, however, requires a coordinated set of interface protocols for information exchange. Even though each satellite may operate semi-independently, it must send specific data —on defined schedules—to the host for consolidation and reporting. Similarly, the host may be required to send data to the satellites periodically. Although the remainder of the host and satellite implementations can be unique, these information exchanges must follow mutually agreed-upon rules.

Database design and the establishment of the database(s) form the "static" portion of database administration (the "dynamic" monitoring and control of database usage are discussed in Chapter 20). Today's centralized on-line systems have been developed around large integrated databases under strong central control. This control is exercised by the database administrator (DBA), or by a database administration staff if the database is very large. The DBA typically resolves conflicting requirements for database content and access. For example, if an integrated database serves both engineering and marketing organizations, compromises may be necessary. Engineering requires detailed drawing-number information for each product, while marketing needs only major product data. In addition, the organizations may refer to the same product by different identifiers, one internal and one external. To make the integrated database workable and provide a unified view of real-world conditions, realistic trade-offs must be made by the DBA.

In contrast to centralized control of an integrated database, a distributed database offers several choices for administration. A hypothetical distributed system with a distributed database is shown in Figure 19-2.

The system includes a partitioned database, in which the data stored at the two hosts collectively form the organization's database. Each partition contains data unique to that location. An organization having this type of system may choose to assign a central DBA, perhaps at City A, to manage the distributed database. Local users at City B could request that certain data elements be maintained, but the DBA would determine whether or not this is done. The DBA would maintain all schemas and subschemas, perhaps creating and validating them at the City A host and then transmitting them to City B via downline load for use there. This

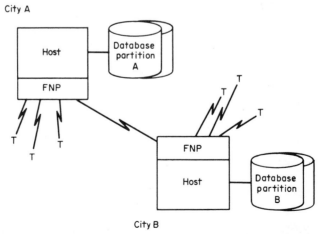

FIG. 19-2 Partitioned database. FNP = front-end network processor; T = terminal device.

approach retains tight central control over the partitioned database and ensures that all of its elements are compatible.

As an alternative, the organization may assign database responsibility to a DBA at each location. Each DBA then controls the local database partition by means of schema and subschema creation. Each database partition can then be designed to best meet local needs. In this case, certain coordination activities are required. For example, if data elements are to be moved between locations, compatible data descriptions must be used, or, if they are not used, data-conversion procedures must be specified and implemented. The best technique to use when database partitions have different structures is the flat-file approach. Data to be moved between locations are handled in terms of logical records, with reformatting as necessary by the receiving processor. The flat-file approach is discussed in more detail in Chapter 14.

19-3. SELECTING A MANAGERIAL APPROACH

Equipment selection, application development, and database installation are the most important elements of "static" managerial control. As the preceding discussions illustrate, available managerial options range from total centralization of control to relatively complete decentralization. Total local autonomy, however, is impractical because certain standards must be defined and enforced to ensure that the distributed system's components can work together successfully.

Once an organization has decided to implement a distributed system, a choice of managerial approach must be made. Because of the importance of this decision, top management may well be involved in the decision-making process.

The distributed information system managerial approach chosen will generally depend on one or more of these three factors:

- Cost
- Managerial philosophy of the organization
- The nature of the application(s) being implemented

Cost is an important factor in choosing a managerial approach. However, this cost is not simply the cost of information-processing equipment. Costs for the entire information system must be considered: computer and terminal equipment costs, data-communications facilities costs, software costs (in-house and external), data-processing-department staffing costs, and end-user staffing costs.

It is particularly important to evaluate end-user costs and the effect which various system alternatives have on these costs. In any large on-line system which serves the mainline activities of a business, end-user costs tend to be much greater than computer equipment and staffing costs. This aspect may be overlooked, because information-processing people often still think in terms of batch systems, and in such systems, computer costs far outweigh end-user costs. In on-line systems, including distributed systems, opportunities to increase end-user productivity and reduce overall system costs should be explored. For example, one large business has implemented a substantial number of new services to its customers while lowering total end-user salary costs. Increased end-user productivity allows a smaller staff, supported by distributed computer power, to more adequately meet customer needs. The Honeywell Information Systems (HIS) plant in Phoenix, Arizona, has increased productivity by implementing a distributed production-monitoring and control system. This has allowed HIS to build a larger number of computers without a comparable increase in the work force.

The choice of a managerial approach for a distributed system should therefore begin by posing questions about the costs of various alternatives. One such question would be: Will a centralized application-development staff be more cost-effective than distributed staffs or will the latter sufficiently improve overall productivity (by meeting local needs more effectively) to offset the added staffing costs? Many questions of this type about the specific distributed system must be formulated and answered in order to evaluate the cost of each managerial alternative. These are clearly difficult questions to answer realistically, but obtaining answers to them is a fundamental step in deciding how to manage a distributed system.

The managerial philosophy of the organization can also affect the distributed-system management approach. Management philosophy in most large organizations—particularly in the United States—favors decentralization, with each local manager assigned full profit-and-loss responsibility for a local segment of the business. However, lacking viable alternatives, many decentralized organizations have until now adopted centralized computing philosophies. Distributed-systems technology today makes it practical to distribute control to match the organization. In general, therefore, an organization which favors decentralized management will tend to prefer this same approach in distrbuted-system control. An organization which favors strong central management will generally retain centralized control of information processing, even when system components are distributed.

The nature of the application will often be the deciding factor in determining how to control a distributed system. For example, it may be practical to distribute the processing and database storage for an airline reservation system, as shown in the Figure 19-3 hypothetical system. However, it would be very difficult to distribute the managerial control of such a system. This is a highly integrated application, all of whose parts must work together in exact synchronization. Otherwise, even though conditions were identical, a customer requesting a reservation in one city might receive a response different from that received by a customer in another city. All aspects of this application therefore require strong central control.

A hypothetical manufacturing-control system involving two factories and a headquarters location is shown in Figure 19-4. In this system, in contrast to the airline reservation system, local control can optionally be exercised at each site, providing specialization in order to best meet local needs. Only data exchange for decision-making and reporting purposes requires standardization under central control.

The complex banking system used as an example earlier (Chapters 3 and 15) is shown again in Figure 19-5. This system might be characterized as falling into a third managerial category. The system structure and implementation require strong central control, for the same reasons as in the example airline reservation system. It would certainly be unfortunate if a customer's balance were reported differently in each bank branch. However, extensive local customization of reporting would be feasible, in order to meet the needs of each bank branch manager more satisfactorily. In this system, a reasonable compromise can be achieved between central and local management control.

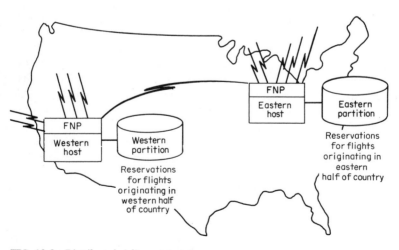

FIG. 19-3   Distributed airline reservation system.

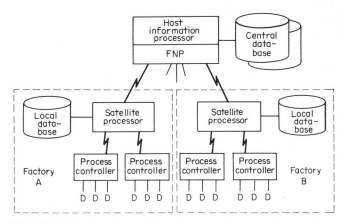

FIG. 19-4 Distributed manufacturing-control system. FNP = front-end network processor; D = device.

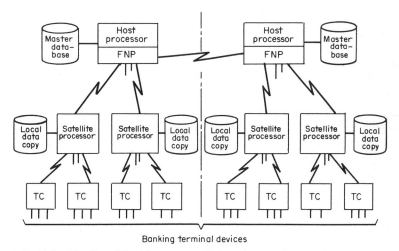

Banking terminal devices

FIG. 19-5 Distributed banking system. FNP = front-end network processor; TC = terminal controller.

Summary

The management of distributed systems is currently the subject of much discussion—sometimes even of much controversy.

In general, information-processing management favors continued centralized control of all aspects of the system: application development, database administration, and equipment selection. Their main arguments focus on economies of scale (particularly in staffing) and the need for control to avoid anarchy. End users and their immediate management, in contrast, strongly favor local control, stressing the need to meet specialized requirements and thereby increase user productivity. Objective analysis, based on evaluation of cost, overall management philosophy, and application requirements, is the best way to make decisions on how to manage a distributed system most effectively.

20

OPERATIONAL CONTROL

Chapter 19 covered the more static aspects of managerial control: those associated with equipment acquisition, system design, and implementation. This chapter covers the "dynamic" aspects of control: those which have to do with managing the operation of the system and adjusting operation to match changing needs. Both static and dynamic control are affected by managerial philosophies. The static aspects of information-system control are more heavily affected by the overall management philosophy of the organization than the dynamic aspects are. Because dynamic monitoring and control deal with very complex technical facets of the system (such as operational errors and performance problems) there is more impact from technical aspects than from managerial aspects. However, dynamic operational control must also be sensitive to management directions or it will not adequately meet organizational objectives.

This chapter is separated into an introductory section on operational monitoring and control, and the information-processing aspects of these functions. A section on database administration discusses the dynamic portion of the DBA's role in a distributed system. Network administration is covered in the third unit, and security and privacy administration is discussed in the last unit of this chapter. In a specific distributed system, not all of these aspects of operational control may be of equal importance, but the system designer should be aware of all of these facets in order to ensure that they all receive consideration.

Throughout this chapter various types of system administrators are discussed, such as the database administrator (DBA), network administrator, and security/privacy administrator. These references do not necessarily mean the functions described are carried out by a single person. In a very large system, a staff may share the DBA duties. In a smaller system a small group may share all system-administration functions. The emphasis is on the functions required, not specifically on staffing to perform these functions.

20-1. OPERATIONAL MONITORING AND CONTROL

In a centralized system, operational monitoring and control functions are usually handled by the console operators of the main computer system. Even in this case, problems such as inadequate response at terminal locations and failures of central site hardware or software are often difficult to diagnose, correct, and/or work around. In a distributed system, there are many more possibilities for problems and failures, and the difficulties involved in diagnosis and correction increase exponentially. These problems therefore deserve a great deal of attention from system designers and operational management.

Monitoring and Control Objectives

The operational monitoring and control functions—which form an important part of system administration—have two basic objectives:

1.   To detect and correct problems and failures.

2.   To analyze operational patterns for possible future problems and/or failures.

For example, if response time to terminal users suddenly changes from two seconds to thirty seconds, the cause must be determined and corrected as rapidly as possible. If a disk device fails at the central system, or at a remote satellite processor, corrective action must be taken to repair the device and reconstruct the stored data. This sort of activity—detecting and acting immediately on short-term problems—falls into the very dynamic part of operational monitoring and control.

Usually the short-term monitoring is performed based upon CRT monitors which display—either continually and/or on request—the status of various parts of the system and/or remote network and processing elements. One or more monitors of this type form part of every large-scale computer center. In the case of a distributed system, it is necessary to extend these facilities so that not only the central-site equipment but remote elements and the data-communications network which links them can be monitored.

The less dynamic aspects of operational monitoring and control involve situations such as the gradual growth of transaction volume (perhaps as the result of improved business conditions). Since at some point steady growth can be expected to degrade response and/or to overload the information system, systems administrators must be able to detect trends of this type by analyzing patterns of operation over time and to take appropriate action before any problems arise. Longer-term pattern analysis is done by collecting statistics in various parts of the system during operation, then collating and analyzing these statistics offline.

Centralized or Distributed Monitoring

Monitoring and control can be centralized: in this case, all monitoring devices and personnel are located at one center. Or, a distributed approach to monitoring and control may be chosen if the system is a very large one. In this case, the monitoring and control equipment and personnel are located at multiple sites, chosen either on a geographical basis or on an organizational basis.

In a nationwide distributed system, the monitoring and control might be done on the basis of geographic region, with an eastern region, a central region, and a western region. Each system-administration center would handle problems in its region. Problems crossing regional boundaries would be handled by means of coordination between the regions.

Alternatively, monitoring and control sites might be chosen on an organizational basis, with each division or department in a corporate-wide distributed system given its own monitoring and control site. The equipment used by a given division would be administered by personnel of that division. A corporate-level administration staff would probably be required to coordinate overall operations and resolve any difficulties crossing divisional boundaries. This type of system-administration pattern is shown in Figure 20-1.

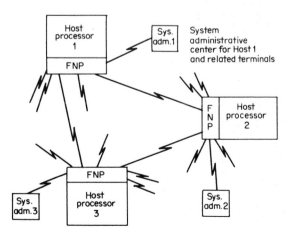

FIG. 20-1 Distributed monitoring and control functions. FNP = front-end network processor.

System Instrumentation

Monitoring and control are only feasible if the components of the distributed system provide the necessary information, interfaces, and functionality. For example, each element in the system must be *instrumented* —it must collect information about its own operation, both for dynamic display purposes and for longer-range statistical collection. An information processor used for transaction processing, for example, ought to collect the following information:

- Number of transactions processed, by type, per time period.
- Processing time required for each transaction, broken down by central-system time, memory residency, and peripheral time.
- Typical multiprocessing depth.
- Location from which each transaction was received, and locations (s) to which each response was sent.
- Database-access information, such as number of accesses per transaction, database area(s) used, delays and/or interlocks encountered.

One of the problems most frequently encountered is that various components may each be instrumented differently, and though the instrumentation of each may be adequate, when the components are used

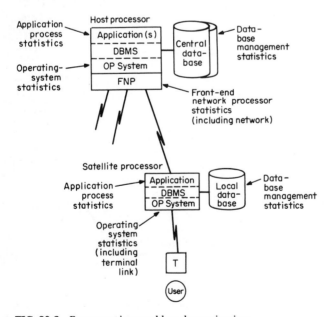

FIG. 20-2   Response-time problem determination.

together it may turn out that their approaches to instrumentations are not only different but incompatible.

For example, if remote satellite processors do part of the processing—and a central host does the remainder—for certain types of transactions, it is necessary to match up the satellite and host statistics to determine the processing and response pattern for the entire transaction. This type of situation is shown in Figure 20-2. If the response is too slow when a transaction is processed by both satellite and host, it may be very difficult to determine which processor(s) may be at fault.

If the implementation approach chosen for a distributed system is a turn-key one, then the system specifications can include the appropriate set of coordinated statistics. If the implementation is built around standard vendor-supplied components, especially if the components are supplied by different vendors, it may be necessary to add statistical collection facilities to the software supplied by the vendor(s). If necessary, much of the statistical-collection logic can be built into the application programs. While this is not the optimum approach, it is usually preferable to modifying system software.

Test and Control Facilities

Dynamic monitoring also requires component test and diagnostic (T&D) capabilities to be effective. Ideally, a system administrator ought to be able to initiate testing of any component—hardware or software or communications facility—suspected to be malfunctioning. More and more hardware components today have self-test facilities built-in, and powerful test facilities are being built into software systems. However, this is another area which needs careful consideration during system design and implementation. If possible, these capabilities should be obtained from the vendor when components are acquired. If this is not practical, at least a minimum set must be added during system implementation. The alternative will be to spend a great deal of money traveling to remote locations to determine the cause of errors, problems, and failures. The time and expense involved in this sort of diagnostic hunt could be the factor which causes a distributed system to be termed a failure.

Dynamic monitoring and control also require that system elements have control interfaces which allow system administrators to change the system's operation in order to enable it to respond to changed conditions more adequately. For example, if an administrator determines that time-sharing response is too slow because too much processing power is being used for background batch work, the administrator must be able to modify dynamically the operating system's priority algorithms so that more resources are allocated to the interactive workload. Or if a specific transaction type is causing system failures, the system administrator must be able to discontinue processing of that transaction type until the problem can be analyzed and solved. In this case, the administrator should also be able to send a message explaining the situation to all affected terminal users.

Control interfaces of this type must be protected by security features which allow their use only by authorized personnel. This can be achieved by allowing activation of these interfaces only from specific terminal locations—usually the terminals in the system administration center(s). However, in some cases, this approach limits flexibility. For example, a system administrator may be at home during off hours, but still be on call for participation in the solution of a complex problem; the administrator should be able to use an at-home terminal in such a case. The best solution to security protection for control functions is to provide *password and privilege protection*—the administrator must supply the correct password (possibly different for each class of control function) and a valid identifier which triggers access to a list of privileges assigned to that administrator. This approach provides great flexibility since lists of privileges can be precisely tailored to the duties of specific classes of administrators.

Information-Processing Monitoring and Control

Operational monitoring and control apply to all aspects of a distributed system, including information processing, database operations, the data-communications network, and security/privacy protection. The latter three topics are covered in following sections; this section briefly covers aspects unique to information processing.

Monitoring and control of the information-processing elements of a distributed system must cover the following areas:

- Error and failure analysis for information-processing hardware and software
- Statistical analysis to detect changing patterns in the use of information-processing resources

Under the first heading are operations such as detection of problems in a host processor or in a satellite processor (problems such as the failure of a tape handler), incorrect processing of certain types of transactions or jobs, or inadequate response for certain types of users and/or for certain types of transactions. All of these problems require prompt analysis and corrective action by the system administrators.

Under the second heading come all of the statistical analysis functions —analyzing system usage, component usage, response-time patterns (peaks, averages), and so on. Appropriate statistical analyses can detect changes in how the system is being used and/or in how it is operating. Such analyses allow corrective action to be taken before changing situations become problem situations.

Since both error and failure analysis and statistical analysis for information processing are extremely similar, functionally, to these operations when performed for database and network functions, specifics of how the system administrative staff operates are supplied in the next two sections.

20-2. DATABASE ADMINISTRATION

The database administrator's role in database design is emphasized as the DBA's major job responsibility in many organizations. However, dynamic monitoring and control of database usage are equally or more important, especially in large on-line systems—whether they are centralized or distributed. The use of a distributed database increases the level of complexity of the DBA's task, especially if the parts of the distributed database are closely interrelated. As in the other aspects of the distributed system (information processing and networking), database monitoring and control have both dynamic and longer-range aspects.

Database-Usage Monitoring

One of the major functions of dynamic database administration is to monitor database usage, including the following items:

1. Number and types of database accesses
2. Access patterns over time:
   a. Per second, minute, hour, day, month
   b. Peak access volume versus average or mean volume
3. Locations which request database accesses

The database-management software must accumulate this statistical information continouously. Dynamic display of database usage should be limited to conditions defined to be outside of the norm. For example, if a given database area is being saturated by access requests, this should be displayed at once for possible DBA action. All other data should also be available for dynamic display on DBA request and must be accumulated for longer-range analysis.

These data can be accumulated and periodically used to create a report showing patterns of access for the DBA. Ideally, the system should retain a set of norms either obtained from accumulated usage over time or provided manually by DBA input. In this case, the reports can highlight conditions which deviate from the norm. If the system does not provide this capability, the DBA must search for patterns which seem abnormal.

When database access patterns change, the DBA must take appropriate action to ensure that these changes do not cause the system to perform inadequately. Actions which can be taken are as follows.

The database structure can be changed (reorganized) to more fully match access patterns. For example, if experience shows that application processes are continually interfering with each other because of the need to access a common record in the database structure, either the structure can be changed to eliminate that interdependency or the logic of the applications can be reorganized to avoid, at least in some cases, access to that record. If new records added to the database require a great deal of processing for linking, index update, etc., perhaps a change in structure will reduce the processing needed. These problems, and their solutions, are identical with those which occur in a centralized database.

The DBA may also determine that the best action in response to new access patterns is to distribute the database. For example, if response is degrading because too many terminal users are accessing the centralized database, it may be possible to partition the database across two hosts. Or, it may be appropriate to replicate some of the data onto remote satellite processors. Either, or both, of these two tactics can improve response when database accesses increase and users are no longer being served adequately.

If the database is already distributed, changes in access patterns may cause the DBA to consider a redistribution of the database. For example, if formerly users heavily accessed data residing at a nearby satellite processor but are now beginning to access data residing at the host more often, perhaps some transfer of data between the host and satellite is appropriate. Or, if the database has been replicated, it may become clear over a certain period of time that some data elements included in the replicated copy are not being used very often. It would then be appropriate to drop these elements from the copy or copies and to retain them only at the central master-database location. A combination of these strategies may also be called for: the DBA must determine what the result of each such action will be and which will be the most appropriate way to respond to changing conditions.

Database-Problem Detection and Resolution

The other major function of the DBA in dynamic monitoring and control is to detect database-related problems and failures and to take appropriate action to correct them.

One problem which the DBA may have to handle is inadequate response to terminal users. (The definition and measurement of system response time are discussed in Unit 18-3.) Response time has many facets, but a major factor is often the time taken to obtain (and possibly update) database information. If response-time difficulties are traced to the database, then it is the DBA's responsibility to resolve the problem. The actions which the DBA can take are basically the same as those described earlier for changing access patterns. A given part of the database can be reorganized or restructured to improve access speed. Some part of the database can be distributed or the distribution of data elements across the system can be changed. The appropriate combination of these actions must be determined by the DBA through analysis of the situation.

A number of conditions can be grouped under the heading of database failures. For example, if the database is being recovered after an application or system failure, but the recovery does not complete successfully, the DBA must take action to correct database content. If the structure of the database is somehow damaged (lost linkages, incorrect or lost indices, etc.) because of software and/or hardware problems, the DBA must determine how to repair the damage. Because the number of situations of this type is potentially almost unlimited, it is extremely difficult to provide automatic recovery or correction methods. Generally, therefore, the DBA must determine exactly what the situation is and select the most appropriate recovery actions. Often recovery actions involve one of these two approaches:

1. Reconstruction of the database from saved copies and "After" journals

2. Manual, often interactive, correction of damaged data

If the problems are severe, it may be necessary to completely reload the database from the most recent saved copy. The system "After" journal(s) can then be used to reconstruct database content to the point of failure. This corrective action, while time-consuming, is sometimes used to recover from a serious disk-device problem—either by reconstructing the database content on the device after the hardware problem is fixed or by reconstructing the data on another device to take the place of the failed one.

Interactive correction, accomplished by browsing through database content in order to determine exactly where the error is, then "patching" it by means of interactive input, is used when relatively small amounts of data are in error. For example, if a database-management software problem exists which causes an index to be improperly updated, this could cause certain data to be inaccessible and/or cause some accesses to be directed to the wrong data. The DBA could use an interactive "patching" facility to locate and correct the invalid index. Of course the necessary interactive tools must be available for the DBA's use in this mode of operation.

The DBA's role in monitoring and control is very similar to the role of the information-processing system administrator and the network administrator. In smaller systems these roles may be combined so that a single system-administration staff handles all dynamic functions. In larger systems, the monitoring and control workload may be so high that specialization is important. In any case, the DBA functions described here are required, and they must be provided for in a distributed system.

These dynamic monitoring and control functions can, in some cases, be integrated into the same terminal facilities used for other system-administration functions; this will often be the most cost-effective method. In other cases, ease-of-use and/or the size of the distributed system may make it appropriate to configure a separate terminal or set of terminals for the DBA's use.

20-3.   NETWORK ADMINISTRATION

Network administration is an important part of distributed-system monitoring and control and covers all aspects associated with the data-communications network facilities and components.

Network-Error Detection and Correction

In the data-communications network, errors and failures must be reported automatically. (As discussed earlier, instrumentation of system elements is vital to the success of these control functions.) Serious errors and failures of any type must be reported immediately to the network administrators; less serious errors, as well as statistics describing network operation, can be reported periodically—usually on an hourly and cumulative daily basis.

Some errors and failures will be reported manually, either by the terminal users or system operational personnel. For example, if an unintelligent terminal has failed, the system may not be able to detect this unless output is waiting for the terminal. The user, however, will discover that the device is inoperative when an attempt is made to send input. Failure notification in this case will take the form of a telephone call to the network-administration staff.

When a problem is noted the network administrator must take appropriate action to resolve it. The location and cause of the error may not be immediately apparent if the network is complex. For example, the inability of a terminal user to access a central host system might be caused by terminal failure, by the failure of the modem at the terminal, by communications-link failure, by failure of the modem at the host's front-end network processor, or by some type of failure in the central-site hardware or software. This situation is shown graphically in Figure 20-3.

The technique most often used to discover the exact location of the problem is the execution of a series of *loop-back tests,* also shown in Figure 20-3. In a loop-back test a message is sent through the network, time after time, progressing each time one step further through the total set of components. Whenever the message fails to complete a loop-back test, the element included for the first time on this test is assumed to be the failed one; diagnostic and/or corrective action is thus localized.

Diagnostic capabilities may be provided in the component, and if they are, these capabilities can be activated by the network administrator. For example, many terminals have self-test capabilities, which can be triggered either by the terminal user or in some cases by remote signal.

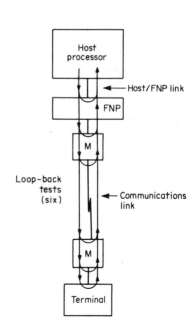

FIG. 20-3 Problem location via loop-back tests. FNP = front-end network processor; M = modem.

Often these self-tests are executed automatically each time the device is powered on, so that many problems are detected prior to use.

If the problem appears to be in the communications network, it may be possible for the network administrator to make use of carrier test facilities, either automatically or by making a phone call to a carrier test center. Usually the carrier or PTT can initiate a variety of tests to determine the condition of a circuit (and sometimes the terminating modems). These tests will generally determine whether or not a particular circuit is operating adequately, and if it is not, the carrier can take the necessary corrective action.

Depending upon the component(s) which appear to be causing the problem, the network administrator can take the appropriate corrective actions. In some cases, it may be possible to diagnose problem cause completely and take action to repair the failed device. (Some users choose to perform their own maintenance to lower overall service costs.) In other cases, it is appropriate to notify the communications carrier, the hardware vendor, or the vendor of purchased software. Problems with in-house software elements must be referred to the in-house staff for resolution.

It is important in any on-line system—whether centralized or distributed—to have specific agreements with the carriers and hardware and software vendor(s) involved so that reaction to problem calls is rapid. Special agreements may be necessary to ensure that parts are stocked on-site or nearby and/or to ensure that adequate response is available during off-hours. Similar agreements may be needed with the in-house software staff, to ensure that coverage is adequate for problem resolution during off-hours. These additional services may entail additional cost, but this is unavoidable if continuous operation for critical applications is to be provided.

Monitoring Network Usage

The network administrator must monitor network usage, just as the DBA does database usage. Items to be monitored include:

1. Traffic patterns
   a. Peak, average volume
   b. Locations from which and to which traffic is sent
   c. Traffic-type distribution
2. Changes in patterns over time (seconds, minutes, hours, day etc.).

In general, statistics of this type need not be reported dynamically to the network administration center unless the numbers accumulated vary dramatically from the norm. For example, on a day when business is very active, a high transaction rate from certain locations may cause slow response and processor overloading. This type of information must be reported immediately in order to permit possible remedial action. Other statistical information should be accumulated and reported periodically (usually hourly) to the network administration center and over longer periods (weekly, monthly) in the form of hard-copy reports. Analysis of these reports can lead the network administrators to increase the number and/or speed of links to and from locations at which traffic is increasing and to decrease the number and/or speed of links to and from locations at which traffic is decreasing. If the network processor(s) in the system are becoming overloaded, network administrators must upgrade them so that they provide more power or add more NPs in order to split up the processing load. If a terminal or terminals cannot handle the volume of traffic experienced, network administrators must see to it that more terminals are added or perhaps that locations of existing terminals are changed so that they will more adequately match traffic patterns. More powerful intelligent terminals may also be called for in order to provide more capability for individual devices unable to handle increasing volumes of traffic.

As in all cases of pattern analysis, the network administrator must be extremely careful not to base decisions on insufficient data and fall into the trap of overreacting. If, for example, a large increase in volume is experienced due to a specific business situation of short duration, it is unnecessary to add communications links and/or terminals to the network. The extra volume can simply be handled with slower-than-desirable response for that period of time. The network administrators should notify terminal users of the situation and of the temporary nature of the problem. Similarly, if a temporary decrease in traffic is caused by vacations or business slack, the network administrator should not remove the temporarily underloaded terminals or links. These cautions apply to the monitoring and control of information-processing and database resources as well as to the communications network.

Monitoring Equipment

The network administrative functions can be made easier by the use of hardware devices which can monitor and, to some degree, diagnose problems in the communications network.

Monitoring equipment can include a simple display panel which indicates the channels and modems currently active. This information is displayed by a series of lights, one per channel and modem, each of which is lighted when the associated channel is active and unlighted otherwise. This type of display is relatively inexpensive and is very help-ful both as a quick check on system load and, by a no-lights-showing condition, as a quick indication of system failure.

An oscilloscope to observe circuit activity on the links may be pro-vided as part of the monitoring equipment. The network administrators must be trained in the patterns to be expected and the meaning of other patterns observed.

Another useful tool is an EIA voltage monitor (EIA stands for Elec-tronics Industry Association, which provides the most common modem-interface standards in the United States). The EIA voltage monitor, which can be equipped with a speaker for audio monitoring, permits monitoring of each of the signals which make up the EIA interface. To activate this monitoring, the terminal or processor and modem are plugged into the two front-panel connectors on the monitor. The moni-tor module is then transparent to data flow while monitoring takes place.

The telecommunications analyzer is another useful tool for equip-ment monitoring. The telecommunications analyzer provides for analy-sis of the analog and digital parameters which affect the performance of a communications link. The following analog parameters must be meas-ured for routine and/or emergency diagnostic operations:

- Amplitude response versus frequency
- Relative envelope delay
- Harmonic distortion
- Phase jitter
- Phase hits
- Impulse noise
- Noise level (Gaussian)

Acceptable limits on each item can be established, for each type of circuit, and it may be appropriate to obtain assistance from the carrier in setting these limits. Measurements outside of defined limits indicate trouble; in many cases, the specific out-of-limit parameter indicates which problem exists.

Public-Data-Network Considerations

If a public data network is used, rather than a private-link network, the majority of these problems can be offloaded onto the carrier. The carrier which provides the network is responsible for its operation and for anal-ysis and correction of problems in the network. Of course, public data networks have a very high level of redundancy in their configurations and therefore are not so vulnerable to link or equipment failure as most private networks are. However, failures can lead to degraded response and the carrier must be able to supply alternate routes.

One potential problem in the use of public data networks is the difficulty of activating remote diagnostic capabilities at terminal or satellite processor locations. For example, in some cases remote testing and diagnosis (T&D) depends upon specific message types being transmitted from the host location. If these message types are not acceptable to the public network, remote T&D cannot be activated this way. If use of a public data network is planned, these aspects should be investigated in detail during the system-design phase.

20-4. SECURITY-AND-PRIVACY ADMINISTRATION

Most data-processing departments did not have a security/privacy administration function during the years preceding 1980, unless they served military or diplomatic organizations or ones engaged in similar operations. In the 1980s, lack of a security/privacy administration function will become increasingly rare.

Security is becoming more important as integrated databases make more and more data vital to an organization available on-line. In addition, there is a definite trend toward interconnecting computer systems operated by different companies or organizations in order to exchange data of mutual interest. In the face of this trend, it is increasingly important to ensure that only defined data are exchanged and that other data are protected from disclosure. Trends toward allowing customers access to the computer system of a business via terminals (e.g., unattended teller terminals) also intensify the need for security protection of data.

Privacy is becoming a topic of increasing public interest. Several countries have legislated restrictions on the use of personal data and measures for the protection of such data. Legislation in the United States so far deals mostly with personal data managed by federal government organizations, but further legislation may extend this protection to all personal data.

These trends make it likely that many on-line systems, and most distributed systems will, in the near future, require a security and privacy administration function even if, except in the case of large organizations and/or those which manage very large amounts of personal data (e.g., insurance companies), a full-time administrator is unnecessary.

Access Control

The most basic security/privacy-protection function is control of access to an information system and /or to its resources. Techniques most often used are the establishment of passwords and/or privilege lists.

Passwords are stored by the system, and a user must supply a matching password to be allowed access. Sometimes a single password allows the user to make use of all of the system's resources. More often, the first password only allows access to the system (a *log-on* password) and other password(s) must be supplied to gain access to other resources such as processes and/or databases. There are many methods for ensuring password security, such as using rotating passwords, encrypting (encoding) passwords through nonreversible formulas, and using time-stamped passwords.

Privilege lists use the technique of establishing a set of functions which a specific user, or class of users, can access. After furnishing a valid individual or group identifier, users are linked to the privilege list and allowed to execute those functions and/or access those resources on their lists.

Most systems use some combination of password(s) and privileges, according to the policies of the organization and the needs of the system users. The security administrator, of course, must also be under control of a higher-level privilege list which prevents change to other areas not under that administrator's control.

The security administrator must also monitor use of the system, to determine if access controls are being violated and if attempted violations have been prevented by the system's control mechanisms. Usually attempted accesses which fail because of security protection are logged, so that the security administrator can determine who is trying to access the system and why. If a pattern of attempted access is discovered, it may be appropriate to alter security-protection methods to deal with the situation more adequately.

Data Protection

The other basic security/privacy-protection function is control of data accessibility. One of the ground rules of security is that the system must have a very high level of integrity to ensure security. A system which cannot protect data integrity cannot—by definition—protect data security. In addition, a system which fails in undefined and unpredictable ways is incapable of providing high security, because security and privacy protection methods may be breached through failures. Naturally this is not an all-or-nothing situation: as every system fails on occasion. However, a high degree of integrity is the base for security and privacy.

Encryption is one method used to protect data from disclosure. Encryption encodes or alters data so that these cannot be understood except by another process which can execute an appropriate decryption algorithm. There is a standard method or algorithm for encryption in the United States, based upon techniques developed by IBM and formalized by the National Bureau of Standards (NBS). Although standardized relatively recently, the NBS methods of encryption are becoming the standard for all systems except those in the military and diplomatic services (which use more complex approaches).

Encryption is most often used to protect data during transmission over a communications network. Data are most vulnerable at this point, since a data link can be tapped relatively easily and inexpensively. However, if the data are encrypted, tapping reveals nothing of use to the intruder.

Data stored on removable storage devices such as diskettes and disk packs are also sometimes encrypted, so that if the device is stolen the data are not revealed. This, however, is expensive, and so often physical protection methods of access control to the disk and tape library locations are used instead of encryption.

Multilevel encryption is also sometimes used, so that if data are misrouted in a complex network, disclosure will not result. An example network of this type is shown in Figure 20-4. If a message is sent from Host A to Host B, but is misrouted and delivered to Host C, link encryption would allow disclosure of the data. However, if the data are encrypted twice, once at the message level and once at the link level, only the link level can be decrypted at Host C, leaving the data still encrypted

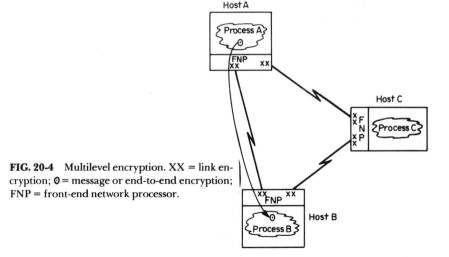

FIG. 20-4   Multilevel encryption. XX = link encryption; O = message or end-to-end encryption; FNP = front-end network processor.

and therefore secure. As more and more complex networks—including public networks—come into use, multilevel encryption will be more common than today.

Public data networks affect the type of data encryption which can be used. If a public network requires header information indicating where each message or packet is to be sent, the header cannot be encrypted or the intelligent components of the public network could not decipher the header information and so could not route the message. However, message-level encryption of the text can be used, so that these data are transmitted through the network in encoded form and decrypted only at the correct receiving location.

The major problem which the security and privacy administrator must cope with is how to manage the encrypting and decrypting keys. Since the NBS standard makes the algorithm used public, only the keys used are private, and the security of the encryption system rests on protecting the keys.

In a private-key system, keys are usually distributed by some method other than data communications. For example, a courier may manually deliver them, or they may be sent by mail or registered mail. In some cases, they may be delivered via data communications, but encrypted using a special and different key than normal messages. The difficulty is to find a scheme of key distribution which is effective, secure, and also cost-effective.

Some researchers* are working on public-key encryption systems, which allow publication of both the algorithm and encryption key. Only a complementary decryption key is kept private. Research such as this may solve the key-management problem, but today this problem continues to cause considerable difficulty in ensuring security and privacy protection by use of encryption techniques.

Security/Privacy Trade-offs

The key to designing adequate security- and privacy-protection methods is to trade off security and privacy against costs correctly. It is pointless to spend a great deal of money and effort protecting data which are of little value. It is equally unsatisfactory to allow vital data to be disclosed and/or altered for lack of adequate security protection methods. A basic ground rule used in these cases is that the cost of protection must not exceed the value of the data and/or resources being protected. Stated another way, from the point of view of the potential system intruder, it is not worth

*"The Mathematics of Public-Key Cryptography," Martin E. Hellman, *Scientific American*, Volume 241, Number 2, August 1979, pp. 146-157.

spending more money to penetrate an information system than the value of the data or resources which will be gained. The trick, therefore, is to make it more expensive for potential intruders to gain access than they believe the intrusion will be worth. Of course, because the value of data and/or resources is often a very subjective question, management guidance in assessing trade-offs is very important.

SUMMARY

21

SUMMARY AND CONCLUSIONS

The potential advantages of distributed information systems are receiving increasing attention within the computer-user community. Recognition of these advantages provides impetus for both theoretical and practical work on distributed systems. On one hand, theoreticians are grappling with the definition of multilayer protocols for information interchange, formulation of rules for system-wide deadlock detection, definition of methods for access to distributed databases, and other similarly complex technical problems. On the other hand, forward-looking computer users are implementing distributed systems in order to enable them to better handle the real-world problems of their enterprises. Early implementations are, as is usual, proceeding in the form of specialized subsets of general capabilities. In this way, the leading-edge users of distributed systems are gaining valuable experience, enabling the computer community as a whole gradually to determine which techniques are feasible and which give the best results.

These bases of theory and experience are necessary if it is to become practical for the majority of computer users to implement distributed systems. The emergence of wider, more general-purpose support for distributed processing and distributed databases over the next several years will make it possible for many computer users to consider the distribution of functionality within their information systems.

Not all applications will use the distributed system structure, however. Many information systems will remain centralized because that form can satisfactorily serve their users' requirements. But other information systems will be converted to—or be created with—a distributed structure, because that will better meet their users' objectives.

The existence of generalized support for both centralized and distributed system structures will give computer users an increasingly wide range of alternatives in meeting the needs of their enterprises. It will no longer be necessary to choose between centralization or decentralization; distributed system structures will provide a range of alternatives between these two extremes.

Distributed information systems and the advantages they offer will therefore represent an important trend, for at least the next decade, in the evolution of information systems.

GLOSSARY

Acknowledgment (ACK) A reply which indicates that the receiver has accepted previous transmissions(s).

Address The name of the destination(s) to which a message is to be delivered.

Administrator, system A person who defines, controls, and manages the information-system environment within which the information-processing activities of an enterprise are handled. Specializations within the system administrator class include database administrator and network administrator.

Advanced Communications Function (ACF) Software available from IBM, which extends Systems Network Architecture (SNA) capabilities to support Multisystem Networking (MSN).

Advanced Communications Service (ACS) A data network planned for future operation by American Telephone and Telegraph Company (AT&T).

Advanced data communications control procedure (ADCCP) A standard protocol for data communications, defined by American National Standards Institute (ANSI). A superset of high-level data link control (HDLC).

Advanced Research Projects Agency (ARPA) An agency of the United States Department of Defense, which engages in research projects. The organization which funded development of the ARPA computer network (ARPANET).

"After" journal A record of database content following updating, to be used for recovery in case of damage to the storage medium.

American National Standards Institute (ANSI) A nongovernmental organization in the United States which defines and publishes standards related to information processing and data communications. ANSI represents the United States in activities of the International Standards Organization (ISO).

American standard code for information interchange (ASCII) A code, defined and standardized by American National Standards Institute (ANSI) in which each character is defined by 7 bits, which may be accompanied by an eighth bit for parity checking.

Application A definable set of tasks to be accomplished as part of the work of an organization; e.g., payroll, inventory control. An application may be partly manual and partly computerized.

Application developer A person who is responsible for tailoring the basic capabilities of the information system into a form suitable for the end users.

Application program A set of statements defining certain tasks associated with an application that are to be executed by a computer.

Architecture A standard set of rules for functional modularity, interfaces, and protocols, which forms the framework for the implementation of products which can operate compatibly together.

Asynchronous transmission A mode in which the receiving mechanism synchronizes at the start and end of each character. Also called *start/stop transmission* (STR), because a start bit precedes, and one or more stop bits follow, the information bits for each character.

Attached Resource Computer (ARC*) The facilities provided by Datapoint for connection of multiple, functionally specialized processors to a common bus, with the ability to connect via data communications to other ARC and/or host processor systems.

Automated-teller machine (ATM) *See* ATT.

Automated-teller terminal (ATT) A device by means of which an authorized bank customer can obtain banking services such as savings/checking withdrawal without a teller in attendance. Also called ATM.

Availability The probability that an information system, or some portion of an information system, will be usable when needed. Typically computed by combining the reliability of the system components and analyzing component interdependencies.

Bandwidth The range of frequencies assigned to a data-communications link, which determines the volume of data which can be transmitted in a given time period.

Batch processing A mode of computer use in which input data (transactions) are accumulated into groups of convenient size before processing.

Baud A signaling rate in data transmission. Sometimes, but not always, equivalent to bits per second (bps).

"Before" journal A record of database content prior to updating, to be used for recovery in case the updating process is unsuccessful.

Binary synchronous communications (BSC) A protocol for data communications defined by IBM, used in their products as well as in many other vendors' products. Also called *bisynch*. Being replaced by synchronous data link control (SDLC).

bps Abbreviation for *bits per second,* the most common way of describing the transmission capacity of a link.

Broadband A communications link with a bandwidth greater than a voice-grade circuit, capable of data-transmission speeds of more than 10,000 bps.

Carrier A company which, in the United States, supplies voice-, record-, or data-transmission services to the public, under control of the Federal Communi-

---

*Trademark of the Datapoint Corporation.

cations Commission (FCC) or other regulatory body. Carriers are classified as "common" or "specialized common" according to the type(s) of services offered.

Cathode-ray tube (CRT)   A term in common use to refer to a keyboard/display terminal, whether or not the display is actually a cathode-ray tube.

CCITT   *See* International Consultative Committee on Telephony and Telegraphy.

Centralized information system   An information system in which all processing logic is located at one site.

Circuit   A means of communication between two points, comprising both "send" and "receive" channels.

Circuit-switched network   A communications network in which each message is transmitted by establishing a physical connection—a circuit—between the sender and receiver and retaining that connection until transmission is complete. The voice-telephone networks are, in general, circuit-switched networks.

Common carrier   *See* Carrier.

Communications controller   *See* Network processor.

Communications network   *See* Data-communications network.

Communications processor   *See* Network processor.

Communications system   In Univac's Distributed Communications Architecture (DCA), the combination of the transport network and the termination system.

Communications-system services (CSS)   The software which, in NCR's Distributed Network Architecture (DNA) provides for end-to-end message control.

Communications-system users   The software packages which provide services, such as database inquiry, to end users (people and application programs) in Univac's Distributed Communications Architecture (DCA).

Concentration   The collection of data from a number of links onto a smaller number of higher-capacity links, with the distribution of the return flow from fewer to more links.

Concentrator   A network processor which performs the concentration function.

Conference on Data Systems Languages (CODASYL)   A standards-definition body in the United States. Responsible for the definition of languages such as COBOL.

Correspondent   The term used in NCR's Distributed Network Architecture (DNA) to refer to an entity which can communicate, such as an application program or a terminal.

Coupling   The function of interconnecting the links of the network to the terminals and/or processors. A data set or modem is a coupling device.

Cross-compiler   A compiler which operates on one type of computer, often a large-scale general-purpose computer, but generates object code suitable for execution on a different type of computer—typically a minicomputer or microcomputer.

Cyclic redundancy check (CRC)   A mode of error detection used in some protocols, such as high-level data link control (HDLC).

Data access protocol (DAP)   The protocol defined in Digital Equipment Corporation's (DEC) Digital Network Architecture (DNA) to provide functions such as remote file access, file transfer, and remote system load.

Data-communications network   The collection of transmission facilities, network processors, etc., which provides for data movement among terminals and information processors.

Data-definition language (DDL)   A means of describing the structure (fields, records, interrecord relationships) of a database or some portion of a database. The concept and the language are defined by Conference on Data Systems Languages (CODASYL). The DDL is used to create a database schema.

Data element, or **Database element**   The content of a field within a file or database. Contrasted with *Database structure.*

Data set   A device which converts digital data at the sending terminal or processor into a form suitable for transmission and reconverts it to the original form at the receiving location. Also called *modem* or *subset.*

Data-manipulation language (DML)   The commands required to create, access, and change the content of a database. The concept and two specific DMLs —one associated with common business-oriented language (COBOL), the other with FORTRAN—are defined by Conference on Data Systems Languages (CODASYL).

Database   A generalized, integrated collection of company- or installation-owned data which fulfills the data requirements of all applications which access it and which is structured to model the natural data relationships which exist in an enterprise.

Database administrator (DBA)   The person or group of people responsible for definition of an organization's database(s) and for the monitoring and control of operations against the database(s).

Database/data communications   The term used by IBM to describe transaction processing.

Database management system (DBMS)   The functions which support the semipermanent storage of user-owned data and provide access to those data.

Database structure   The field, record, and interrecord relationships which collectively define the format in which data are stored. The content of the structure is made up of data elements.

Database synchronization   The process of ensuring that the component parts of a distributed database are logically consistent.

Datagram   A technique for sending messages in a data network, in which each message/packet contains all of the information necessary to reach its destination and is handled independently of all other messages/packets. *See* also Virtual circuit.

Decentralized information system   Two or more sets of information-processing equipment, operated by the same organization, but without any implied coordination among the sets.

DECnet   The overall capabilities provided by Digital Equipment Corporation (DEC) for distributed systems and networks. The architecture which supports DECnet is the Digital Network Architecture (DNA).

Dedicated link   A communications link which is continuously available to the user. Also called *private* or *leased*.

Destination   A logical location to which data are moved, a data receiver. A destination can be a terminal, a person, or a process.

Dial link   A communications link which is shared with other users and therefore available only when not already in use. Access is achieved by dialing. Also called *switched*.

Dialogue   The term used in Digital Equipment Corporation's (DEC) Digital Network Architecture (DNA) to describe a logical connection between two objects—such as an application program and a remote file access software package—for data exchange. Generally equivalent with session. (*See* Session.)

Digital data communications message protocol (DDCMP)   A protocol for data communications defined by Digital Equipment Corporation (DEC) and used in their products.

Digital Network Architecture (DNA)   The architecture defined and used by Digital Equipment Corporation (DEC) in providing product capabilities for networks and distributed systems.

Distributed database   A single logical database which has been implemented in more than one physical segment, attached to more than one information processor.

Distributed Communications Architecture (DCA)   The architecture defined and used by Sperry-Univac in providing product capabilities for networks and distributed systems.

Distributed Communications Processor (DCP)   The Univac network processor which, in conformance with the rules of Distributed Communications Architecture (DCA), operates as a front-end, concentrator, or network-switching processor.

Distributed information system, or **Distributed system**   A coordinated set of information-processing capabilities implemented in two or more relatively independent resource centers such as computer sites, terminal locations, and so on.

Distributed network   *See* Meshed network.

Distributed processing   A technique for implementing one logically related set of information-processing (application-related) functions within multiple physical devices.

Distributed Network Architecture (DNA)   The architecture defined and used by NCR in providing product capabilities for networks and distributed systems.

Distributed Systems Architecture (DSA)   The architecture defined and used by Honeywell Information Systems (HIS) and Cii Honeywell Bull (CiiHB) in providing product capabilities for networks and distributed systems. *See* also DSE.

Distributed Systems Environment (DSE)   The overall capabilities provided by Honeywell Information Systems (HIS) and Cii Honeywell Bull (CiiHB) for distributed systems and networks. The architecture which supports DSE is the Distributed Systems Architecture (DSA).

Distributed Systems Network (DSN)   The architecture defined and used by Hewlett-Packard company (HP) in providing product capabilities for networks and distributed systems.

Domain   In IBM's Systems Network Architecture (SNA) the set of processors, terminal controllers, and terminals assigned to a specific processor's System Services Control Point (SSCP) for access control and session establishment.

Downline, or **Down load**   The transmission of a program or data from one processor (usually a host) to another (usually a satellite), for execution and/or retention there.

Electronics Industry Association (EIA)   A trade association in the United States which defines and publishes standards such as those required to interconnect computer and communications equipment. There is considerable overlap between the activities of EIA and of the International Consultative Committee on Telephony and Telegraphy (CCITT).

Encryption   The process of converting data into an encoded form, undecipherable except to a processor or human which possesses the correct decryption formula.

End point   A logical or physical entity at the end of a branch of a network. End points can include application processes, terminals, and people at terminals.

End user   A person who utilizes an information system during the performance of his or her normal duties. End users include bank tellers, retail store clerks, managers, engineers, factory workers, etc.

Enterprise   An organization (business, governmental, educational, etc.) which (in this context) makes use of information-system resources.

Extended binary-coded decimal-interchange code (EBCDIC)   An 8-level (8 data bits) code for information processing and data communications.

Fallback   A procedure or facility which provides for continued operation, perhaps in degraded mode, when failures occur.

FCC   *See* Federal Communications Commission.

Federal Communications Commission (FCC)   A board appointed by the President of the United States under the Communication Act of 1934, having the power to regulate all interstate and foreign electrical communication systems originating in the United States.

File   A named increment of storage. Also, an unstructured or user-structured form of data storage. Often restricted to one user or one application, and possibly existing only as long as that user/application is active.

Flag A character which designates the beginning or end of a transmission increment in protocols such as high-level data link control (HDLC).

Flow control The function of preventing overload within a data-communications network by limiting data flow according to some algorithm(s). Also called *pacing.*

Four-wire A communications circuit which includes four wires, two for each direction of transmission. Four-wire facilities are always full-duplex (FDX). Usually written *4-wire.*

Frame A transmission increment in high-level data link control (HDLC) and similar protocols. Generally synonymous with *Packet.*

Frequency-division multiplexor (FDM) A device which multiplexes multiple data streams onto a single link by assigning different frequencies within the total bandwidth of the link to the various data streams. *See* also TDM.

Front-end network processor (FNP) A network processor which provides communications control and network access to one or more associated information processors. Also called a *front-end processor* (FEP).

Full-duplex (FDX) The characteristic of a communications circuit which allows transmission in both directions at the same time. A full-duplex circuit can support either two-way simultaneous or two-way alternate operation.

Fully connected network A meshed network in which every processor is directly connected to every other processor.

Global catalog An association of the names of objects (e.g., files, end points, processes) and the location(s) at which each object exists. Also called *global directory.*

Global directory *See* Global catalog.

Global object-type descriptor The term used in Digital Equipment Corporation's (DEC) Digital Network Architecture (DNA) to describe a global catalog which contains the location and attributes of each resource (an object) of global interest.

Half-duplex (HDX) The characteristic of a communications circuit which allows transmission in only one direction at a time. A half-duplex circuit can support only two-way alternate operation, not two-way simultaneous.

Hierarchically distributed processing A distributed system in which the logical relationships among the components—information processors, terminal controllers, real-time device controllers, etc.—form a graded series, or hierarchy. Also called *vertically distributed processing.*

Hierarchical network A data-communications network structure which forms a graded series, or hierarchical, pattern of connections. The simplest form of hierarchical network is a star network.

High-level data link control (HDLC) A standard protocol for data communications, defined by International Standards Organization (ISO).

Horizontally distributed processing A distributed system in which the information processors cooperate in an equal partnership. Also called *peer-distributed processing.*

Host processor An information processor (IP) which provides supporting services and/or guidance to users and/or to satellite or intermediate processors and terminals. A host processor is generally assumed to be self-sufficient, and to require no supervision from other processors.

Hybrid distributed processing A distributed system which includes both hierarchically distributed processing and horizontally distributed processing.

Information network An interconnected set of hardware and software components, including communications facilities, configured to meet (some part of) the application workload requirements of an enterprise. *See* also Information system.

Information processing The hardware and software functions which provide computation, decision making, and data manipulation, supporting the execution of computerized applications.

Information system An interconnected set of hardware and software components, configured to meet (some part of) the application workload requirements of an enterprise. May or may not include communications facilities. *See* also Information network.

Integrity The prevention of, and/or recovery from, failures and errors in such a way that data and/or processes within an information system are neither lost nor damaged.

Interface A set of rules by which services can be requested and provided. In layered architectures, an interface defines how one functional layer can request services from the next lower layer, and how that layer must respond. *See* also Protocol.

Interface message processor (IMP) The name applied to the network processors which control the Advanced Research Projects Agency (ARPA) network.

Intermediate processor An information processor which fulfills a subsidiary role in a hierarchically distributed processing system. Typically a smaller version of the host processor, rather than a minicomputer; hence, distinct from *Satellite processor.*

International Consultative Committee on Telephony and Telegraphy (CCITT) An association of communications carriers and postal telephone and telegraph authorities (PTTs), which recommends common methods of transmission and interconnection.

International Standards Organization (ISO) A multinational body which formulates standards related to information processing and data communications.

Isochronous transmission A mode of data transmission in which characters are delimited by start-stop bits, as in asynchronous mode, but are transmitted with a constant time interval between successive characters/bits, as in synchronous mode.

Job control language (JCL)   The set of commands which defines required operations—e.g., compile, execute, access a file—in batch processing.

Journal of Development (JOD)   The publication in which Conference on Data Systems Languages (CODASYL) work is reported.

Journal   A location for the storage of information retained for later recovery and/or auditing purposes.

Leased link   Synonymous with *dedicated link.*

Line   A link implemented as a physical connection, such as a wire or group of wires, as contrasted to a microwave or communications satellite link.

Link   The interconnection between two nodes of a network. A link may consist of a data-communications circuit or of a direct-channel connection (such as a cable or bus).

Load leveling   The function of allocating a given workload evenly over some number of processors or transmission facilities.

Logical unit (LU)   In IBM's Systems Network Architecture (SNA), a port logically associated with an application to allow communication with other applications (including terminal control applications).

Loop multipoint link   A data-communications link which begins at a processor, extends to connect two or more terminals, and returns to the processor.

Mean time before failure (MTBF)   The length of time a hardware or software element can normally be expected to operate before a failure occurs.

Mean time to repair (MTTR)   The length of time normally required, after failure, to return a hardware or software element to operation.

Meshed network, or **Distributed network**   A data-communications network structure in which the links provide multiple connections between any two processors.

Message   A collection of data to be moved as a logical entity.

Message switching   Computer-controlled transfer of messages from a terminal to other terminal(s).

Microcomputer, or **Micro**   A computer built around a "processor on a chip."

Microwave   Any electromagnetic wave in the radio frequency spectrum above 890 megacycles per second.

Minicomputer, or **Mini**   A "small-scale" information processor, capable of operating in office or hostile environments; i.e., with minimal environmental control.

Modem   A contraction of *modulator-demodulator.* A form of coupling device. Synonymous with *data set.*

Multidrop link   A data-communications circuit which extends past two or more terminal devices, each of which is connected to the link by a "drop."

Multipoint link   A data-communications circuit which allows connection of more than one terminal device. Can be configured as a loop multipoint or a multidrop.

Multiplexing   The support on a single physical link of two or more logical data streams.

Multiplexor (MUX)   A device which performs the multiplexing function.

Narrow-band   A communications link which can support data transmission only in the range of 300 bps or less.

National Bureau of Standards (NBS)   An agency of the United States Department of Commerce, involved in setting standards in many areas, including certain computer-related areas.

Network addressable unit (NAU)   In IBM's Systems Network Architecture (SNA), a location to which data can be sent.

Network Control Program/Virtual Storage (NCP/VS)   Software provided by IBM for operation in their front-end and remote communications controllers, managing the physical network facilities. NCP/VS can operate in Systems Network Architecture (SNA) mode, in non-SNA mode, or in a hybrid environment.

NCR Data link control (NCR/DLC)   A protocol for data communications defined by NCR and used in their products. Similar to high-level data-link control (HDLC).

Network processing   The hardware and software functions which support the definition, establishment, and use of facilities for data movement among (usually physically separated) information-system components.

Network processor (NP)   A hardware device or set of devices, under the control of a single set of operating-system software, which provides the functions needed to control data-transmission facilities.

Network services protocol (NSP)   The protocol defined in Digital Equipment Corporation's (DEC) Digital Network Architecture (DNA) to establish and manage dialogues between pairs of objects.

Node   An end point of any branch of a network, or a junction common to two or more branches of a network. In an information network, nodes include information processors, network processors, terminal controllers, and terminal devices.

Object   The term used in Digital Equipment Corporation's (DEC) Digital Network Architecture (DNA) to describe any distributed system resource, such as a program, a file, or a database.

Pacing   *See* Flow control.

Packet   A transmission increment in a packet-switched network.

Packet-switched network   A data-communications network in which messages to be transmitted are separated into packets (usually short and of fixed length), each of which may travel a different route to reach the desired destination.

Partitioned database A distributed database formed by splitting up the total set of data elements and attaching the resulting partitions to two or more processors.

Password A private code which must be supplied by a user or device to satisfy a predefined access-control validation procedure.

PDN *See* Public data network.

Peer-distributed processing *See* Horizontally distributed processing.

Physical unit (PU) In IBM's Systems Network Architecture (SNA), the device interface between the network and a host, communications controller, terminal controller, or terminal.

Poll and select The method by which a processor controls a multipoint link, polling to obtain input or selecting to send output.

Postal, telephone, and telegraph authority (PTT) A general term used to refer to the governmental authority which, outside of the United States, controls voice-, record-, and data-transmission services. The authority may or may not have this exact title.

Privacy The ability to protect data or other resources belonging to one user or user group from access, use, or modification by other users.

Procedure A series of operations performed in a regular sequence to accomplish a stated purpose. Procedures may be either manual or computerized; a program consists of computerized procedure(s).

Process A computerized procedure which has been activated for execution. Can be an application process, defined to perform some part of the processing needed by a specific application, or a system process, supplying some part of the system logic.

Propagation delay The time required for data to travel over a communications circuit. Proportional to circuit speed and distance.

Protocol A set of rules for the exchange of information. In layered architectures, a protocol defines rules for cooperation between two copies of the same functional layer, each resident in a different processor. *See* also Interface.

Public data network (PDN) A network primarily designed for data transmission and intended for sharing by many users from many organizations. Analogous to the public voice (telephone) networks.

Reliability The ability of an information-system component (hardware or software) to operate continuously without failure. Typically expressed in terms of mean time before failure (MTBF) and mean time to repair (MTTR). Reliability is one of the elements required to calculate availability.

Remote network processor (RNP) A network processor which is not directly connected to an information processor.

Replicated database A distributed database formed by copying at least some of the data elements at two or more processors.

Remote job entry (RJE) A mode of computer use in which jobs to be executed are submitted from terminals, usually remote from the information processor.

Request for proposal (RFP) A formal request for proposals to provide specific hardware and/or software and/or services. Also called *Request for quote* (RFQ) or *Request for bid* (RFB).

Response The speed with which output follows input. Typically measured from the depression of the "transmit" (or equivalent) key until the first character or line of the reply is visible at the terminal.

Resource An information-system component (hardware or software) which can serve a user requirement. Example resource are databases, disk devices, language compilers, processes, etc.

Resource sharing The ability to make unique resources (which exist at only one or selected locations) accessible by users or applications at other locations.

Routing The function of selecting the appropriate path(s) for the movement of data within a network, ensuring that all data are directed to the appropriate destination(s).

Satellite, communications A device which, when placed in orbit around the earth, reflects back transmissions directed to it. All ground stations tuned to the satellite receive all transmissions.

Satellite processor An information processor (IP) which is arbitrarily assigned a subsidiary role in a distributed system, communicating with—and perhaps depending to some degree upon—a host for supporting services and/or guidance. Typically a minicomputer; hence the distinction with *Intermediate processor*.

Schema An explicit declaration of the interrecord and intrarecord relationship structures of a database.

Security The function of controlling access to, and/or the use of, resources within an information system.

Session The term used in IBM's Systems Network Architecture (SNA), and in some other contexts, to describe a logical connection between two processes— such as an application program and a terminal controller or two application programs—for data exchange.

Sink In data communications, synonymous with *destination*.

Site A physical location for the housing of information-system equipment.

Source A physical and/or logical entity (process, person, or terminal) which originates information to be moved within an information network.

Specialized-communications common carrier A common carrier which provides only certain specialized services, rather than a full range of voice, data, and/or record services as provided by the conventional common carriers.

Star network A data-communications network structure in which links radiate from a central information processor to surrounding terminals and/or terminal controllers. The simplest form of hierarchical network.

Subschema A description of a logically consistent subset of a database, defining the areas to be accessed by a specific program or set of related programs. A subset of a schema.

Subset (or **digital subset**) Synonymous with *data set.*

Switched link Synonymous with *dial link.*

Synchronous transmission A mode in which the receiving hardware synchronizes at the block level, by recognition of special character(s) preceding the transmission block.

Synchronous data link control (SDLC) A protocol for data communications defined by IBM and used in their products, and in certain other vendors' products. Similar to high-level data link control (HDLC).

System A collection of components which is under a single unified management.

System administrator *See* Administrator, system.

Systems Network Architecture (SNA) The architecture defined and used by IBM in providing product capabilities for networks and distributed systems.

System Services Control Point (SSCP) In IBM's System Network Architecture (SNA), the software entity which provides essential control functions, such as the establishment of sessions between pairs of network addressable units (NAUs).

Tariff In the United States, a definition of a specific service or services to be offered by a carrier, with the associated cost to the user. Tariffs for interstate services must be approved by the Federal Communications Commission (FCC), while intrastate or local services are approved by state or local agencies.

Telecommunications Access Method (TAM) Software provided by NCR, in accordance with Distributed Network Architecture (DNA) rules, which allows application programs to send and receive messages.

Telecommunications Access Method (TCAM) Software provided by IBM for use in their general-purpose computer systems. TCAM controls the interface between applications and remote terminals. TCAM can operate in Systems Network Architecture (SNA) mode, in non-SNA mode, or in a hybrid environment. *See* also VTAM.

TELCON The software provided by Univac to control the Distributed Communications Processor (DCP) and manage the data communications facilities.

Telecommunications A term used by IBM and some other vendors to refer to network processing.

Teleprocessing The term used by IBM to refer to information processing plus data communications.

Terminal A device which embodies a set of interface functions between people and systems, such as a teleprinter or keyboard-and-display cathode-ray tube (CRT) device.

Terminal controller A device which provides detailed control for one or more terminal devices.

Termination system   In Univac's Distributed Communications Architecture (DCA), the software which provides network management functions such as message fragmentation/reassembly and flow control.

Time division multiplexor (TDM)   A device which multiplexes multiple data streams onto a single link by assigning time slices on the link to the various data streams. *See* also FDM.

Time sharing   An interactive mode of computer use in which multiple terminal users concurrently access the same set of computer resources.

Transaction   An event (sale, order, payroll change, etc.) of interest to the organization. Also, a computer-processable record of that event.

Transaction processing   An interactive mode of computer use in which each event of interest (i.e., a transaction) is entered into the computer for processing at the time that the event occurs.

Transmission facilities   Links, switching centers, and all other equipment by means of which a communications common carrier or postal, telephone, and telegraph authority (PTT) provides a stated type of service.

Transmission subsystem interface (TSI)   In IBM's Systems Network Architecture (SNA), the software which interfaces the network addressable units (NAUs) to the transmission subsystem, hiding the specific details of the network/terminals from the NAUs.

Transparency   Having the property of masking details from the "observer." For example, terminal transparency indicates that only generic terminal characteristics, not device specifics, are visible to application programs.

Transport network   The term used in Univac's Distributed Communications Architecture (DCA) to describe the data-communications facilities plus any communications processors used to control those facilities.

Two-way alternate (TWA)   A mode of data communications in which either sending or receiving takes place on a specific link at any given point in time.

Two-way simultaneous (TWS)   A mode of data communications in which both sending and receiving can take place on a specific link at exactly the same time.

Two-wire   A communications circuit which includes two wires. Usually written *2-wire*.

Universal data link control (UDLC)   A protocol for data communications defined by Sperry-Univac and used in their products. Similar to high-level data link control (HDLC) and advanced data communications control procedure (ADCCP).

Upline dump   The transmission of memory content, following a problem or failure, from one processor (usually a satellite) to another (usually a host) for problem analysis.

User   A person known to the information system by means of a unique identification (name, password, etc.), who can act in one or more roles (end user, application developer, system administrator), and who has a defined set of access rights to system resources.

Value-added network (VAN) A data network operated in the United States by a specialized common carrier which obtains basic transmission facilities from the common carriers (e.g., the Bell System), adds "value" such as error detection and sharing, and resells the services to users.

VAN *See* Value-added network.

Vertically distributed processing *See* Horizontally distributed processing.

Virtual circuit A technique for sending messages in a data network, in which a logical connection (the virtual circuit) is established between the sender and receiver. The physical transmission path may vary (depending upon the implementation), but related messages/packets are associated with the virtual circuit until the logical connection is terminated. *See* also Datagram.

Voice-grade A communications link which is suitable for the transmission of speech; i.e., in the frequency range of 300-3400 Hertz. Capable of data transmission at speeds up to, and in some cases beyond, 10,000 bps.

Virtual Telecommunications Access Method (VTAM) Software provided by IBM for use in their general-purpose computer systems, which controls network access and conforms to the rules of Systems Network Architecture (SNA). *See* also TCAM.

BIBLIOGRAPHY

Adiba, M., et al: "Issues in Distributed Data Base Management Systems: A Technical Overview," *Proceedings of the Fourth International Conference on Very Large Data Bases,* Berlin, September 1978.

Andrews, F.B. and Chris G. Cooper: "Probing NCR's Distributed Network Architecture," *Data Communications,* April 1978, pp. 49–59.

Bachman, Charles W: "The Programmer as Navigator," 1973 ACM Turing Award Lecture, *Communications of the ACM,* Volume 16, Number 11, November 1973, pp. 653–658.

Becker, Hal B: *Functional Analysis of Information Networks,* Wiley, New York, 1973.

Becker, H.B: "The Distributed Environment—A Formal Structure for Its Definition and Design," *IEEE Digest COMPCON '76,* IEEE Computer Society, Piscataway, N.J., Fall 1976.

Berglund, Ralph G: "Comparing Network Architectures," *Datamation,* Volume 24, Number 2, February 1978, pp. 79–85.

Bernstein, A.J. and A. Shoshani: "Synchronization in a Parallel Access Data Base," *Communications of the ACM,* Volume 12, Number 11, November 1969, pp. 604–607.

Booth, Grayce M: "Distributed Data Bases," *Distributed Data Processing,* Infotech State of the Art Report, Infotech International, Ltd., Maidenhead UK, 1977.

Booth, Grayce M: "Distributed Information Systems," *Proceedings of the National Computer Conference,* New York, 1976, pp. 789–794.

Booth, Grayce M: *Functional Analysis of Information Processing,* Wiley, New York, 1973.

Booth, Grayce M: "Honeywell's Distributed Systems Environment," *Proceedings of the Fourth International Conference on Computer Communications,* Kyoto, Japan, September 1978, pp. 347–351.

Booth, Grayce M: "The Use of Distributed Data Bases in Information Networks," *Proceedings of the First International Conference on Computer Communications,* Washington, D.C., October 1972, pp. 371–376.

Canning, R.G: "In Your Future: Distributed Systems?" *EDP Analyzer,* Volume 11, Number 8, August 1973.

Cerf, Vinton G. and Alex Curran: "The Future of Data Communications," *Datamation*, Volume 23, Number 5, May 1977, pp. 105–114.

Champine, G.A: "Six Approaches to Distributed Databases," *Datamation*, Volume 23, Number 5, May 1977, pp. 69–72.

Combs, Paul G: "Needed: Distributed Control," *Proceedings of the (First) International Conference on Very Large Data Bases*, Framingham, Mass., September 1975, pp. 364–375.

Conant, G. and S. Wecker: "DNA: An Architecture for Heterogeneous Computer Networks," *Proceedings of the Third International Conference on Computer Communications*, August 1976.

Chu, W.W: "Performance of File Directory Systems for Data Bases in Star and Distributed Networks," *Proceedings of the National Computer Conference*, New York, 1976, pp. 577–587.

Dappe, M.E. and J.P. Fry: "Distributed Databases: A Summary of Research," *Computer Networks*, Volume 1, Number 2, September 1976, pp. 130–138.

Davis, G: "AT&T answers 15 Questions About its Planned Service," *Data Communications*, February 1979, pp. 41–60.

des Jardins, R. and George White: "ANSI Reference Model for Distributed Systems," *Proceedings of the IEEE COMPCON '78*, pp. 144–149.

Diffie, W. and M. Hellman: "Privacy Authentication: An Introduction to Cryptography," *Proceedings of the IEEE*, Volume 67, Number 3, March 1979, pp. 397–427.

Erskine, S.B: "Access to Packet Switching Networks," *IEEE Digest COMPCON '76*, IEEE Computer Society, Piscataway, N.J., Fall 1976.

Feistel, H., W.A. Notz, and J.L. Smith: "Some Cryptographic Techniques for Machine to Machine Communications," *Proceedings of the IEEE*, Volume 63, Number 11, November 1975, pp. 1545–1553.

Foster, J.D: "Distributive Processing for Banking," *Datamation*, Volume 22, Number 7, July 1976, pp. 553–555.

Gray, J.P. and T.B. McNeil: "SNA Multiple-System Networking," *IBM Systems Journal*, Volume 18, Number 2, 1979, pp. 263–298.

Helgeson, W.B: "Distributed Data Bases—Networks bring DP to Source of Data," *The Data Communications User*, December 1975, pp. 39–41.

Hellman, Martin E: "The Mathematics of Public-Key Cryptography," *Scientific American*, Volume 241, Number 2, August 1979, pp. 146–157.

Kawaoka, T., T. Abe, and A. Shiraishi: "A Logical Structure for a Heterogeneous Computer Communication Network Architecture," *Proceedings of the Fourth International Conference on Computer Communications*, Kyoto, Japan, September 1978, pp. 519–524.

Kleinrock, Leonard: *Queueing Systems, Volume 2: "Computer Applications,"* Wiley, New York, 1976.

Kopf, J: "Tymnet as a Multiplexed Packet Network," *Proceedings of the National Computer Conference,* Dallas, 1977, pp. 609–613.

Lehon, A., R. Negaret, and G. LeLann: "Distribution of Access and Data in Large Data Bases," Groupe Reseaux, IRISA, Universite de Rennes, France, March 1976.

Lohse, E. and J.S. Foley: "General Purpose Computer/Terminal Network Architecture—Its Natural Structure and the Implications on Interface Standards," *Proceedings of the Fourth International Conference on Computer Communications,* Kyoto, Japan, September 1978, pp. 427–432.

Loveland, R.A. and C.W. Stein: "How DECnet's Communications Software Works," *Data Communications,* January 1979, pp. 49–65.

Mahn, T.G: "What Will Congress Do to Change Data Communications?" *Data Communications,* June 1979, pp. 57–64.

Martin, James: *Design of Man-Computer Dialogues,* Prentice-Hall, Englewood Cliffs, N.J., 1973.

Martin, James: *Systems Analysis for Data Transmission,* Prentice-Hall, Englewood Cliffs, N.J., 1972.

McFadyen, J.H: "Systems Network Architecture," *IBM Systems Journal,* Volume 15, Number 1, 1976.

McGovern, J.P: "DCA—A Distributed Communications Architecture," *Proceedings of the Fourth International Conference on Computer Communications,* Kyoto, Japan, September 1978, pp. 359–367.

Meadow, C.T: *Man-Machine Communication,* Wiley, New York, 1970.

Munz, R: "Gross Architecture of the Distributed Database System VDN," *VDN Report 15/78,* Technical University of Berlin, West Germany, 1978.

Palmer, Ian: *Data Base Systems: A Practical Reference,* Q.E.D. Information Services, Inc., Wellesley, Mass., 1975.

Patrick, R.L: "Decentralizing Hardware and Dispersing Responsibility," *Datamation,* Volume 22, Number 5, May 1976, pp. 79–84.

Pouzin, L: "Virtual Circuits vs. Datagrams—Technical and Political Problems," *Proceedings of the National Computer Conference,* New York, 1976, pp. 483–494.

Pyke, Jr., Thomas N: "Assuring User Service Quality in a Distributed Computer Network," *IEEE Digest COMPCON '76,* IEEE Computer Society, Piscataway, N.J., Fall 1976.

Roberts, L.G. et al: "The ARPA Network," in *Computer Communication Networks,* Abramson and Kuo, Editors, Prentice-Hall, Englewood Cliffs, N.J., 1973.

Sammet, J.E: *Programming Languages: History and Fundamentals,* Prentice-Hall, Englewood Cliffs, N.J., 1969.

Small, D. and W. Chu: "A Distributed Data Base Architecture for Data Processing in a Dynamic Environment," *Proceedings of the IEEE COMPCON '79,* IEEE Computer Society, Piscataway, N.J., Spring 1979.

Sussenguth, E.H: "Systems Network Architecture: A Perspective," *Proceedings of the Fourth International Conference on Computer Communications*, Kyoto, Japan, September 1978, pp. 353–358.

Tominaga, H., S. Tajima, and K. Saito: "Trade-off of File Directory Systems for Data Base," *Proceedings of the Fourth International Conference on Computer Communications*, Kyoto, Japan, September 1978, pp. 405–410.

Van Rensselaer, Cort: "Centralize? Decentralize? Distribute?" *Datamation*, Volume 25, Number 4, April 1979, pp. 88–97.

American National Standard programming language COBOL, ANSI X3.23, American National Standards Institute, Inc., New York (updated periodically to reflect current language status).

Data Base Directions: The Next Steps, U.S. Department of Commerce, National Bureau of Standards Special Publication 451, 1976.

Datacomm Advisor (periodical), International Data Corporation, Waltham, Mass.

Distributed Databases, Infotech State of the Art Report, Infotech International, Ltd., Maidenhead, U.K. 1979.

Distributed Processing Newsletter, International Data Corporation, Waltham, Mass.

Distributed Processing Tutorial, IEEE Computer Society, Long Beach, Calif., 1978.

Distributed Processing Systems, Infotech State of the Art Report, Infotech International, Ltd., Maidenhead, U.K., 1977.

Distributed Systems, Infotech State of the Art Report, Infotech International, Ltd., Maidenhead, U.K., 1976.

HP3000 Computer Systems—General Information Manual, Hewlett-Packard, Santa Clara, Calif., 1978.

Public data networks, CCITT Orange Book, Volume VIII.2, International Telecommunication Union, Geneva, 1977.

RXS/IAS DECnet System Manager's Guide, Digital Equipment Corporation, Maynard, Mass., 1978.

INDEX